March 2014,

Jeff,

Thank you for trusting me with your health and wellness. It's a pleasure taking care of you. May God/life/the universe grant you love, joy/laughter, and fulfillment in all things.

Love,

Micah Han

A JOURNEY OF DISCOVERY

Published by BookLocker.com, Inc., Bradenton, Florida.

While all of the incidents in this book are true to the author's best knowledge, some of the names and personal characteristics of the individuals involved have been changed in order to protect their privacy. Any resulting resemblance to persons living or dead is entirely coincidental and unintentional.

All information in this book is provided for your information and inspiration only and may not be construed as medical advice or instruction. No action or inaction should be taken based solely on the contents of this information. This book is not intended as a substitute for the medical advice of a physician. The reader should consult appropriate health professionals on any matter relating to their health and well-being.

Editor: David Garnes
Cover designer: Carol Bigl
Back photo credit: Michael Kealey; Bement Bridge, Bradford, NH

Printed in the United States of America on acid-free paper.

Booklocker.com, Inc.
2012

First Edition

A Journey of Discovery

True stories
of love, loss, laughter, and hope
from a family practice physician

Minh Han, M.D.

Dedicated to my grandmother By Quy Nguyen, an inexhaustible source of love and wisdom

Acknowledgements

There are so many people in my life that deserve my heartfelt thanks for helping me to get where I am. I thank my mother and late father for sacrificing everything to get our family out of war-torn Vietnam and give us a better life. You loved me, encouraged me, and prodded me to strive for excellence. Thank you to my step-father, Giao Hoang, M.D., whose medical practice I took over after residency. You gave me a place to land after my training and a set of wonderful patients.

Thanks to all my teachers and mentors from Hastings, Rice, Baylor, and Roanoke. Your lessons and example were not lost on me, even if they seemed to at the time. I fully recognize I had quite a number of rough edges and character flaws. Without you, I would have neither knowledge nor wisdom. Thank you for exemplifying both.

A tremendous thank you to David Dachner, Bob Posey, and all the staff and volunteers at *Discovery! Austin*. You all astound me with the depth of your giving, taking hurting, broken people and helping them find hope and love. That also applies to my *Discovery* Class, who have stuck with me through my personal journey of discovery. I love you all.

Thanks go out to all the patients who have entrusted their lives—and more importantly, the lives of their loved ones—to my care. It is with great honor and humility that I serve as your physician. I take that responsibility very seriously, and I commit to doing my utmost to help you have the best quality of life possible for the longest time possible. You are the reason that I get up every morning and go to work loving my job.

Finally, I thank my life partner Michael, who has supported me during the challenging years of residency, moved to Connecticut with me, and helped me establish a thriving practice. You have seen all those flaws no one else gets to see, and yet you've still stuck around. I love you, and I look forward to a lifetime of years together.

Minh Han

Table of Contents

Preface

This collection of stories began as two different projects which have been combined into one work. A number of years ago, I realized that I regularly encountered situations throughout my medical career that made me laugh hysterically. I started to write down as many stories as I could remember from my medical training and then jotted down humorous situations as they arose in my office. Every now and then, I would reread those stories to remind me of life's funnier moments. It helped me break out of the cynicism that the grind of a medical practice invariably produces.

The second part of the project began as a series of e-mail exchanges with a group of people I met in Austin, Texas from the program *Discovery!*. *Discovery! Austin* and its sister program *Discovery! Dallas* are non-profit organizations that seek to help individuals find more joy, self-worth, clarity, and purpose in their lives. By the invitation of a close friend, I attended the three parts of *Discovery!* from January to March of 2011. Even as a physician with nearly twenty years of clinical experience, I found the life skills imparted during *Discovery!* to be immensely powerful and effective, both for myself and my patients.

During the third session of *Discovery!*, trainees craft a Mission Statement, which helps give self-guidance and purpose. My Mission Statement is *"to help those who cross my path find greater physical, emotional, and spiritual health through my life experiences and my profession as a physician."* The e-mails detailing my attempts to live out my Mission became the seed for the stories included in this book. Therefore, *Discovery!* is often featured in these stories.

The names and/or identities of the individuals involved in these stories have been changed to protect patient confidentiality, or the individual has given permission to disclose information regarding his/her care. The photographs included in this book were either taken by me or supplied by the patients in the stories.

These stories are all true and are accurate accounts of patients' lives and challenges, which invariably are messy and often not pretty. To honor the patients and their difficulties, the stories are not scrubbed and sanitized. Yet in the midst of great pain and struggle there is also faith, hope, and love. Ultimately, these stories are about overcoming the bumps in the road of life. I hope as you read them, you will find your own path to a life of greater fulfillment, purpose, and passion.

Respectfully,

Minh Han, M.D.

SERVICE

"Everybody can be great. Because anybody can serve. You don't have to have a college degree to serve. You don't have to make your subject and your verb agree to serve.... You don't have to know the second theory of thermodynamics in physics to serve. You only need a heart full of grace. A soul generated by love."

~Martin Luther King, Jr.

A Night in Ben Taub

When I was attending medical school at Baylor College of Medicine in Houston, the curriculum consisted of eighteen months of intensive class work and lectures followed by clinical rotations starting the second half of the second year. The advantage of this system was that it afforded an extra six months of clinical rotations. Students could spend that time exploring various specialties before deciding on one that for all intents and purposes would lock them into that specialty for the rest of their lives.

There were, however, several disadvantages to this arrangement. During the eighteen months of Basic Sciences, students had essentially no contact with actual live patients. Because there were no names, faces, or stories to attach the information to, all the class work was overwhelming and frequently became rote memorization of huge lists. Also, students were thrown into the proverbial lion's den at the beginning of clinicals, without even the first clue of basic hospital procedure.

In an effort to break the humdrum of an endless series of classes and get some clinical experience, some students decided to spend several hours during a midnight shift at the Ben Taub General Hospital emergency room. Ben Taub was a community hospital serving almost exclusively an indigent population. Spanish was the predominant language spoken, but so many other nationalities were represented that it was more like a United Nations of sick people. Houston also had a very active "knife and gun club," with almost daily stabbings and shootings. As a *Level One Comprehensive Trauma Facility*, many of these patients were brought to Ben Taub for evaluation and stabilization. Car accidents and other major traumas rounded out the list of issues presenting to the ER. Thus, in any given night, one could have a patient with a hang nail or a multiple-car pileup. The Ben Taub ER was many things, but it was never boring.

The administration knew that first- and second-year medical students were "moonlighting" in the ER. The practice was neither encouraged nor sanctioned. Maybe the school's insurance policy did not cover students unless they were doing a specific clinical rotation. Maybe they wanted us focusing on the studying first and worry about the clinical aspect later. Or maybe the chief residents complained of having a clueless medical student wandering around the ER looking for exciting things to do and see. Whatever the case, it was an open secret, and until the school specifically barred the practice, students would continue doing it.

I decided to take a Saturday night to experience Ben Taub's ER first hand. For some reason, the medical students called it "going commando." I guess it was the predominance of traumas that were seen in the ER. My plan was to get to the ER at 11 PM and stay until about 3 AM. That way, I would miss all the people who came during the day and used the ER as a clinic for frivolous matters. Bars were also winding down at 2 AM, so maybe I would be lucky and get to treat a car accident victim or a stabbing. Basically, I was hoping to profit from someone else's misfortune. My notion of the ER was based on the stylized scenes from Hollywood and my own preconceptions. My imagination was far from reality.

When I walked into the ER from the tunnel that connected the school to the hospital, the place was unusually quiet. A bunch of fires were just put out, and there was nothing going on at that moment. I found the surgical chief resident in charge of the trauma side of the ER. I introduced myself to Chuck and told him what I was doing. He chuckled and nodded his head. I'm sure he had seen plenty of first year medical students *going commando* before. Chuck was an atypical surgical resident: he was personable and pleasant. He took me around the surgical side with the nurses' station, the five trauma bays, and the small exam rooms along the back hallway for minor surgical procedures such as suturing lacerations.

Chuck then pointed with his whole arm through an open door. I could see an expansive open room filled with patient stalls, each separated by a thin curtain for the barest semblance of privacy. "That's the medical side of the ER," Chuck said. I had this image of Yoda pointing to the cavern and saying to Luke Skywalker, "That place is strong with the dark side of the Force."

Shortly after the tour, the intercom blared, "MVA five minutes out."

"The EMS calls the ER to let us know when they're bringing in a person from a car accident," Chuck explained. "That way, we can get the team together before they arrive." There was only one injury, and word was that it wasn't too serious. Sure enough, the nurses and medical technicians sauntered to the trauma bay, relaxed but ready to take action. When the ambulance arrived with the patient on the gurney, the trauma team came together with practiced efficiency. The patient was transferred to the trauma table, his clothes were sliced off with bandage shearers, and his vitals were recorded. His neck was immobilized by a cervical collar, and Chuck examined his neck to determine if it was broken. After Chuck was confident that there were no cervical injuries, the C-collar came off. He was then sent for X-rays and other tests. The entire encounter took a surprisingly short time.

That man was only the first car accident victim. There were several more, some in much more serious condition. But it was not only car accidents that ended up in the trauma unit. While Chuck and his team were working on one patient, another was being tended to in the adjacent bay. A fifteen-year-old boy was just brought in with a self-inflicted shotgun injury to his head. He missed the lower part of his brain, so the heart and lungs were still pumping. But his pupils were blown, and he was completely unresponsive. The X-ray of the boy's head was on the viewer. The metal shot lit up white against the dark field of his brain. It was like looking at a nightmare sky with deadly stars. There was no hope for the boy's survival. The Spanish translator was called in to explain to the parents what the prognosis was and to ask them permission for organ donation. People could hear the mother's agonized wails throughout the ER.

Over the course of four hours, dozens of patients were seen in the surgical side of the ER. Most of them were minor lacerations or fractures, but a few were major traumas. Fortunately, other than the young teenager, no one lost his life for the rest of the shift. At the end of my stint, I thanked Chuck for his time and teaching, and I prepared to leave.

On my way out of the ER, I decided to poke my head into the medical side. The room was packed! All the curtained bays were full, and patients lined the walls, sitting on plastic folding chairs. I made a quick sweep and decided to walk through the room because it was more convenient. Near the exit, I could hear Vietnamese being spoken from behind a curtain to my left. Everyone else was speaking Spanish, so the Vietnamese sliced right through the din. A woman was talking to a man, who I assumed was her husband. She was lamenting the fact that he was so sick, and she could not understand what the doctors were saying.

I found my steps slowing down, and I decided to speak to her. I got her attention and said, "I am a medical student, and I speak Vietnamese. What is going on?"

The woman's eyes lit up and she pointed to her husband lying on a stretcher. His skin and eyes were yellow, and his stomach was distended. Frankly, he looked terrible. "My husband has liver problems, and he's been sick for a long time. Now, he can't eat or drink. I took him here, but we don't understand English. I think he's dying."

"I'll see what I can do," I assured her. I asked for the nurse in charge of the patient, and I met an attractive middle-aged woman. She was both thankful and relieved to run into someone who could translate for her.

"The patient has liver cancer from Hepatitis B," she told me. "He's in critical condition. He's not a candidate for further treatment because he's under hospice care. We don't think he's going to make it."

I relayed this information to the wife, and she was not surprised, but more resigned. "I thought so," she said.

I asked her if there was anything she needed or that I could do for her. She said, "There is one thing. It's so noisy and crowded here. Is there somewhere we could go for some privacy? If my husband is going to die soon, I don't want it to be here."

When I relayed the wife's request to the nurse, she was chagrined that she had not thought of that herself. "Of course, I'll get right on it." Fifteen minutes later, she came back and led us to a private room that even had a couch. How the nurse managed to find a room like that when the entire hospital was filled to the rafters was beyond me.

The wife was very pleased with the room, and she said "Thank you, thank you," to the nurse over and over in her thick accent.

"There's not much more to do," the nurse told me. She took stock of the bag I had in my hand and correctly deduced that I was heading out. "Why don't you go home?" She suggested.

"No, I can stay for a while," I said. "If the couple needs something, I can help translate."

I helped the nurse fill out a few forms and dealt with minor requests, and I tried to make myself both available yet unobtrusive. I sat waiting quietly on the comfy couch. It was close to six AM, and I had been up all day and night. The adrenaline from the hectic night was wearing off. At some point, my head leaned back and I nodded off.

I woke up to a gentle nudge by the nurse. She was the only other person in the room. "I'm sorry to wake you," she apologized. "You must be beat. I wanted to let you know that Mr. Tran passed away a short while ago. We saw you were sleeping, and we didn't want to wake you up. I really appreciate everything you did for that couple. It could have been much more difficult if you hadn't been around. You should really go home and get some good rest. You deserve it."

I somehow made it back home without an accident. My whole body was aching from sleep deprivation. I ended up sleeping until early afternoon.

When I started the evening at Ben Taub, I was referring to patients by their ailments. "The gunshot wound in Five." "The head-on collision in Two."

But behind each of these ailments was a person. Each had hopes and dreams, I daresay much like mine: stability, happiness, health. These people were much more than the ailments that caused them to seek medical attention. That night, I came face to face with the humanity and the tragedy of illness. I wish I could say I never again referred to patients by their illnesses, but I did. Through medical school and residency, it was easy to slip into that depersonalizing medical shorthand. But I would correct myself quickly and tried to respect the patients who trusted their lives to my care.

The Khmu in Thailand

When I was a third-year medical student, I received a phone call. "Hi, Minh. My name is Jerry. I got your name from the director of the Medical Center Christian Student Union. Joyce said that you have done some medical mission work in the past and might be interested in helping me out. I'm not a doctor, but I would like to put together a medical mission trip to Thailand in about six weeks."

"Well, Jerry," I told him, "You have a whole lot of work on your hands then." Typically, a medical mission trip takes many months to prepare. Contacts in the country have to be established. Visas have to be obtained. An itinerary has to be planned. Plane tickets have to be bought. Medicine donations have to be procured. The thought of doing all of this in less than two months was staggering. Jerry had started some of this process already, but there was still much that had to be done.

I told Jerry I would help him get the medicines together through the contacts I had in the medical center. Although I never said I would do anything more than help Jerry prepare, he made the assumption that I would be joining him and proceeded merrily along that path. As it turned out, I was able to raise the several thousand dollars I needed and get the time off from my medical school rotations to join Jerry and the small team of people he cobbled together to go to Thailand.

Although I had done short-term medical trips to Mexico, Venezuela, and Trinidad before, this was a whole different animal. For Thailand, just the travel to Bangkok took 26 hours. Thailand is a tropical country, famous for its lush jungles and elephants. We went in the middle of summer and were greeted with the country's equally-famous heat and humidity as we stepped off the plane. We boarded a connecting flight to Chiang Mai and then endured a five hour van ride up windy mountain paths to get to our destination. Travelling both north and up into the mountains, I noticed the temperature dropped significantly. Days were still hot and humid, but not stifling. Nights were cool enough to need a long-sleeve shirt. We were in a part of the country that saw very few tourists.

We went to Thailand to work primarily with the Khmu, a people of about a million, spread throughout the regions of northern Thailand, Laos, Cambodia, and Myanmar (formerly Burma). It was generally known that out of all the various ethnic groups in the region, the Khmu were the most downtrodden, with the least access to basic standards of living. Less than one percent of Khmu were literate. The life expectancy was very short, and infant mortality high. Drugs, smoking, and alcohol were serious concerns affecting a large segment of the population.

We four Americans met up with Sionh Chan, a Khmu missionary, and his team of helpers and translators. For months, Sionh had been sending out messages through his short-wave radio broadcasts, by runners, and through word of mouth that a team of Americans was bringing medicines and supplies to help the Khmu people. Each day, our team visited one and sometimes up to three villages to listen to people and treat their medical problems. Often, we would hear of people who got word of our team, traveled three days through the jungle of Laos, and hitched rides on boats down the Mekong River to get to our clinic sites.

It would not be uncommon to have almost a hundred patients waiting for us when we arrived in a village. One by one, I examined patients and treated them the best I could. Common complaints were back aches and other musculoskeletal issues, headaches, gastritis, malnutrition, infestation with worms and other parasites, and lung issues from poor air quality and smoking.

I gave out the medicine we had, and when we ran out, we went to the pharmacy in a nearby town to buy more. Although I knew that the pain medicines I was giving out would only last a short while, the fact that we were able to touch these people's hearts and show our caring went far beyond the medicines we handed out.

Some patients had serious medical problems that our team was not equipped to treat. One young man approached Sionh and told him that he had made a terrible mistake by sleeping with prostitutes and now was diagnosed with HIV. He asked us if we had any HIV medicines to give him, which we of course did not. We took up a collection from the team for the man to get to the city for some further care.

In another instance, an older gentleman came to the clinic with both of his feet wrapped in dirty bandages. When he removed the bandages, most of his toes were down to nubs, and the green flesh and terrible smell clearly evidenced gangrene. The man originally told the translator that he had leprosy. Upon further history, we found out that the man had seen a city doctor many years ago and was diagnosed with diabetes. He bought and took a month's supply of diabetes medicine, but because that did not "cure" him, the man stopped his medicine and could not afford to go back to the doctor. Over time, the diabetes worsened, causing bad circulation and decreased feeling in his feet. Because of poor hygiene, an infection set in and rapidly spread. By the time the team saw it, there was not much that could be done. The man needed to have both his legs amputated, likely above the knee. When I told him the prognosis, he shook his head and hobbled away, unwilling to consider my suggestion.

Patients frequently got to the clinic site many hours before the team arrived. They then stayed all day until they were seen, never complaining. What a contrast to American patients getting bent out of shape about having to wait more than ten minutes for their appointment! While the people waited for their turn, Sionh used the time to educate the people about lifestyle choices that could affect their health, especially alcohol and smoking. The team also used a pictorial flip chart to improve literacy. Being Khmu themselves, Sionh and his team had an intimate understanding of the challenges and cultural inertia the people faced that kept them in a state of poor physical and social health.

Other than providing medical care, the medical team spent a good deal of time giving basic health education. The villagers needed to cook their meat fully to decrease the burden of worms and other parasites. Fertilizing with human waste was discouraged for the same reason. Walking with shoes or sandals decreased infections as well as worms burrowing through people's feet as they walked. All of the people, but mostly the women, had to carry heavy burdens through the day. We taught them how correct lifting techniques and better posture could save their sore backs. We also had generous donations of clothes and toys, and we passed those out during our clinic days.

The two-week trip was such a huge success that the team was invited back the next year. Because word had spread and demand was higher, Jerry recruited a physician to join the team. Dr. Bruce Bell and I split the patients for the day, giving me a reprieve from the hectic schedule. Non-medical team members also joined the trip and played a valuable role in numerous ways. One young man was an electrician by trade, and while the medical team was working with patients, he helped put electrical wiring up for a village to improve their quality of life.

Many of the villages also did not have running water, and so baths consisted of ladling cold water over yourself. Still, I particularly enjoyed the several evenings the team stayed in the villages. We slept on grass mats under thatched roofs alongside the villagers. It was an eye-opening experience to see how the villagers lived their daily lives. It was these times when the differences of nationality, socioeconomic class, educational level, and language melted away. We were all people living and sleeping under the same sky, trying to help ourselves and help the world be a better place.

During this trip, we had a morning devotional on the story of Jesus exemplifying servant leadership by washing His disciples' feet. Joe Balena, a retired gentleman on our team, and his grown son, John, decided to take this lesson literally. That day, they spent time washing the feet of the people coming to the clinic. John and Joe are the quintessential football player types: well over six feet and muscular. When the patients saw these two big Americans stooping down to wash their feet—the dirtiest parts of their body—words could not express how touched they were.

Jerry continued to take teams of people to Thailand on an annual basis, although I missed a number of trips because I entered residency. After residency, I felt a calling back to this part of the world and again joined Jerry on a team. This time, Mike and his nine-year-old son Egan joined the team, along with a retired social worker from the church named Marie. With multiple generations represented on the team, many people were impacted by everyone's contribution. I will never forget seeing Egan's straw-blond hair bobbing up and down in the middle of a sea of black-haired Khmu children, laughing and running after Egan like the proverbial pied piper. By seeing such poverty in the world, Egan's life was forever changed, teaching him appreciation for all the things he had. At the same time, even with next to nothing, these Khmu kids were truly happy. That showed that material possessions do not equate to happiness.

In 2004, Jerry's organization Innovative Mission Opportunities sponsored one last trip to Thailand. Because he could not go, I led the trip. Mike and Egan again came along, as did my nurse Melinda and a few other Texas team members. Again, we went from village to village, treating patients. On this trip, however, we also had a home base. From the beginning of the trips started in 1997, funds steadily accrued to help the Khmu. At first, a suitable site was found that could become a clinic that would serve the entire region. Money was raised to buy the land. The foundation was then laid and walls erected, using donated funds and villagers volunteering their labor. Sionh found the brightest, most educated Khmu villagers and had them trained in nursing and basic medical care. With a permanent clinic, people came from all over the surrounding area and even from Laos for medical treatment. Records could be kept, and some continuity of care was established. Although more serious cases still had to be sent to the city, at least this clinic was equipped to help many who would otherwise get no medical care. Also, any donated medicines and supplies could be sent and stored at the clinic to help people through the year.

The Khmu people now had a clinic as well as a chance for a better life. The responsibility lay with Sionh, his team, and his people to continue the work that was originally helped by Jerry and his organization. Although I have not been back to Thailand, a part of my heart will always be with the Khmu, who taught me so many lessons about patience, gratitude, and the joy of living a simple life.

Caring for a young father and his child on our first mission trip to Thailand

Egan playing with a group of Khmu children

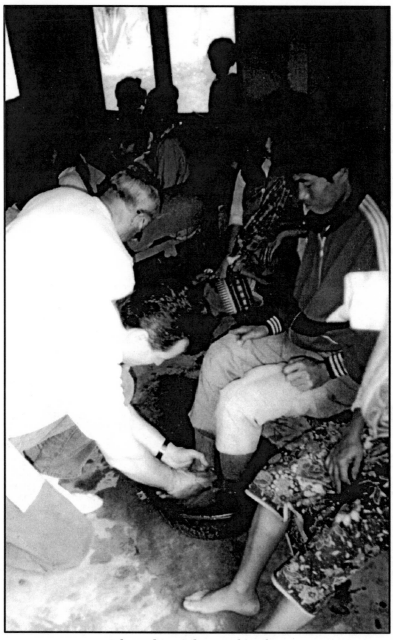

John and Joe Balena washing feet

Sionh's team talking to the Khmu village about a better way of life

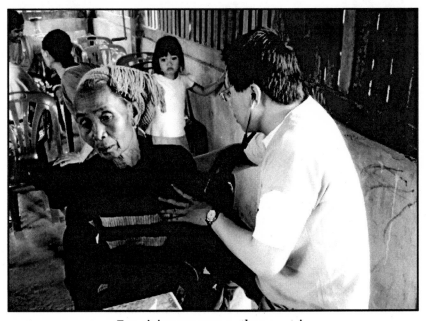

Examining a woman on the 2004 trip

Waiting patiently in line for a medical consultation

Me on the 2004 trip

Weaving thatch for a roof

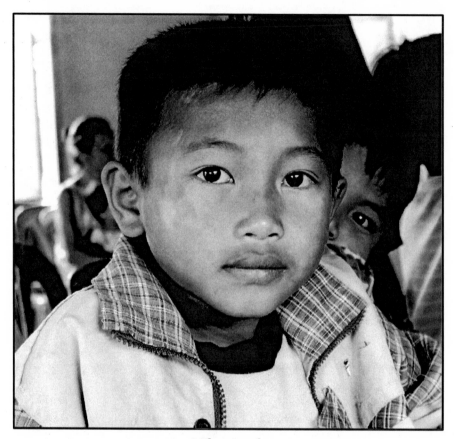

A Khmu youth

The Thief of Memory

Gertrude was in her seventies and had already been with the medical practice for fifteen years when I took it over. She didn't come in very often because she was so healthy, with only a bit of arthritis and some high cholesterol. She maintained a slim figure with regular exercise. Coupled with a short, modern hair cut and a quick wit, one could easily believe she was decades younger than her actual age.

At a routine physical several years ago, Gertrude and her husband Clarence mentioned offhandedly that her memory might not be as sharp as it once was. She was having a harder time finding the right words in conversation. Alzheimer's was a possibility since her mother had Alzheimer's when she was around the same age. Gertrude did not seem overly concerned about the situation; it did not seem to affect her daily life much. I suggested that we could discuss this again when she came back next time.

Six months later, Gertrude and Clarence came back for her follow-up for her regular problems. This time, Clarence was much more concerned with his wife's memory and ability to find words. She called the pharmacy for a med refill and could not remember the word "prescription," keeping the pharmacist on the phone as her mouth worked to say a word she could not find.

More than just finding words, Gertrude was repeating things and asking the same questions over and over. Because her husband handled the household affairs, she didn't have to drive, balance the check book, or perform other activities. It was more her general interactions with Clarence that showed she was not "as sharp as a tack" as she once was. Her writing, once very elegant and legible, had started slanting uphill and getting smaller. Clarence was also worried that his wife might had decreased self confidence and be depressed.

I performed a Mini-Mental Status Exam (MMSE) to evaluate her cognitive function. Gertrude did well with language, understanding, and following commands, but her short-term memory was clearly impaired. She could not spell WORLD backwards or count back from 100 by 7's. Although she could name common objects, she could not recall what she had named after a short period of time. When I asked her to draw a clock that read "a quarter before five," she drew a very small clock on a large sheet of paper that read 3 o'clock instead of what I instructed.

Through my conversation with her, I did not think Gertrude was depressed. I suspected what Clarence was noticing was that Gertrude did not have the vivacity that she previously showed in abundance. Her countenance was more subdued, more flattened. Based on my findings, I confirmed Clarence's suspicion that Gertrude did indeed have moderate Alzheimer's disease. I started her on two different Alzheimer's medicines and asked that they follow up in a month.

When they came back, the couple was very pleased. Gertrude's word finding skills were much better, and she seemed to have more energy than before. She was getting back to her old self. I was glad of her improvement, but I cautioned them about the inexorable course of Alzheimer's.

"Alzheimer's is like a boulder rolling down a hill. Once gravity takes effect, it is a force of nature, and nothing can stop that from happening. Clarence, your wife is going to get worse. Now, medicines can help. Instead of rolling down a steep mountain, I can shallow out the slope, so it becomes more like a gentle hill. I can't stop the boulder, much less push it back up to level ground. But what I can do is buy you another 18 to 24 months of better memory and function. Without the medicines, Gertrude would get much worse much more quickly."

Clarence considered the extra expense of the medicine to be well worth the extra quality time he would have with his wife. Over the next several months, I tried to gradually increase the dose of her medicine. Half way through the titration, Gertrude started developing significant nausea and vomiting. Although this side effect was common, it was usually self-limiting. Gertrude's symptoms, however, would not go away and just got worse. She had no appetite, dropped from an already-petite 116 lbs to 108, and was crying all the time. The couple was forced to stop her medicine.

Over the next year, we worked on trying to find Gertrude the right combinations and dosages of medicines that could improve her memory yet not cause undue side effects. I also managed the other effects of her Alzheimer's. Before her illness, Gertrude was bubbly, sanguine, and the life of the party. As her illness progressed, she lost much of her positive personality. Clarence mentioned a few times that she was argumentative, particularly when she had forgotten something and insisted otherwise. I'm sure it was a daily occurrence, and I held a deep respect for Clarence for the patience he showed to his wife.

During her office visits, Gertrude no longer smiled and cracked jokes. She wore a mask-like facial expression, glassy-eyed and slightly slack jawed. It took her several moments to hear, understand, and respond to questions. Her voice became softer and more monotoned as well. It was clear that her brain was not making all the connections necessary to interact fully with the world around her.

In an effort to make mental connections that were no longer there, Gertrude began hallucinating. She saw family members who were long dead, or she heard people in the house who were not there. She had a time when she forgot where she lived, thinking she was still in the house of her childhood. Gertrude asked Clarence repeatedly when they were going to go home, and had to be told that she was already at home. Of course, that caused her to be belligerent, and Clarence had a difficult time mollifying her.

As her condition progressed, more and more parts of Gertrude's brain were affected by the ravages of Alzheimer's. Her autonomic nervous system stopped running smoothly. Her blood pressure fluctuated tremendously. She stopped having any sort of appetite, and her weight continued to drop. I encouraged Clarence to give her three cans of Ensure Plus a day to get some calories into her.

She also lost her bladder control and became incontinent. I recommended medicine and timed voiding. At three and six AM, Clarence set the alarm to get up and take Gertrude to the bathroom. Apparently, every night was a fight. "I don't need to go! I've already gone!" Gertrude would tell her husband. It took cajoling to get her to the bathroom and empty her bladder. If not, Gertrude would empty her entire bladder contents into the bed. Even adult undergarments were not enough to stop the leak.

As Gertrude's mental capacity worsened, it was clear that Clarence could not continue to take care of his wife by himself. Although they had lived alone for decades, Clarence agreed to move in with his daughter, who was a nurse and could help her mother. They also hired a live-in caretaker to help with domestic tasks. Their daughter lived out of state, so they had Gertrude's medical records transferred to a doctor who was closer to where they now lived. I shook Clarence's hand and put my arm lightly around Gertrude's frail shoulders, wishing the both of them the best.

Gertrude and Clarence taught me so much during their time in my office. I witnessed amazing courage as Gertrude faced the inevitability of her Alzheimer's and what would be a terminal illness. More tragic than cancer, she knew Alzheimer's would rob her of her most precious asset: her quick mind. I saw Clarence extend to Gertrude unconditional love in spite of very difficult circumstances, even when she did not know who he was or what he was doing. Alzheimer's was the ultimate thief, stealing a lifetime of memories one by one, until the barest husk of a person was left. Yet in spite of this, I saw in Gertrude and Clarence indomitable spirits, united by bonds of love and decades of marriage. I do not know if Gertrude is still alive, but I hope that when she gets to the end, she will be able to look back on a life incredibly well lived with a husband and family who love her.

Braille Without Borders

The mission trip to Tibet did not go at all as planned. For months, the team prepared for a research project on the genetic factors of Kashin-Beck Disease, a debilitating arthritic condition affecting ten percent of Tibetans. Although the Chinese ministry of health approved of the project, but when the team arrived, the officials did everything they could to stymie our efforts. As it turned out, the roadblocks the Chinese officials put up became a blessing in disguise. Among many other things, we had a chance to work with Braille Without Borders.

A couple of days before the flight, Mike scheduled a massage from Paul Allen, Connecticut's only blind massage therapist. When Mike mentioned offhandedly that he was going to Tibet, Paul told him, "Then you've got to look for the massage therapy school for the blind that I've heard about." Mike had no particular intention of doing so because he did not know what the itinerary would allow.

Because the Chinese officials would not work with the team, the bulk of us went to the English Club to talk to Tibetans and Chinese and allow them to practice their English skills. As it turned out, when the room broke into small groups, Mike was sitting next to Jampa, a blind Tibetan. Seeing Jampa sparked a memory, and Mike asked him about the massage school for the blind. Amazingly, not only did Jampa know of the school, his sister Keela, who was also blind, was running the school. "I will take you there tomorrow morning," Jampa promised.

Mike told the team about the invitation to visit the school. Carol, a fellow team member, had randomly picked up a book called *My Path Leads to Tibet* at a Half Price Book Store right before leaving for Tibet. The book told the story of how Tibet's first and only school for the blind got started, the very school Jampa was taking Mike to. Mike and Carol recruited two other team members, and the next day, the four of them went to the blind school to meet the kids and learn more.

In the summer of 1997 Sabriye Tenberken, blind herself, travelled within Tibet to investigate the possibility of providing training for Tibetan blind and visually impaired people. In May 1998, she and her partner Paul Kronenberg started the Rehabilitation and Training Centre for the Blind, otherwise known as Braille Without Borders, in Lhasa, Tibet. Armed with the Tibetan Braille script Sabriye had developed in 1992 to help her own study of Tibetology, she and Paul gathered six Tibetan children from all over the region. The children boarded at the school and learned Tibetan, English, Chinese, and Braille, as well as several different vocations, including massage therapy, farming, cheese making, and fiber crafts. Over time, the school grew to house around forty children and young adults.

While visiting the school, Mike heard heartbreaking stories about how the children were treated before arriving at the orphanage. Tashi lost his vision as a child, and his parents sold him off to people who forced him to beg in the streets. When he did not bring in enough money, they tied him to the bed post and beat him. While on the streets literally begging for his life, Tashi heard about the blind school. He found the courage to run away from his owners and went to the school. Although Tashi was of Chinese descent, he at first pretended to be Tibetan because he thought the school only accepted Tibetans. At the school, he learned a wealth of skills to make him a productive member of society. More importantly, he found a family who cared about him.

Many children had similar stories of abuse and neglect. Parents did not know how to deal with handicapped children, and financial circumstances did not allow for the parents to stay home to attend to the children's needs. Many children were trapped in their houses all day until an adult came home from a long day of work. Many were made to beg on street corners. Even for those families who cared for their children, no public social services existed to address the needs of the blind. If not for Braille Without Borders, the children would have spent their lives in abject poverty and complete dependence on family that was ill-equipped to care for them.

The culture they came from did not help their plight. Many of the small villages where the children came from believed that they must be possessed by demons that caused their blindness. Thus, not only the children but the entire family was shunned by the rest of the village. Furthermore, Buddhist tradition taught that the current difficulties in one's life were caused by sins in a past life. Tenzin, another young man at the school, has said that he must have been a terrible person, maybe a murderer, in his past life to deserve being blind in this one. I was raised Buddhist as a child, and much of the Buddhist philosophy of living life in moderation and doing no harm to others I agree with. But it breaks my heart to think that this precious young man felt that he somehow deserved his handicap because of something he did in a previous life.

The four members of the mission team chatted with Keela and the students at the school. They were told that several of the kids had medical problems that could be addressed by our medical team, and so we were asked to come back the next day. Before going back, they were led across town by Tenzin through the busy streets of Lhasa to the massage center, where they all got excellent massages by the blind massage therapists who had graduated from the school. Walking through the city and across eight lanes of traffic would test the memory and courage of anyone, but to experience being led through the twists and turns of the city by a blind person completely from memory must have been impressive indeed.

The following day, I and a group of seven team members went back to the school and met Sabriye and Paul, who had just returned from out of the country. They were very excited to have a physician visit them. We set up a makeshift clinic in the kitchen area and provided medical care for any of the kids and workers who had problems. Most of the children had relatively minor ailments and skin conditions. Sabriye did a phenomenal job caring for the children's physical needs as well as their general education.

However, there were a few children with some serious issues that needed to be addressed. Sabriye asked my opinion on the deplorable case of a young blind woman who was raped multiple times. There was a question of whether she might have contracted HIV. When Sabriye brought this to the Chinese health department, she got the reply, "The girl cannot have HIV because HIV does not exist in China." They refused to test her for the virus. Another young man was coughing and likely had active tuberculosis. Again, the authorities refused to treat him or even test him for TB.

It was generally known that across all sectors of life, including health and medicine, Tibetans received far substandard care compared to the Chinese nationals. I gave Sabriye what advice I could, but the Chinese government staunchly refused to allow any collection of blood samples from any Tibetan. There was little I could do for these two unfortunate young adults.

While the doctors and nurses worked at the medical clinic, several others passed out donated Beanie Babies to the kids. The children examined their gifts with their hands and deduced what animal they received. Seeing the joy on the faces of the children who now had a soft, cuddly "friend" to play with was priceless.

Rachel, a team member who lived five minutes from the beach in Florida, brought a bag of sea shells and passed them out to the kids. She also told them that they could hear the ocean in the sea shells. Unfortunately, only a few of the shells were conch-shaped. Many of them were flat and would not produce that ocean sound. So some of the kids were frustrated, walking around shaking their flat shells, hoping to hear the ocean. When they discovered that not all of the kids had the round shells, those that did walked around to their friends and held up the shells to their ears so that everyone could hear the ocean. The children taught me a valuable lesson of consideration and gift sharing. Their vision might have been lost, but their hearts were fuller than those of most people I know.

Many sighted people would consider blindness as a handicap that would be next to impossible to overcome. Indeed, most of the children at the school had faced nearly insurmountable odds before and during their time at the school. Yet, overcome they did. They spoke not one, but three, languages. They mastered vocations that would be difficult for anyone, much less those who were blind. And they displayed a memory that was nothing short of prodigious.

To prove this point, Sabriye and six blind teenagers climbed the formidable 23,000-foot Lhakpa Ri Mountain, a sister to Mount Everest. The entire adventure was recorded in the documentary *Blindsight*, which won numerous awards and critical acclaim.

Since the beginning of the school, the first set of students recruited by Sabriye have graduated and assumed significant leadership roles in the running of the school and the various vocational programs. It was never Sabriye's intention to remain in Tibet forever. Sabriye and Paul hope to hand the school over to the Tibetan graduates within the next few years and move to India to start a similar school there. As the tag line of *Blindsight* says, "They lost their sight, not their vision."

Denam and Choden with their Beanie Babies

Receiving Beanie Babies

Jampa at the English Club

Keela at Braille Without Borders

Listening to the ocean

Closing the Curtains

Wyns Lee was born to ethnic Chinese parents and grew up in Vietnam. Like any other child, he laughed, played, went to school, and spent time with his parents and siblings. But at fifteen, something started happening to his vision. His eyes were becoming particularly sensitive to sunlight. They were tearing all the time. It took his eyes a long time to adjust going from outside to indoors. All the blinking and squeezing of his eyes were causing headaches. And then Wyns noticed that his vision was getting worse and worse. It was like curtains were being closed, the brightness of the world darkening.

Wyns' parents took him to a doctor. "Your vision isn't *that* bad," he told Wyns. "Here's a shot of medicine. Come back in a week for another shot, and your vision will get better." The doctor continued to give Wyns shots and empty promises, all the while taking as much money as he could from the family. Meanwhile, Wyns' vision continued to deteriorate. Wyns gave up on that doctor and tried another. That doctor diagnosed him with glaucoma. Unfortunately, the doctor was fleeing the country because of the imminent threat of the *Việt Cộng* forces, so he could not do the surgery.

By sixteen, after less than two years of symptoms, Wyns had lost basically all of his vision. In Vietnam, there was no support for the blind. Wyns practically did not leave the house for a year. He could not go to school. He instead listened to the radio, dreaming of leaving Vietnam and going to the U.S. When he did venture out, he encountered youngsters who insulted him and ridiculed him. Every now and then, he felt a rock hit him.

But there was nothing he could do, so he did his best to ignore the taunts. Although those insults and rocks did not hurt him much physically, they hurt his spirit tremendously.

By God's grace, Wyns and his family were able to flee Vietnam when the communists took over. In 1983, when Wyns was seventeen, he and his family came to the U.S. When he arrived, he spoke no English, he was blind, and he did not know Braille. Wyns had three eye surgeries to salvage any portion of his vision, but his optic nerves were too damaged. After the multiple surgeries, the only thing the doctors could do was spare a small corner of his left eye to sense some changes in brightness. The rest of the vision was completely gone.

Although Wyns was seventeen, he had not had any schooling for years. He was put immediately into the ninth grade. To facilitate his education, he had an English-Vietnamese bilingual tutor. At the same time, he studied Braille. Because he was older when he started learning, and English was still a language he was trying to master, it took Wyns a whole year to learn Braille.

Wyns stayed in high school for all four years. Everything was much more difficult for him than for other students. Subjects took him longer to learn than other people because he had to struggle with not just the reading material but also the combination of the language barrier and his blindness. All quizzes and tests had to be sent out for translation into Braille. Wyns then read and responded in Braille. His answers then had to be transcribed back into written format for the teachers to grade. If the subject or test required an essay response, Wyns sat with a transcriptionist who wrote down what he said. Regular school work and homework were difficult, but standardized tests were especially challenging. His SAT took 8 hrs, almost triple the usual time.

When Wyns finished high school, he applied to Manchester Community College. Because of the extra time he needed for studying and tests, it took him five years to finish his associate degree in computer science. In 1992, his father died, and Wyns went through a period of depression. He stopped pursuing a bachelor's degree at that point and never went back to school.

To find some social activities and help him snap out of his depression, Wyns volunteered for the National Federation of the Blind (NFB). On occasion, Wyns went to the office for several hours and helped stuff envelopes. As he spent time at the NFB office, he made friends and felt good that he was making a bit of a difference in people's lives.

One day, Vichhyka Shelto, a social worker from Catholic Family Services, called the NFB. She was looking for some information and help for a client of hers. A Vietnamese woman who was blind had just immigrated to the U.S. The woman could not speak any English, and the worker had no idea what resources were available for the blind.

That day Wyns happened to be volunteering at the office stuffing envelopes when Vichhyka called. Wyns overheard the conversation and thought there couldn't be a more perfect match for this girl. He immediately agreed to volunteer his time to do home visits. Over the next several months, Wyns helped translate for her and introduced her to the social services available to the blind. Because of Wyns' help, the woman improved her English and developed the necessary skills to handle her disability.

Because of the success of helping the blind woman, Wyns continued his relationship with Vichhyka. Vichhyka spoke Mien and Cambodian, while Wyns helped translate for the Vietnamese and Cantonese refugees. What they found was that the various Asian immigrants had very little support from state and local governments to access social services and integrate into society. In the 1970's during the influx of refugees from the

Vietnam War, immigrants were given thirty-six months of public assistance and free language training. Now, the time has been shortened to about six to eight months. Every minute counted to help immigrants understand and access available services as soon as possible.

More than just financial services and language skills, Vichhyka and Wyns identified a tremendous need for mental health counseling. Post-traumatic Stress Disorder, depression, and anxiety were all too common. Furthermore, it was not culturally acceptable to talk about one's feelings or discuss details of domestic violence or neglect. The language barrier isolated many immigrants, and even years later, many did not have a basic working knowledge of English. Because of these emotional and social stresses, alcoholism, compulsive gambling, and domestic violence were all too common.

Vichhyka and Wyns addressed these challenges through several avenues. First, just the fact that they were Asian broke down barriers to communication. Between the two of them, they could speak five languages. This meant that they could communicate with the clients in their native tongue, thereby removing the greatest barrier to care. Also, being Asian, they understood the cultural sensitivities and appropriate behavior of the population. For example, they bowed to the clients and showed respect for the elderly. Vichhyka was a licensed clinical social worker and was qualified to provide professional counseling for her clients. Wyns was intimately familiar with the services available for handicapped individuals because of his own personal struggles.

In 1996, Vichhyka founded the non-profit organization Asian Family Services (AFS) to address the physical, social, and emotional needs of the Asian community. Wyns continued to work with Vichhyka and played a major role in the organization as an assistant. AFS recruited more multilingual workers and provided counseling, case management, psychiatric services, medication management, English classes, and preparation for citizenship. To expand their reach even further, in 2007 AFS merged with the Community Renewal Team, the largest non-profit provider of human services in Connecticut.

In June 2000, Wyns was sworn in as an AmeriCorp/VISTA volunteer, primarily doing his service through AFS. For two years, Wyns donated 35 hours a week, working as a community educator responsible for scheduling, interpreting, planning and reviewing programs and activities, managing the extensive database, and providing client advocacy. Because of Wyns' selfless acts of caring, he has been presented with multiple awards through the years. In 2006, he was nominated for Outstanding Naturalized Immigrant and received Connecticut's Immigrant Award.

In my own office, Wyns has always been a breath of fresh air. He is constantly agreeable and in a good mood. He is quick to laugh and treats me, the staff, and the other patients in the office with kindness and respect. He also has an amazing memory. As he checks out and the nurse gives him his next appointment, he never has to get a reminder card or even write it down. He just remembers the appointment and always shows up for it.

Wyns has faced numerous difficulties in his life. He did not have many family members to help him through his blindness, and he had to find most of the community resources himself. When he lost his sight, he had to relearn everything. He had to learn how to use his cane, navigate the bus routes, keep track of money by folding each denomination differently, label everything in Braille, cook for himself, and a million other tasks sighted people take for granted. Wyns' goal has always been to be self reliant and not dependent on other people for his basic needs. Not only has he accomplished this goal for himself, but he has used his knowledge to help countless other people find independence as well. Wyns has said to me,

"Life gives you difficulties, but you try the best you can, that's it." It seems Wyn's best has been pretty impressive.

I asked Wyns what he remembers from his time when he was sighted. He responded, "I remember the trees, the grass, and some colors. I also remember learning how to ride a Honda motorcycle. Now, I can still ride the motorcycle, but I can't see where I'm going, so I guess I better not ride." As always, Wyns has a gift for making me laugh.

Wyns as a young man

Wyns at work

Wyns in 2013

Responding to a Call

One day, I received an urgent company-wide e-mail from the office manager of a busy multi-doctor practice a few towns over. Several decades ago, the practice was started by the Smiths, a husband and wife physician couple. He took care of the adults, while she saw the children. Over time they grew the practice, adding both patients and doctors, developing the office into one of the cornerstone practices in their town. Everything was going well, and the Smiths planned to hand over their leadership roles to younger partners and retire in a few years.

All of their plans changed in one terrible moment. Mrs. Smith was stepping over the dog gate at the top of the stairs when her foot caught in the fence. She tumbled down the stairs and heard a snap. She had broken her neck. Luckily, her husband was home and heard the commotion. He rushed out of the bedroom and looked down, finding his wife at the bottom of the stairs, her head at an odd angle to her body. She was struggling weakly but was unable to move her legs. Mr. Smith immediately called 911, and in minutes, Mrs. Smith was transported to the ER trauma center.

While in the emergency room, Mrs. Smith's condition grew worse. Her speech was getting hoarse, and she started losing what little function she had of her upper limbs. A stat CT scan of her neck revealed that swelling was damaging her throat and spinal cord. To protect her airway and decrease any further movement that might worsen her condition, the doctors paralyzed her with medicine and put her on a ventilator. The situation quickly went from treating her injury to fighting to save her life.

Mr. Smith immediately dropped his patient load and spent every moment day and night by his wife's side. As he took a leave of absence to help her, both the adult and pediatric practices were short a doctor. Although the pediatricians could rearrange their schedule to absorb the overflow, the adult doctors were already flat-out busy. The office sent out an urgent e-mail request through the whole company to see if anyone would help out. Out of almost 200 providers throughout the state, I was the only one who responded. Although I was already busy in my own practice, I rearranged my schedule. One day a week, while my staff stayed in the office and got paperwork done, I went to Palisades Family Practice to help with overflow patients.

I was greeted very warmly by the doctors and staff at Palisades. They were all surprised that I was the only one who was willing to help. After all, I was lending my assistance, but I wasn't doing it for free. They were paying me a fair wage for my services. I quickly learned the office's work flows and integrated myself into their daily schedule.

At first, I saw all the acute office visits, freeing up room for the other doctors to see established patients. Over time, I developed my own small set of patients who liked my practice style and planned their visits to coincide with the Thursdays that I would be working. I tried to treat the office like my own, bringing patients back to the exam room and doing the procedures that I would normally do in my own office. Apparently, this did not go over very well with the nursing staff. I was derailing their normal routines. My requests for blood draws and injections were balked at. My suggestions of adding minor office surgical procedures were met with, "That's just not how we do it here." A few months of friction brought about a meeting between me, the senior physicians, and the office manager. I was told to stop all the procedures I was trying to do and just concentrate on seeing the patient for the problems they presented with.

I was incensed at first. My office was doing very well financially, and my patients appreciated the care I gave. In my office, my decisions were the law of the land. Now, at Palisades, I had *nurses* telling me what I could or could not do, and then "tattling" to the doctors when they didn't get their way. Well, if they didn't want me to work, then that was just fine and dandy with me. They were paying me by the hour, after all. I would do just the minimum necessary and skate on by. What would it matter to me if the practice did not do well financially, as long as I got a pay check?

I quickly realized, though, that I had the wrong attitude about the whole situation. I was there to help Palisades, after all. Yes, it was a job that I got paid to do, but it was more than that. Trying to do the least work possible because my feelings were hurt just compounded the frustration and resentment. I had to learn to give up my agenda, even if it was to help the practice, and operate within the work flows that the office had long established. I needed to work to the best of my ability, not for them, but for me, because I'm a person who finds great satisfaction in a job well done. A busy work day helps make the time go more quickly, and sitting around doing nothing is really no fun.

As my perspective changed, my outlook and countenance improved as well. I got along much better with the staff. They supported my fund raising efforts for my medical mission trips by buying candy bars and flower bulbs. One woman donated hundreds of Beanie Babies that she had collected during the Beanie Baby craze. They were in mint condition, including the plastic tag protectors. We promptly ripped off all the tags before stuffing them into our duffels. The Beanie Babies were given to children at Braille Without Borders, the Dickey Orphanage, and the various villages we visited in Tibet.

One day, I went out to the front desk during a lull in the patient schedule. Next to Candice was an entire plate of scrumptious-looking cupcakes. It was well past mid-morning, so I was already hungry. "Oh, can I have one?" I asked, as I reached out my hand.

"No, you can't," Candice said tersely as she looked at me from the corner of her eye. I quickly snatched my hand back and walked away, nonplussed.

Later in the day, Candice came to find me. "Dr. Han, I'm so sorry about earlier. I hope I didn't hurt your feelings. Those cupcakes are from Mrs. Johnson. She means well, but all of her baked goods are just terrible. We wait until she goes home, and then we throw her stuff out. We just have never had the heart to tell her that we don't really like any of her food. She's the sweetest person, but a terrible cook. I just wanted to save you from having an upset stomach for the rest of the day."

That situation really taught me that at times, outward appearances and actions might not always explain underlying motivations. On the surface, it seemed to me that Candice was being selfish and rude. It was only after understanding more of the situation that I discovered she was looking after my best interests. I realized that this is often the case. Before jumping to any hasty conclusions about people or situations, I should investigate further. Chances were good that everything would make more sense once I had more information.

For two years, I went to Palisades once a week to help out. During that time, Mrs. Smith made a slow but steady improvement. She spent several months in the ICU on the ventilator, several more months in the hospital after that, and then transitioned to a hospital rehab facility. She had 24-hour nursing care, physical therapy, and occupational therapy. Eventually, she came home with close supervision. It seemed like for the better part of a year, Mrs. Smith was in one facility or another. Finally, she was able to go home with her husband, who took attentive care of her.

Mr. Smith's leave of absence also lasted about a year. Mostly to give himself a break from the daily routines at the house, he came back to work for two half-days a week. He happened to be working on Thursdays as well, so I occasionally asked about his wife's progress without being too obtrusive. Several months after her accident, she was again able to breathe on her own and swallow, so she could come off the ventilator and gastric tube.

Mrs. Smith also regained some function of the fingers on her right hand. This was a major milestone in her rehabilitation because she was then able to operate an electric wheelchair and regain a modicum of independence. The occupational therapist worked on some contraption to allow her to feed herself, but I don't know if it was successful. Even with all of these significant improvements, Mrs. Smith had to rely on someone to help with the most basic activities that most people take for granted: bathing, toileting, teeth brushing, grooming, and dressing. Of course this did not touch on shopping, going to her doctor visits, or any other general activities of living.

Palisades Family Practice had a tradition of thanking all of the doctors, nurses, and staff for their hard work for the year by hosting a dinner event. Small gifts were passed out, groups of people did funny skits, and words of thanks and encouragement were given. But the most memorable event of the evening was seeing Mrs. Smith come through the door in her electric wheelchair, her husband by her side. She was much thinner than before, with tired-looking eyes due to the late hour. However, her face was radiant, and she wore an elegant black dress that sparkled as she wheeled herself around the room greeting everyone like an accomplished hostess.

Mrs. Smith's accident made me reflect on both the frailty of life and the indomitable spirit. The poet Robert Burns wrote, "The best laid schemes of mice and men/ Go often awry." Their whole lives, the Smiths did all the right things and had their plans all set up for retirement. Literally, one missed step changed the paths of their lives forever. Once that tragedy struck, the Smiths had a choice to make. Either they were going to give up and become bitter at the terrible turn of events, or they were going to tackle head-on the challenges life had thrown at them. Although I am sure they each had times when life became overwhelming, overall it seemed they were doing fairly well. I am honestly not sure if I could maintain as positive an attitude as they have if I were faced with the same set of circumstances.

Both the Smiths and my time at Palisades taught me great life lessons. I learned the necessity of more humility. I improved my skills as a team player. I fought for things that were essential and let go of things that were not. Mostly, I found joy in helping out someone who really needed the help. I can only hope that if I ever encounter such an incredible life challenge, someone will stand by my side when I need the help myself.

Srafa Aboano and Ekumfi Abuakwa

In late 2011, Eric Thepsiri, a sophomore at the University of Connecticut, asked me to consider joining his group on a medical mission trip to Ghana, Africa in May 2012. Eric had gone with me on previous trips to Mexico and Honduras, and so I knew his competence and dedication well. I agreed to join the team as the group's physician.

Eric introduced me to UConn's chapter of Global Brigades (GB), the world's largest student-led global health and sustainable development organization. UConn GB had sent teams to Honduras before, but this trip was the first one to Ghana. I worked with Kevin Haines, then-president of the club, as well as the rest of the club's leadership to prepare for this medical brigade.

Through the following months, we worked on the myriad logistics for the trip. The students raised money for their individual trip expenses as well as funds to buy medicines and supplies. I requested medication samples from my colleagues and brought large trash bags of meds to the club's weekly meetings for the students to consolidate and inventory. We held web conferences with in-country advisors to prepare us for the trip. The team got shots and medication for malaria prophylaxis. We planned as much as we could, and on May 8, our team of 28 students and four medical providers started our day-long journey to West Africa.

After twenty hours of travelling, we landed at the airport in Accra, the capital of Ghana. We stepped off the plane and walked the short distance across the tarmac to the airport entrance. The large green sign read, "*Akwaaba!* Welcome to Ghana." The country is situated on the hump of the West African coast just north of the equator, so even at mid-morning when we disembarked, the air was already hot and muggy. By the time the team got through the several-hour process of immigration, baggage claim, and introductions to the in-country staff, everyone was ready for the air-conditioned bus ride to Weda Lodge.

Weda was a two-hour drive west of Accra and one and a half hours from the community the team was going to be working with, Srafa Aboano. The lodge was on top of a hill, providing breathtaking views of the ocean on one side and lush greenery on the other. With large dorm rooms and communal spaces, it was the perfect team-building location.

The team spent the first day getting to know one another better while sorting medicines for the upcoming clinics. Then the village invited the team for the welcoming ceremony. Children surrounded the buses even before they came to a stop. Each person getting off the bus immediately had both their hands clutched by children in dirty clothes and face-splitting grins with every white tooth flashing. Drummers led the way as the procession of several hundred people carried our team through the village.

We ended at the central square where tents had been erected to provide shade for the American team. The Ghanaians, however, seemed unaffected by the relentless sun as they enjoyed their favorite activity: dancing. From the youngest child to the elderly, these people seemed to have an innate grace and sense of rhythm as they gyrated to the *azonto*, a national dance involving leg shaking and fist pumping. We were invited to participate multiple times in the dancing, and we did our best until we were wilting from the heat and our exertions. Our team then introduced ourselves individually, and the chief of the village, dressed in ceremonial *kente* cloth, officially welcomed us to the village. By the end of the two-hour welcome ceremony, everyone's shirts were plastered down with sweat.

Because of Global Brigades' focus on partnership with the community and sustainable development, instead of diving right into medical clinics, the team spent a day assessing the needs of the village. Splitting into small groups, each with a translator, team members walked through the village, met with people in their homes, and asked them what they thought were their most pressing concerns. The villagers cited the need for a clean water supply, dealing with parasites, difficult farming, and more. In this way, rather than a foreign team coming in and dictating what needed changing, the villagers took responsibility for assessing what their issues were that the team could help address.

When we did start the medical clinics, the patients I saw were some of the sickest of all the mission trips I had been on. Children were brought in by their parents, their bodies struck by a particular form of malnutrition called Kwashiorkor. The lack of protein and imbalanced amount of carbohydrates caused stick-thin limbs, protuberant bellies with large livers, and brown, brittle hair. Chronic parasitic infestations contributed to the malnutrition and caused anemia, with eyelids a pale white instead of the normal rosy hue. Patients presented with old broken bones that were not properly set, causing permanent disability. Open wounds were not cleansed and were allowed to fester. The flies which were attracted to the wounds were innumerable. The moment one's hand stopped waving the flies away, they landed again. So, the villagers allowed the flies to crawl around, further contributing to infections.

I also saw tropical diseases I would never encounter in the U.S., like elephantiasis, caused by *filariae* worms burrowing through lymphatic channels of an infected person, causing horrible swelling of the affected limb. Patients also presented with malaria, leprosy, and a host of other tropical conditions. These diseases I had only read about in medical school and seen pictures of, and now patients were in front of me afflicted with these diseases and hoping for a chance of treatment. I treated the conditions I could, referred some patients to regional facilities for more intensive care, and consoled those with conditions I could not reverse.

I also treated patients with tragic stories during those clinic days. One woman was twelve years old when both her parents died. She was "taken in" by an older man who impregnated her. Before she was twenty, she had already had multiple children. In an even worse situation, a young girl of nine was brought in by her grandmother. She had been savagely raped the year before. Since the attack, the child could no longer hold her urine or stool. I told the grandmother that I needed to examine her. When the grandmother tried to lie the child down and lift her dress up, the girl became terrified. She screamed and fought uncontrollably, and then she went completely limp like a rag doll. Her exam revealed what I had feared. Her anatomy was ravaged, with fistulae, unnatural connections, between her bladder and colon to her female parts. After seeing what was done to her, I experienced the strongest burning anger against a person I had ever had. For the whole previous year, the girl told her family that she did not know who had done this to her. After the tender care our team showed her, she revealed that her attacker was actually a man in a nearby village, but she had been afraid to tell anyone. We reported the case to the staff of Global Brigades as well as authorities, who promised to follow up on the allegations.

Around 850 patients had their physical needs addressed during our clinic days. Many had arthritis from long days of backbreaking labor. Others had chronic conditions like high blood pressure or diabetes that were not treated. Everyone received vitamins to replenish what the parasites had taken. Quite a few patients had stories of diminished quality of life due to a lack of access to adequate medical care.

More important than the medications we handed out, we provided education on health and hygiene. Simple concepts like only drinking purified water, washing one's hands, and taking steps to minimize the spread of infection were all new to these people. For the farmers, we taught better bending and lifting techniques as well as stretching exercises to save their backs. A group of students worked with children, teaching them the importance of flossing and brushing, while the dental team extracted teeth that were too far gone. The team had raised funds to buy Life Straws, household water filtration devices that can provide a five-member family clean drinking water for three years. These Life Straws were sold to villagers at 10% of their value, making them much more affordable. Long after the medicines are gone, the education the villagers received will endure and help improve their overall quality of life.

For the students, the brigade provided invaluable experience regarding the various aspects of medical care. Every student rotated through the triage station, pharmacy, doctor consultation, and public education. Some also spent time in the dental or OB/GYN stations. These college students saw more patients in one week of clinics than many medical students see in two years. For some, it affirmed their calling to the medical field. Overall, the brigade gave all the students a much bigger world view and a passion for helping the underserved at home and abroad. In particular, Kevin and his friend and co-leader Kyle Putman decided to apply for positions with Global Brigades as in-country advisors in Ghana. Because of the incredible success of their leadership, they were both accepted to a year-long internship.

The following year, while Kevin and Kyle helped other schools from around the world plan for trips to Ghana, Eric was overwhelmingly elected as president of the club. Another team was formed, and in May 2013, I again joined UConn GB for its trip to Ghana. Some of the 32 students were veterans of the first trip, but for most, this trip was their first experience doing medical mission work.

For this brigade, our team was assigned to the community Ekumfi Abuakwa. In contrast to Srafa Aboano, which had never had a brigade before ours, Abuakwa had two previous brigades come through. Thus, the people were a bit healthier. Also, while Aboano had only a depression in the ground collecting contaminated water as their sole water source, Abuakwa was situated by a stream. It was not big and fairly muddy, but it was better than standing water.

Again after the opening ceremony and requisite hours of dancing in the hot sun, the team set up the clinic. The community outreach revealed joint pains and infections as the most common issues, and we certainly saw much of those during the clinics. But this mission trip provided its own share of difficult stories. A young boy was brought into the clinic, his gait revealing a weakness on his left side. The mother told the story of how some thieves with guns had come to the village two years ago when the boy was six. The next day, during a re-enactment of the commotion, the gun accidentally went off, striking the boy in his right eyebrow and going through the back of his skull. Miraculously, the boy survived, but the injury had damaged the left side of his body, causing loss of motor control. We had to tell the mother there was nothing we could do to restore his neurological function.

Situations during this brigade helped prove how anyone and everyone could play a vital role to help bring healing to others. During a conversation with Omar Ghannam, he told me that as a chemical engineering major, he did not feel like he had as much to contribute to the team as the pre-med majors could. I listed his strengths and assured him he was indispensable, but Omar remained skeptical. The next afternoon, Omar joined my small group as we headed into the village to do house calls for those too ill to get to the clinic site at the top of the hill. An old man was at the first house we came to. He had pencil-thin legs that clearly could not support his weight. He had to move around by sitting on the floor and scooting on his rump with sandals on his hands.

The man came out to the front step. He told us his story about how he lost the strength in his legs six years ago and it was worsening. After a careful exam, I had some bad news to give. The man had symptoms consistent with amyotrophic lateral sclerosis, Lou Gehrig's disease. I told the translators his poor prognosis, and they were reluctant to inform him. The man could see the concern on our faces and deduced it was not good news. He wanted to know, however bad it was, so the translators told him. He accepted the news with stoicism.

I then moved from my squatting position and sat beside him. I said, "I have no medicines to give you back the strength in your legs. But I could offer someone to pray for you. Do you follow any particular religion? Are you Christian or Muslim?"

"I am Muslim," the man replied through the translator. This was unusual, because the village was predominantly Christian.

"I have a member of my team who is Muslim," I told him. "Would you like him to pray for you?" He nodded his head. I pointed with my arm to Omar, standing with the small group of students and the two translators. "My team member is right here.

"Omar, would you consider praying for this man?" I asked.

Omar grinned nervously and said, "Yeah, I guess so." He sat on the man's left side as I sat on the right. Omar put his hands out, palms and fingers facing up in a gesture of supplication. He then gave a *du'a* and prayed in Arabic, "*'As'alu Allah al 'azim rabbil 'arshil azim an yashifika.*"

(I ask Allah, the Mighty, the Lord of the Mighty Throne, to cure you.) As Omar continued his prayer, the man murmured assent after each sentence. After the prayer, Omar and the man held each other's hands and said thank you to each other.

I turned to the man and said, *"Madase,"* *thank you* in Fanti. And then I said, *"Salaam alaikum,"* *peace be to you* in Arabic. We took pictures together and left him smiling on his front step. As we walked away, I commented to Omar how there was no one else on our team who could have done what he just did for that man. What were the chances that Omar would happen to join us for that jaunt through the village, and that he would be uniquely qualified to provide what the man needed the most?

Throughout the week, the team addressed the various needs of Abuakwa. At the same time, we took care of one another. As a 24-hour stomach bug raced through most of the team, people got sick and were cared by those who were well. Students felt comfortable sharing their more personal issues as well as raising some of the difficult questions of life during evening free time. I had a chance to mentor the students, not just in medicine but by being honest and real with them regarding my strengths and faults.

Ultimately, the people in Abuakwa and in Aboano the previous year were the greatest teachers. They had little health and fewer possessions, yet they danced in joy for what they did have. They bore great burdens on their heads and did not complain. They showed such wonderful gratitude for just a bit of medicine and a small prayer. They lived together in one village as Christians, Muslims, and animists, and yet they all seemed to get along.

Although I and the rest of the UConn team went to Ghana to provide a service, we were the ones more richly blessed. It is this consistent truth that drives me to continue to do medical mission work around the world.

A Journey of Discovery 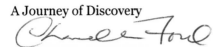 Srafa Aboano and Ekumfi Abuakwa

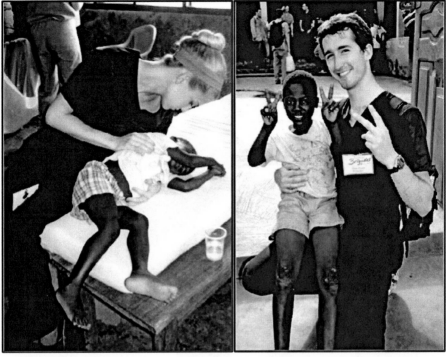

Chandler Ford and sick child, Ekumfi Abuakwa   Tom Presti, Ekumfi Abuakwa

David Ryan and Anthony Josie at Triage station, Ekumfi Abuakwa

Kyle J. Putman

Kyle Putman taking notes at Triage station, Srafa Aboano

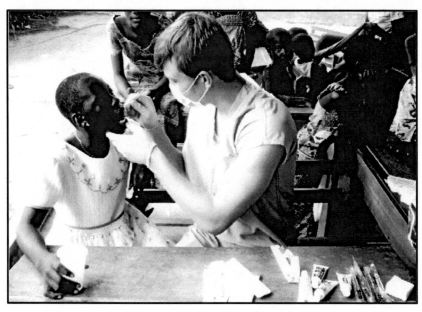

Eugene Mironets applying fluoride, Srafa Aboano

Left to Right: Brittany Duffy, Shannon Hayes, Kyle Putman, Michelle Whelan, Kreshnik Jusufi, Jordan Billings. Welcome ceremony at Ekumfi Abuakwa

Steven Graf. Welcome ceremony, Ekumfi Abuakwa

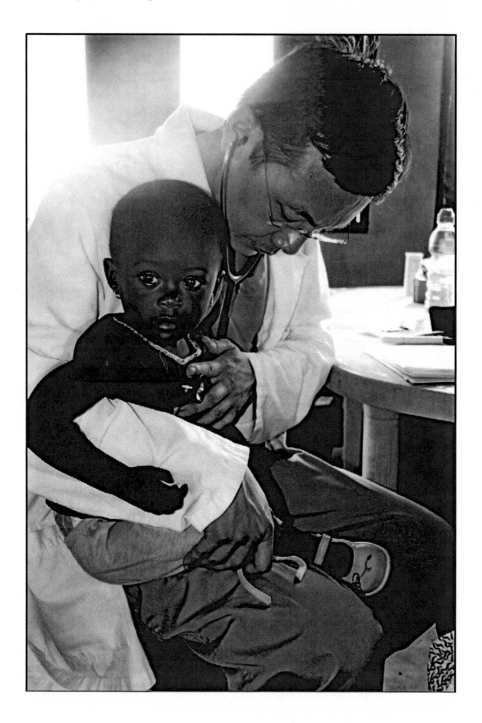

Laughter is the Best Medicine

In medical school I had my obstetrics rotation at Ben Taub Community Hospital in Houston, where the vast majority of the women delivering there were Mexican and could only speak Spanish. Like most mornings, the entire team of residents and medical students got together for hospital rounds, seeing patients who had been admitted to the service the previous night.

Walking into a room and seeing a dark-skinned woman, the chief resident immediately began asking the woman in her best broken Spanish what brought her to the hospital and when her due date was.

The woman listened intently without saying a word. And then she said in perfect English, "I have no idea what you just said. I'm from India."

****

"Are you still sexually active?" I asked Sterling as part of my standard set of questions for a complete physical.

"Are you kidding? I'm eighty-four years old. Those times are long gone."

"Sex doesn't have to end at any age, Sterling," I rebuffed.

He replied, "At this point, I'd get more thrills from a nice dinner, and it would last longer too."

****

On a medical mission trip to Venezuela, I was trying my hand at seeing patients without an interpreter, relying instead upon my three years of Spanish that ended in tenth grade. One of my patients that afternoon was an infant brought in by her mother. The mother said that the child's skin was dry and she seemed to scratch at it often. Upon examination, the child clearly had atopic dermatitis, a condition of dry, sensitive skin. The best treatment is the use of moisturizers and gentle soap. So, I told the mother in my best Spanish, "Lava tu bebé en sopa suave."

The mother looked at me quizzically. "Sopa?" She asked.

"Sí, sopa. Sopa suave," I replied. It was clear that I was not getting my point across. So, I gave in and enlisted the help of one of the interpreters. I explained the situation, the diagnosis, and the treatment, saying that I told the mother to wash her child in gentle soap, "sopa."

The interpreter started laughing. "Sopa isn't soap. It's *soup!*"

Well, I didn't try working without an interpreter for quite a while after that.

****

During medical school, I served as a Vietnamese-English translator. As anyone who is multilingual can attest, it is sometimes difficult to translate things without a subtle yet dramatic shift in meaning.

I was asked to translate for a woman who was going for surgery and needed general anesthesia. I wanted to say, "The doctors are going to give you this medicine, and it will put you to sleep." I told her in Vietnamese, *"Bác sĩ sẽ cho cô thuốc mê, để cô ngủ luôn."* Well, the woman clearly did not get my drift.

Later in the day, I happened to talk to my mother and explained the situation and what I said. My mother said, "Son, you told her, 'The doctors are going to give you medicine to put you to sleep for good.'"

Oops.

****

On my way out of Trinidad from a medical mission trip, I was stopped at the airport X-ray machine. The security officer was a black man, at least 6'4", with shoulders a mile wide and biceps bigger than my thigh. "Sir, I need to see what's in your duffel bag," he said in a deep gravelly voice.

Shoot! He probably saw the Trinidad coke bottle I was trying to smuggle out. I opened my bag and took it out. "Is this what you're looking for?" He waved his hands to keep on going. Puzzled, I continued to pull out the contents one by one. I took out my stethoscope, my otoscope, my toiletry bag. Soon, all I had left were dirty socks and underwear.

"Alright, that's fine, you can go." He motioned for me to repack my bag.

Now I was curious. What was he looking for? "Sir, was there something I had that you were concerned about?"

The officer pointed to my otoscope. It was a hefty piece of equipment, with a rechargeable battery in a metal sleeve. Now it made sense to me. He probably couldn't see through the metal and wanted to make sure I was not bringing a weapon or explosives onto the plane. I could not have been far from the truth.

He told me, "I saw that metal cylinder and thought it was a dildo. I wanted to see what it looked like."

****

Medical students routinely rotate through my practice. It gives them the opportunity to see primary care lived out on a daily basis, and it forces me to keep up with the basic science I would otherwise neglect.

Usually, either I or the medical student will ask the patient what brings her into the office, and then we examine the patient together. I will take one side as the medical student stands on the other side, and we both listen to the lungs. Since there is only one heart, I will listen first, and then the student follows.

On this particular visit for a physical, things were moving along smoothly until I got to the heart exam. As I was listening to her heart, I heard a very loud, "Thump, thump!" Startled, I continued listening, and there it was again. "Thump, thump!" Thinking the patient was having some sort of heart arrhythmia, I took off my stethoscope to inform her.

It was at that point I realized the medical student, in an effort to be efficient, had begun the neurological exam. While I was listening to the heart, he was tapping on her knees.

****

A number of my patients are Spanish speaking, and I do my best to speak both Spanish and English with them, a mélange of two languages I affectionately term "Spanglish."

During the final part of a complete physical for Pedro, one of my older Puerto Rican patients, I told him I needed him to drop his pants for me to do the "turn your head and cough routine" and examine his "serpiente grande," his big snake.

"Doctór," he laughingly replied, "Mi serpiente es grande, pero se murió." (My snake might be big, but it's dead.)

I thought that was so funny that, with his permission, I went out to the waiting room and told Pedro's wife—also my patient—what he had just said. She cackled and said, "It's true!"

****

In my third year of medical school, I participated in a medical mission trip to Venezuela. I confided in my attending that I was afraid I would make a fool of myself in front of an attending physician or a patient.

"Oh, don't worry, it'll happen," he told me. "Let me tell you one of mine.

"I was post-call after staying up all night delivering babies during my residency. The next day, I had a full schedule of women to see in the clinic. While I was listening to one woman's heart, I closed my eyes to better focus on her heart. That's when I fell asleep with my stethoscope pressed to her chest. I didn't wake up until she said, 'Doctor, is there anything wrong with my heart? You've been listening to it for a very long time.'"

****

François was an elderly French Canadian who had been coming to the office long before I inherited the practice from my step-father. We were having our routine three-month visit, and Francois was detailing his multiple medical complaints.

In the middle of the conversation, he stopped mid sentence and interjected, "Doctor, I know they call this 'the golden years,' but the only thing golden about it is my urine."

INSIGHT

"Once I knew only darkness and stillness... my life was without past or future... but a little word from the fingers of another fell into my hand that clutched at emptiness, and my heart leaped to the rapture of living."

~Helen Keller

Perception

In his eighties, Isaac Silverstein had not gone to a physician in several years before coming to my office. I'm not even sure how he chose my office as a place to establish a medical home. My first impression of Mr. Silverstein was that he looked like Mr. Magoo. He was short and overweight, with a band of short gray hair around his head and a bald pate, squinty wizened eyes, and hanging jowls that wiggled as he talked. He was also extremely hard of hearing, in spite of the hearing aids he was wearing. I had to raise my voice by several decibels and speak directly into his ear for him to make out what I was saying.

Isaac's initial complaint was dizziness, along with a pounding in his head. He told me that both were significantly worsened by his neighbors in the apartment complex. They were constantly yelling at him, insulting him, and telling him to get out of his apartment. It happened at all hours of the day and night, and he couldn't sleep at all. Furthermore, although he was Jewish, his neighbors insisted on preaching Christianity to him, which really bothered him. They kept telling him, "You gotta go to Jesus! Just go to Jesus!"

Isaac was very distraught over all the things he had to face. On top of his belligerent neighbors, his terrible hearing, and his relatively poor health, he also had to care for his daughter, who had significant physical and mental disabilities. He went into great detail about all the things he had to contend with in life, and how it really brought him down. In short, Isaac was a sourpuss. Still, I honestly felt terrible for the man, who had to endure so much abuse from the people around him.

But my entire perspective of Isaac changed in an instant. As Isaac continued to relate his woes with his neighbors, he exclaimed, "I can hear them yelling at me right now!"

His sentence stopped me dead in my tracks. "Mr. Silverstein," I asked. "Did you say that you can hear your neighbors right now, yelling at you? You can't even hear me well, and I'm standing less than a foot from you. Do you realize that you are many miles away from your apartment right now?"

"Yes! Isn't that terrible?" He responded. "They yell at me all the time, trying to get me to move out of my apartment. I think they want more room for their kids. Do you know, I don't even think they're married! Not only that, but I swear they must have bugged my apartment with some sort of fancy devices. They say to me, 'Isaac, are you doing such-and-such?' And you know what? They're always right! They're watching me all the time! It's creepy!"

As Isaac was telling me all of these things, I had to completely reassess the entire office visit through the lenses of this new information. It was obvious that Isaac was very distraught over his perceived circumstance, but did he have the insight to see his issues were self-fabricated? Would he be willing to follow my recommendations? I wrote a prescription for an antipsychotic, and I sent him to the audiologist for the ringing in his ears. I asked that he return in a week or two to go over the audiology results and talk about the voices he was hearing.

Several hours after the office visit, Mr. Silverstein stormed back into the office. "I looked up that medicine you gave me, Doctor. That medicine is for crazy people. I'm not crazy! My daughter might be crazy, but I'm not crazy!" I tried to encourage him to trust me and take the medicine, but he obstinately refused. He did not have any problems. His neighbors were the ones with the problems. He just wanted something to help with the pounding in his head and something to help him sleep through all the racket they were making. When I assured him the medicine would help do those things, he wouldn't hear any of it.

I finally had to tell Mr. Silverstein that I was treating him the best way I knew how. Although I couldn't make him take the medicine, I sincerely hoped he would trust me enough to take the medicine I gave him. He still refused, said he wouldn't be back to the office, and stomped out the door.

I didn't hear from Mr. Silverstein for almost a year. One day, a police officer built like a giant walked into the office, asking to see me. He had to bend his blond head down to fit through the door frame. My heart started racing, partly from concern of why a police officer would want to talk to me and partly at the sheer size of the man. I ushered the officer into a room and asked him what I could do for him. He sat down in the chair as it creaked underneath him. Speaking in a quiet voice that belied his size, he asked, "Do you know a Mr. Isaac Silverstein?" I told him I did, but I could not divulge too much information about my patient. "I was hoping you could help us out," he replied. "Mr. Silverstein has called us numerous times complaining about his neighbors, but when we go out there, we can't find anything wrong. He mentioned he has seen you as a patient."

"He's come to my office complaining of the same thing," I confirmed. "I suggested that he take the medicine I prescribed and come in for a follow up, but he refused to do either. I haven't seen him in quite a number of months."

I asked the officer if it seemed like he was a danger to himself or others, and the officer said that he didn't think so. I told the officer that if Isaac was not in imminent danger of hurting himself, I could not legally commit him to the hospital against his will.

"So is there anything you can do?" The officer asked me. I suggested that he encourage Mr. Silverstein to come back to my office to be seen. The officer thanked me for my time and showed himself out. I did not expect to hear back from either police officer or patient.

A few weeks later, I was surprised to find Mr. Silverstein's name in my schedule. When he came to the office, I asked him what prompted him to come back. "I think something must be wrong with me," he replied. "I asked my friend Ron to come by to see if he could hear the neighbors. My daughter already said that she couldn't, and the police said that they couldn't. I trust Ron, and he told me the same thing. Maybe I really am just hearing things."

I realized that was what Mr. Silverstein needed. He needed someone who he could trust to give him an honest answer before he would reconsider his position. I latched onto this chink in the wall of Isaac's delusion, and I gave him a different antipsychotic medicine to try. We made a one month follow up appointment for him.

The next month, Isaac showed up as scheduled. Much to my delight, he did say that the voices were much better. Unfortunately, his delusional thinking wasn't quite cleared up. He attributed the decreased voices to the fact that his neighbors knew his lease was coming up, so they weren't bothering him. "Have you been calling the police?" I asked.

"No. Those police don't help anything anyway," he scoffed. He then showed me his prescription bill. "I'm not taking those medicines any more. They charged me $44 for my medicine, and my daughter only pays $5. That's too expensive, and I'm not going to pay it."

I looked at the prescription sheet. Sure enough, he was charged $44. But what he failed to mention was that the full medicine cost was actually $450, and he only had to pay a miniscule portion. I tried pointing that out to him but he was again stubborn and refused to take his medicine. Even with my cajoling, he was obstinately refusing. I tried warning him that if he did not take the medicine, the voices would get worse again. Mr. Silverstein got belligerent. "They're the problem! I'm not the problem! Why are you pestering me?"

"OK, OK, Isaac." I tried to mollify him. "If you need me, you are welcome to make an appointment to see me. I'll send that medicine to the pharmacy just in case you change your mind."

"Don't bother," he replied. "I'm not going to take that medicine. It's too expensive." I sighed and showed him out.

I don't know if Isaac is going to be back. Either way, he taught me that our experience is colored by our perspective. Sometimes, it takes a friend or person you can trust to tell you the truth, even when you know you're right, and help you see something in a different light. Maybe Isaac's friend Ron will visit him again and encourage him to take his medicine. I hope that bond of trust stays intact until Isaac can be completely treated to reach a therapeutic dose of his medicine. But ultimately, I can only give him good advice. I will have to rely on others to help me get him to a better place in his life.

Isaac might not be a danger to himself, but he is living a life of self-imposed bondage to his irrational fears. They are literally keeping him awake at night, causing him frustration and anger. They are affecting his quality of life, preventing him from enjoying life to his fullest.

So what are your irrational fears? What is keeping you up at night, worrying about things that shouldn't be worried about? Who in your life do you have a line of communication and trust with? Who can tell you the truth in love, even when you don't want to hear it? What steps do you have to take to be rid of your fears, even when those steps seem crazy to you and do not make sense? The answer to those questions might greatly improve your quality of life and silence those pesky voices inside your head.

Mis-Wired

I first met Melissa as a young girl in fourth grade. She was incredibly sweet and smart, with blond hair and a fiery disposition. Missy excelled at school and had incredible artistic talents as well. Even in the fourth grade, she showed an unusual ability to analyze data and interpret situations. When she took the state-wide mastery tests, she scored at the top percentage for the math and reading, but she totally flunked the writing portion. Knowing that writing was one of her strongest points, the principal called her in and asked her what happened. Missy responded, "Did you even read that prompt they gave? That was the stupidest prompt I've ever read in my life. And the test is just there to show that teachers are doing their job anyway." The principal had to give Missy credit for higher level thinking, but explained to her that sometimes, one had to comply with expectations, even stupid ones.

In the fall of Missy's fifth grade year, her father was deployed to Iraq with the Army. Kyle was gone for a year and a half. Although the whole family missed Kyle during his absence, none did more so than Missy, who was Daddy's girl through and through. When Kyle did return from his tour of duty, he was suffering from post-traumatic stress disorder, and he had a hard time reconnecting with his family and society in general. Missy took her father's difficulties very personally, and that further compounded the distance between them that time apart had created.

Possibly as a response to the emotional disconnect she felt, or maybe to explore her personal identity, Missy developed a group of friends from the Emo/goth crowd in the seventh grade. She wore all black clothes and make up. Missy started expressing and asserting herself, but not always at an appropriate time or venue. Missy did fine academically through the rest of middle school, but she had a rapid change the month before her ninth grade year.

Throughout her childhood, Missy had always exhibited a fun-loving, independent spirit. The summer before ninth grade, Missy developed a mean streak. She started treating with disdain anyone following reasonable, accepted social norms. Missy's relationship with her younger sister soured. She started referring to Becky as the "Abercrombie and Fitch Girl." The name-calling and hurtful words got worse. Missy would say to her parents and sister, "I hate you all. You're all just *lemmings*, following one another off a cliff."

Missy's emotional lability culminated in her running away from home in the middle of her first semester of ninth grade. For six weeks, her parents looked for her everywhere, fearing the worst about her safety. Early one morning, the police caught Missy climbing out of a second story window. She had been staying in the bedroom of a friend, without the knowledge of the girl's parents. Missy was brought home by the police and then admitted to the behavioral unit of the hospital for depression and anxiety. For several days, the psychiatrists and counselors worked to stabilize Missy's emotional state with medications and therapy. They did as much as they could with the limited time and resources available before discharging Missy back home.

Missy showed some improvement after the hospital stay. The psychiatric medicines and intensive outpatient counseling seemed to help. But after a period of calm in the house, Missy decided she was "all better" and stopped both the medications and therapy. This led to a quick downward spiral of her interactions with her family. She exhibited a narcissistic component, doing whatever she wanted regardless of others' desires or expectations. Missy had extreme defiance, rapid mood swings, and fits of rage. Things came to a head one night when Missy was screaming at the top of her lungs and smashing things in the house. Kyle and Debbie had no choice but to call the police and have Missy taken back to the hospital for psychiatric evaluation.

This became a regular cycle for Missy. Over two years, Missy was hospitalized five times. She went home on medications but never stayed on them for long. Her eccentric, immature, and occasionally bizarre behavior would resurface. Then she would crash, and EMS or the police came to the house to take her back to the hospital.

Through this time, Missy came to my office on occasion for treatment of self-inflicted wounds. She shared with me that she was incredibly depressed and at times suicidal. To deal with her emotional angst, she cut herself. Missy pulled up her sleeve to show me the multitude of shallow slashes in her forearm. Missy also became very fond of piercings. She pierced her eyebrows, lips, nose, and hips. Most of the piercings she did herself, under less than sanitary conditions. After the wounds got red and swollen, she would come to the office for an evaluation and antibiotics.

During these visits for her infections, I tried to touch on the underlying emotional maelstrom that was causing the outward behavior. Every now and then, Missy had moments of clarity. She knew she had impulse control issues, and getting along with family was a daily challenge.

"I have really low self esteem," Missy told me once. "I don't like what I see in the mirror."

"Do you have anyone you can talk to?" I asked her.

"No, no one."

I reminded her of the therapists as well as her parents, but she scoffed at both. When I asked what she could do, she said she wrote in her journal to process her thoughts. I encouraged her to continue and reminded her that she could talk to me if she felt like it. Sometimes, I was able to speak a bit of truth into her life. Other times, Missy chose to misconstrue even my most benign comments and became a wall of obstinance. Those times, I stopped the session, because I knew Missy was not going to hear another word I said until she calmed down.

In between one of Missy's cycles of hospitalization, she started at the town's alternative high school for troubled youth. Her grandparents also found her a place to stay with one of their friends. This helped alleviate a number of pressures for everyone. Missy's parents and sister had some breathing room from the daily conflicts with a loved one dealing with mental illness. This also gave Missy a greater sense of independence by not having to be under her parents' thumb. At the same time, Missy was still under the supervision of trusted adults.

Everything seemed to be going well until she met a heroin addict who was just out of jail. Missy detailed what she perceived was her terrible life and impossible parents, and Sean decided to "save" her by taking her away. Sean then called Kyle and Debbie and said he wouldn't give her back unless they met him in a dark parking lot alone. Of course Kyle and Debbie refused this and called the police instead. Because Missy was a minor, they treated the incident as a kidnapping. The police contacted Sean and coordinated Missy's return.

Missy ended up in a group home for young adults, and life seemed to settle into a period of relative calm. Unfortunately, this calm did not last. Debbie got a call one morning from the police department. Missy and her friends were caught "car shopping," breaking into parked cars to steal valuables and resell them. Missy received nine charges, five of which were felonies for burglary.

At first, the police considered giving Missy a "promise to appear," in which she would be let out of jail without bond on the promise that she would show up at court. But because of her co-conspirators and their previous felonies, as well as the concern that Missy was not able to connect actions with consequences, Missy was not released. The bail was set at $25,000 cash, a sum Kyle and Debbie could not possibly pay. Missy spent three months at the state penitentiary waiting for her court appearance. On a regular basis, Debbie visited Missy while she was incarcerated. Every time, Missy would beg Debbie to get her out of jail, but of course, that was impossible.

After her release from prison, Missy moved back home, by mandate of the court. The family had initial fears that this would mean turmoil and disaster. But everyone was pleasantly surprised at how smooth the transition was and how well Missy behaved. Of course, things got a bit rocky when Missy ran out of medicine and could not get an appointment with a psychiatrist for three months. I saw Missy back in my office, reinstated her medications, and got her back on track until her psychiatrist appointment.

Debbie has come to the conclusion that Missy's mental illness does not allow her to connect behavior with consequences. In some ways, mental illness reverts people back to a childish way of thinking and relating to the world. One can't just say to a child, "The stove is hot, you're going to get burned." He has to burn his finger, and the fear of being burned keeps him from doing it again. Missy was unable to understand that certain actions like car shopping might land her in jail. Rather, it took the experience of being in jail and the fear of having to go back that keeps Missy in line.

I see some forms of mental illness as a mis-wiring of the brain. That mis-wiring can sometimes cause substantial disability with daily social functioning. But sometimes, that same mis-wiring can lead to surprising insight and occasionally strokes of genius. One such example is animal psychologist Temple Grandin, who lives with an autism spectrum disorder. Although Grandin has a more difficult time interacting with people, she seems to have an uncanny intuition regarding animal behavior. Her observations have helped transform numerous areas in animal husbandry.

As for Missy, since childhood, she has had uncommon empathy, particularly for animals and less fortunate people. Although Missy has difficulty interacting with authority figures and most of her peers, she seems to excel in working with animals, young children, and people with mental illness. After getting out of jail, Missy found a job as a part time nanny. Missy helps the couple cook dinner, clean the house, and care for their young daughter, who has oppositional defiant disorder and a few behavioral challenges herself. The couple has commented how Missy seems to be able to communicate to their daughter at a level they could never hope to match.

Since the incarceration, Missy still has had bouts of behavioral challenges that have required professional intervention. But there is greater hope for her now than there was before. She has enrolled in hairdressing school and hopefully will make a place for herself as a productive member of society, fully utilizing her particular set of strengths and skills in a positive way.

Loving a Stranger

Peter and his ex-partner were looking for an open and affirming office where they could be themselves as gay men and get good, sensitive care. They were referred to our office by a nurse at the Hartford Gay and Lesbian Health Collective. Neither had had a physical in a while, and they wanted to start taking care of themselves since they were now in their forties.

Peter and Thomas had an interesting dynamic between them. Although they were clearly well acquainted with each other, there was a definite distance between them. They also contrasted each other on so many levels. Thomas spoke effortlessly and was quick to joke and laugh, while Peter was more subdued, his words coming out more haltingly in a flat voice. Peter, with dark hair and the Italian features of a strong brow and Roman nose, was carrying more weight on him than necessary. Thomas, on the other hand, had perfectly coifed blond hair, expertly highlighted of course, and large muscles as evidence of many hours spent in the gym. My first impression was "homebody" and "party boy."

I got along well with both the guys through their new patient physicals. Following my typical approach, I had a relaxed conversation with the two of them while I did my exam and documentation. The two had been a couple until several months previous. While Thomas was back in the dating scene, Peter had not considered entering into any relationships yet. Because they were no longer monogamous, I did an STD screen for both of them to establish a new baseline. I also found it interesting that neither cared to have the other step out of the exam room when the genital and prostate exams were being done. I knew there was much more to the story of the relationship between Peter and Thomas. However, I did not think it was the right time to inquire further. I knew that one or both of them would clue me in when the time was right.

Both of their labs came back fine. Thomas was content to see me annually, but Peter had issues he still needed to address. He came to the office barely a week after his physical. The reason was written down as "lump in breast." Peter said Thomas thought he was born without part of his chest muscle. Indeed, when looking straight at him, Peter seemed to have an indentation in the left side of his chest. I told Peter that it was not serious, but there was nothing I could do.

Of course, that was the stated purpose of the visit but not the real reason Peter wanted to see me. Peter frowned, looked down at his interlocked fingers in his lap, took a deep breath, and told me what was on his heart. "I'm really depressed," he said. "Thomas and I have been together for thirteen years, and he told me a few months ago that he was leaving me. He said the fire was gone, and he wasn't that attracted to me anymore.

"I've always had a poor self image, and this has only made it worse. Thomas said he wanted to be friends, but I don't think I can do that. I feel this huge sense of rejection."

"Peter, can you fill out this form for me?" I gave him the depression screening form. When he handed it back, nearly every symptom was listed at "more than half the days" or "nearly every day."

When I asked him about any thoughts of suicide, Peter said, "No, but I wish I could just disappear."

It was clear that Peter needed some sort of treatment for his depression. When I asked him if he had taken anything in the past, he said he had tried Prozac, Zoloft, and Paxil, and none of them helped, so he stopped. I thought it was still a good idea for him to take a medicine, and he agreed to give one a try.

I knew, however, that medicine was an appropriate stop-gap measure but not really what Peter needed in order to experience healing for himself. Peter needed to know to the core of his being that he was cared for, that his feelings were important, that he mattered. Peter had just faced rejection from the most important person in his life of the past thirteen years. He now needed some sort of affirmation from someone. I told him, "We have only met twice now, but I can tell you have an incredibly giving heart. I thought it was wonderful that you would plan on going with me on my next medical mission trip after just hearing about it at your physical last week. I don't think anyone has ever done that before.

"I think you're a handsome guy. You have an amazing smile. Are you carrying more weight on you than you should? Honestly, yes. But that's something you can change. I know that Thomas leaving you really hurt you badly, but that's not who you are. You are so much more than your relationship with him." The whole time I was talking, Peter barely looked at me. He shook his head in rejection of the compliments I was giving him, like it was impossible for anyone to see anything positive about him.

I continued, "I would like to write down a web site for you to look at. It's about a program in Texas called *Discovery*. It's a place where you can take an honest look at yourself—good and bad—and assess where you are as well as where you want to be. And it's one of those rare places where you can experience unconditional love. I think you've been lacking that in your life for a long time, maybe forever. It would do you a world of good to experience that sort of love in your life."

I wrote down the web address on a slip of paper and handed it to him. He took it, but noncommittally. Well, it was all I could do. I gave Peter the tools, but it was up to him to use them. There was one more thing I could do for him though.

"Peter, do you think you could use a hug?"

Peter's thick eyebrows furrowed together and his lips pursed as he said, "Yes." He and I both got up, and I grabbed Peter in a tight hug. I held the hug for a while to let it soak in, and I slowly let him go. An hour had gone by since Peter walked in, but it seemed like just a few minutes. I asked him to come back in a month and let me know how he was doing.

Peter came back for his follow up a bit later than planned, at the six week mark. "I was not doing well with that medicine. It was making me too tired and it wasn't working. I stopped it two weeks ago." He looked down and sighed. "I don't think anyone cares about me. Well, you might, Dr. Han, but that's about it."

I reminded Peter about *Discovery* as a place to experience overwhelming unconditional love. Peter said, "How do I know they're not just acting? I don't want to pay for someone to care about me."

"You're paying me a co-pay today," I responded with slight amusement in my voice. "So do you think that's why I care about you?"

He started and stopped a couple of times, opening then closing his mouth. Dabbing tears from his eyes, he said, "And that is the really sad part, when the only one who cares about me is someone I have to pay to do it."

"Peter," I asked, "Do you really think that is the only reason I care about you?"

He said, "No, but you're different than everyone else."

"I sure hope so," I told him. "I'm not sure this world could take two of me." Peter smiled. "Peter, I see you as a little boy, who longs to have someone wrap their arms around you and hold you to their chest, in complete trust and love. You so desperately need that right now. Yes, you pay me a co-pay to be your doctor, but I care about you completely separately from that. If you believe my care for you is genuine, then you're just going to have to believe me that the love you will experience in *Discovery* is just as genuine."

"How could someone just love a stranger like me?" He asked tremulously.

"That is the beauty of *Discovery*," I told him. "There are precious few places in the world to find unconditional love and trust. I just happen to know *Discovery* is one of them." Before he could expresses any other doubts, I said, "Just think about it. As a doctor, I use whatever tools I have to get you to better health. Right now, I think *Discovery* is the thing that will help you. I don't recommend it to everyone, but everyone who I have recommended it to who has gone has found great benefit. When the time is right, maybe you'll take my suggestion. The next session is in a month. Either way, I want to see you back in a month to see how the medicine has worked."

I stood up, and he followed suit. I had my hands in my pockets, and his arms were folded across his chest. "Anything else?" I asked.

"I guess not," Peter said.

"Could you use a hug?" I asked.

"Yes," he exhaled deeply. I put my arms out, and we gave each other a long, warm hug.

When I let go, I put my hands on his shoulders, looked him directly in his eyes, and said, "Peter, you are a person of great worth and potential. You just need someone to show you how much worth you have and learn to accept the love they offer."

I gave Peter a month's worth of samples of a different antidepressant, and I walked him out to the front to make his follow up appointment. I'm hoping he'll sign up for *Discovery*. I wonder if it would encourage him to sign up if I told him the hugs I gave were nothing compared to all the hugs he'll get during a *Discovery* weekend.

Peter on a sunset cruise in Naples, FL

Image

I walked into the exam room, and Kara was sitting on the exam table. She was looking good as always, with light-colored eyes, high cheekbones, and the flawless complexion of a young woman in her twenties. As was typical for Kara, she was dressed in athletic garb, with a wind breaker, sweats, and running shoes. She had not changed for the past several years that she had been coming to the office. That was precisely the reason why I asked her to come in. Earlier, I got a note from a staff member that Kara wanted a nutritionist referral. I wanted to determine Kara's motive for asking for one.

When I asked Kara to explain her reasoning for requesting a nutritionist referral, she said, "I've been trying to lose weight for two years, and I can't. I work out five to six days a week, with spinning, weight lifting, and then the insanity work out. I've had three personal trainers. I've completely revamped my diet without any dairy or gluten. I don't know what I'm doing wrong."

"How tall are you?" I asked.

"Five-foot four."

"How much do you weigh now?"

"One hundred thirty," Kara replied.

"So how much do you want to weigh?"

"One hundred twenty."

I got up and pulled my Body Mass Index wheel from the drawer. I dialed her weight on the wheel and aligned it with her height. Kara's BMI was 22, smack in the middle of the healthy range. I showed her the wheel. Before I could say anything, Kara's eyes welled up with tears. "I know what you're going to say. Everyone else says it. 'Kara, you're fine!' Well I don't feel fine. What does it matter what other people say if I don't feel that way?"

"Why do you want to lose ten pounds?"

Kara said, "That's what I weighed two years ago. I started drinking heavily and gained these ten pounds, and now I can't get it off. My muscle mass has changed, but my weight hasn't."

"But muscle is more dense than fat," I pointed out. "You have traded some fat for muscle."

"But what about this *gut*?!" Kara lifted up her shirt and pointed to the barest hint of a roundness on her abdomen. "My mother has the same thing, and I am built exactly like her. We both have these skinny chicken legs and arms, and then this belly. I don't want to be this way!"

"Kara," I soothed, "You're not fat. In fact, if anything, you're doing so much better than most of America."

"So if everyone else doesn't want to care for themselves, do I have to be like them?" Kara countered. "Am I bad for wanting to take care of myself better than everyone else does?"

"Of course not, Kara. But you're doing all the right things, and you're doing a darn good job at it. So, I don't know why you're beating yourself up about it. Kara, are you doing anything like avoiding eating or bringing up food to try to get skinny?"

Kara scoffed, "No! I'm eating more than I was before. I eat small meals five or six times a day. That's what I was told would help, but it's clearly not working." Kara blew her nose into the tissue, the fourth since the start of our conversation.

I paused for a few seconds before I continued. "Kara, I think you have a body image problem. You can't see yourself in an objective light. What you see and what other people see are totally different. You've heard of the young woman who is anorexic. She's nothing but skin and bones, but she still thinks she's fat, and she can eventually kill herself. Did you see the movie *Twilight: Breaking Dawn Part 1?*" Kara nodded. "Bella is being eaten alive from the inside out, and she looks like a Holocaust victim. Everyone can see that she's barely alive, but the anorexic would still see that as fat. That is the quintessential example of a body image issue.

"But that doesn't have to be the only way body dysmorphic disorder can present. I want to tell you something, and I want you to take it the way I mean it. Kara, you are a very attractive, well put together young woman. There is absolutely nothing wrong with you."

"So are you telling me I should just give up and eat whatever I want, because it doesn't matter?" Kara threw her hands up.

"No, I'm not saying that, and you know it." I leaned back in the stool and rested my back against the wall to look into Kara's tearful, frustrated eyes. "You should continue exercising and taking care of yourself. But that's not what's going to make you feel better about yourself. The problem is not your body; it's how you see it.

"Sure, you're ten pounds heavier than you were two years ago. But you were younger two years ago, and bodies *change*. It's like the fifty-year-old woman complaining about how her breasts don't stick straight out like they used to when she was twenty. It's called aging and gravity." Kara laughed.

"See," I pointed out. "You get my meaning. It makes sense when I give you the extreme examples. Believe me when I tell you it's the same way with you."

Kara looked down and away from me. "I don't like what I see when I look in the mirror," she said softly, her tears dropping from her cheeks.

Kara's confession was like a door opening to reveal the wounded soul inside her heart. I felt my own heart breaking for this young woman in front of me.

"Why would you ever think that, Kara?" I asked gently.

"My father and older brother make fun of me and tell me I'm fat." Kara couldn't stop crying.

"Kara, you shouldn't listen to your father or brother when they tell you you're fat, because you're not. Clearly, they have some issues in their lives. They don't know how to build themselves up, so the only way they can feel better about themselves is to make people feel worse than they do. And they must have some pretty serious problems if they're attacking you, their own blood, like that.

"I've been taking care of you for a few years now, and I think you know by now that I care about you, and I want the best for you. If there is something I think you need to hear, or something you need to do, I would not hesitate to let you know. So, I'm telling you that you need to surround yourself with people who will build you up and not tear you down. Your father and your brother have their own issues, and they need to be the ones to deal with them. Don't take their issues upon yourself.

"As for the nutritionist, if you really want to see one, I can do the referral. But it sounds to me that you have a very good grasp on nutrition. And if I do send you, I'm going to be honest with them and let them know my feelings about your body image issue. They might give you some insight on that as well. More than the nutritionist, you need to know from the top of your head down to the tips of your toes that you are a beautiful woman inside and out, and you are greatly loved. Do you still want to go to the nutritionist?" I asked.

"No, I guess not," Kara replied.

"Think about the things I've said. Come back if you want to talk some more. I'll be here." Kara thanked me and walked out.

Life as a Fraud

When Rick came to the office, he had not been to a primary care doctor in quite a long time. He was getting his testosterone replacement therapy from a specialist, but he had up to that point neglected his general medical care. He was going out of the country for a trip and needed travel counsel. With my extensive overseas medical mission work, I had a good idea of what Rick needed for this upcoming trip.

Along with the travel counsel, we spent the first visit getting to know each other. Rick was a nurse at a nearby hospital. A divorcee with two children, Rick was currently in a same-sex partnership for two years. He didn't have too many chronic medical problems other than low testosterone and high cholesterol. I suggested at the end of the visit that he make an appointment for a general check up and blood work.

Rick came back for his physical. Other than being overweight, Rick was in pretty good shape for a man in his fifties. The last part of the physical was the hernia check, so I asked Rick to stand up and drop his pants. When I tried to examine his genitals, I found his testicles were set so far back and up close to his body that I had to ask Rick to widen his stance. Once I finally got to the testicles, they felt very small and hard, not at all like what I would normally expect.

I continued to carefully examine the area as I tried to formulate what to say. "Rick, your testicles don't feel completely normal," I finally said.

Rick leaned down towards me. In a lowered, almost conspiratorial, voice he replied, "That's because they're silicone."

My eyebrows and head rose as I slowly withdrew my hands. I leaned back into the stool as Rick pulled his pants up and tucked his shirt in. "You know, Rick, you could have given me some sort of warning that the anatomy wasn't completely standard before you pulled your pants down."

"Well, I just didn't know how to start the topic," Rick said, mildly defensive.

"So, now that I've done my exam, how about telling me the story behind it all," I requested. And that's when Rick began the story of how he started life as a fraud.

****

Rebecca was raised in the Midwest by two loving parents, with two older sisters and one younger brother. The family was a picture of standard middle-class suburbia. Ben and Judy were deeply religious. While Ben provided for the family as the manager of a clothing store, Judy stayed home with the children.

Everything seemed great, but there was one problem. Rebecca was convinced she was a boy. She thought and felt like a boy. The first time Rebecca even considered that she might not be a boy was when she was four years old and saw another boy's anatomy, finding it not the same as hers. "Well, they say I'm a girl, so that's what I must be," Rebecca thought to herself. But somehow, that didn't seem to settle quite right.

Rebecca was too young to really understand what it all meant. She just knew that although she had Barbie dolls, she preferred catching frogs and chasing her mother around the house with worms. Rebecca hung out at the dairy farm, climbing trees and chasing cows with the other neighborhood boys. When Rebecca got to pick out clothes from the hand-me-down pile, she always chose the boys' clothes. Her preferred attire was jeans, an oxford shirt, and ratty sneakers. Although this was tolerated at home, Rebecca's parents would never allow her to go to school in boys' clothes. When she tried to ease out of the house in jeans, Rebecca would be marched back up to her room to put on a dress like a proper girl.

Rebecca's young childhood was filled with confusion. She always felt out of place, not comfortable in her clothes or even her own skin. Rebecca frequently sneaked into the boys' bathroom at school or in the grocery store because that's just what felt right to her. At eight years old, she started stuffing socks and underwear into the front of her pants to make the area look bigger. For the life of her, Rebecca could not figure out why she even thought about doing that. "I guess I'm just weird," was her only conclusion.

One day when Rebecca was nine, she was passing the time at her father's store. Rebecca's friend Jessica walked in, pulled her aside, and excitedly said, "Hey Rebecca, I'm getting boobs! Have your boobs started to pop out yet?" Rebecca's immediate reaction was to put her hands to her chest. Jessica probably thought Rebecca was checking to see if there was any development yet, but Rebecca was actually trying to push back anything that might be growing where in Rebecca's mind it shouldn't be.

Due to a combination of Rebecca's Puritanical upbringing and her innate discomfort with her own body, Rebecca had no concept of female anatomy, much less the birds and the bees. A few months after her alarming conversation with Jessica, another girlfriend found Rebecca's naïveté unfathomable and said, "You know you have a hole down there, right?"

Actually, it never occurred to Rebecca to wonder what was "down there." She quickly went to check and was horrified. When the school-sponsored sex education courses rolled around in sixth grade, Rebecca kept on feeling like she was in the wrong class. The thought of developing breasts and getting a period every month nauseated her. Rebecca spent most of sex ed with her head down or her eyes closed. Maybe if she didn't see it, it just wouldn't happen to her.

Puberty did finally catch up with Rebecca when she turned 14 and started having periods. She wished to God they would stop, but they didn't. While she watched her friends long for a curvaceous figure, the last things Rebecca wanted were curvy hips and big breasts. The whole thing skeeved her out. Her terrible self-image drove Rebecca to become an anorexic as a way to minimize any fat on her body. The only good thing was that her breasts did not develop any more than an A-cup, but even then Rebecca was mortified by them. She was always trying to hide them. There was not one part of Rebecca's body that she was comfortable with.

High school is generally known to be difficult for all teens, but for Rebecca all of the challenges of self-acceptance and social interactions were magnified. No matter how she felt inside, her body just would not cooperate with her.

Rebecca finally decided to embrace her femininity. She wore dresses rather than jeans, grew her hair out, and wore earrings. Rebecca learned how to play the part of a woman very well. But for Rebecca, it was all a charade. For Rebecca, life felt like a play in which she was an actor, but she didn't know the part, the plot, or the conclusion.

Rebecca woke up every morning and pretended to be a girl, but she always felt like a fraud. She was not comfortable masquerading as a girl at all, and she was sure someone else could see right through her. So, Rebecca kept to herself as much as possible and did her own thing. She did some sketching, but her biggest passion was reading. Rebecca rarely went anywhere without a book from the Weekly Readers book club, and every one of them were about boys and their adventures. Rebecca never touched a book about girls, dresses, parties, or romance.

One thing Rebecca knew without a doubt was that she was attracted to men. It was the one aspect of herself that she did not have to hide from her few friends. But Rebecca was deathly afraid of anything to do with dating or sex because she did not want anyone seeing her body. And although she was attracted to men, when she had sexual dreams, it was with a girl. Ironically, Rebecca was always the one in the dream with the penis, while the girl in the dream had no breasts or even a face. All of these things were incredibly confusing to her. "Am I gay?" Rebecca would ask herself, but she didn't really even know what "gay" meant. As a result, other than a brief platonic dating relationship with a guy in college, Rebecca never had a serious relationship all the way through college and nursing school.

Rebecca had graduated and was working as a nurse when she was dragged over to meet Charlie, the guy who lived in the apartment across the parking lot. Rebecca had a dog at the time who hated all people, but for some reason she decided she loved Charlie. Charlie was outside fixing his car as Rebecca took Sophie out for a walk. Sophie saw Charlie and pulled Rebecca over to him, her tail wagging like a flag in a storm. That started a conversation which then led to a dating relationship. A year later, they got married.

It was in the middle of dating Charlie that Rebecca lost her virginity to him. The excitement of having sex for the first time was overwhelmed by apprehension over Charlie seeing her body. But once their clothes came off and they got to business, Rebecca found the whole thing ridiculous. All she could think was, "I can't believe I bothered waiting 29 years for this." The whole time, she was bored out of her mind. Charlie seemed like he was having fun, but it wasn't doing anything at all for Rebecca. Over the course of their relationship, Rebecca had to find other ways to enjoy the act.

After getting married, Rebecca brought up the topic of having kids. Rebecca always wanted to have a family and children, even if she never saw herself in the role of a mother. Charlie wasn't keen on the idea of raising children, but he eventually warmed up to the idea. The couple tried for over a year without success. They ended up at an infertility clinic and started looking into the cause of why they couldn't conceive. During the investigation, the doctors found abnormalities of Rebecca's reproductive system. She had a malformed uterus and only one ovary. Most notably, Rebecca had "embryonic mineralized remnants" in her reproductive tract. Rebecca was actually intersex, with mostly female organs but also a part of an undescended testicle. Rebecca went on ovulation hormones and then had a successful intrauterine insemination. The pregnancy was uneventful, and Rebecca delivered a healthy girl named Lisa. Because it seemed impossible to conceive without medical intervention, Rebecca and Charlie didn't bother afterwards with birth control. Four years after Lisa was born, somehow Rebecca got pregnant naturally and had Bryson.

Rebecca and Charlie had split work schedules to care for the kids. Charlie worked during the day, while Rebecca did her nursing duties in the evenings and on weekends. Although this worked well for childcare, it widened the relationship gap that had started only a year into the marriage. Rebecca felt like Charlie was so kind and considerate during the courtship. But after the marriage Charlie became more controlling, complaining, and grumpy. He had severe mood swings, in one moment the happy and playful man Rebecca fell in love with, and then in the next moment he was insulting and condescending.

During this time, Rebecca had her own problems. After Bryson's delivery Rebecca became severely clinically depressed and had to take antidepressants for several years. Most people assumed it was prolonged postpartum depression, and certainly that was a factor. But the issue was bigger than that. Rebecca loved her children, but she found playing the maternal role very disconcerting and stressful. Rebecca had to take her kids for play dates and then hang out with the other mothers, but she really wanted to be with the dads. Yet again, Rebecca felt like she had to play a role she was not cut out to play. It all felt very painful to her.

Although they had their issues, Rebecca and Charlie both wanted to keep the family together for the sake of the kids. They tried to get along with each other as much as possible. Eventually, however, it was just easier to avoid each other. There were days when Rebecca had this irrational hope that Charlie would just not come home. Rebecca put up with Charlie's sour moods when they were directed towards her, but she put her foot down when Charlie started being mean to the children. He would yell at them and spank them for inconsequential issues. This went on for quite a while until Rebecca had as much as she could stomach. She packed up the kids and moved in with her brother. Within a month, Charlie served her divorce papers, ending a 15-year marriage.

During the divorce process, Rebecca found a therapist who helped her work on herself, her relationship with Charlie, and her issues with her mother. That helped make the divorce amicable, with shared custody of the kids. Yet throughout the whole counseling process, it never occurred to Rebecca to share with the therapist the thoughts she had lived with for her whole life. Rebecca tried to get back into the dating scene, but it did not work well. With her extra time, Rebecca started to seriously examine her childhood and weird feelings for the first time. She poked around the internet and discovered sites about intersex and transgender people. The strange thing was that Rebecca had heard about hermaphrodites and even saw examples of such on the farm, but it never occurred to her that this might actually apply to herself.

As Rebecca continued to gain a better understanding of her condition, she decided that it was the root of why she was so depressed. Rebecca started visiting various doctors and considered a gender transition. She cut her hair short. She threw out all of her dresses, pumps, and make up. She ditched her purse and got a wallet. She bought khakis, button-up shirts, and dress shoes—all men's clothes.

Her daughter Lisa couldn't help but notice the dramatic change and asked her mother about it. As it turned out, Thomas Beatie, "the world's first pregnant man," was in the news at the same time Rebecca was going through her transition. This became the perfect lead in for the "big talk." To Rebecca's relief, Lisa didn't mind at all and was completely supportive. When Rebecca talked to Bryson about the gender transition, he felt exactly the same way. Both kids were totally blasé and didn't care at all. Rebecca started testosterone shots, grew a beard, and chose the name Rick. For the first time in his life, Rick felt comfortable in his own skin. He no longer felt like a fraud.

As Rick understood himself better, he started looking for a life partner. The problem was that Rick did not feel like he was in any way a stereotypical gay man. He was not into clothes and fashion, musicals, or "Queer Eye for the Straight Guy." The other dilemma was when to reveal that he was intersex. Rick decided not to post anything about his past on his online dating account because he didn't want to be prejudged. One day, as he was perusing people's profiles, he came across one that made him laugh his ass off. "I have got to meet this guy," he said to himself.

Rick and Wilson had a first date that was immensely successful. They were the proverbial two peas in a pod. They both agreed on a second date and spent several hours at a restaurant talking more than eating. As they traded random silly questions, Wilson asked out of the blue, "So are you transgender?"

Rick looked at Wilson like a deer in the headlights. "Noooo." Why would he ask that? Rick wondered if Wilson had done some sort of research on him before the date.

Wilson continued, "I just thought I would ask because you kind of look like this guy at my job who's transgender. It didn't matter either way. I was just wondering, that's all."

The rest of the date went without any further surprises. Rick really liked Wilson, and truth be told, he really wanted to get into Wilson's pants. But he didn't want Wilson to be surprised at his tiny penis. So, on the third date, Rick found the opportunity to tell Wilson his story about how he started life as Rebecca, had a remnant testicle, and identified with the male side of himself. Wilson didn't have problems with any of those things. After that, their relationship deepened. Rick found his life partner, with the emotional connection and the opportunity to express it physically. It took half his life, but Rick was finally living as the person he saw himself: a gay man.

Of course being true to oneself doesn't necessarily make life easier. Rick still has issues with his mother. Their conversations follow a typical pattern. "The doctors said you were a girl, and that's what you are. Why can't you be like Ellen DeGeneres?"

"No, Mother," Rick would respond. "I'm a man. And Ellen is a woman who likes women. I'm a *man* who likes *men*."

"I just don't understand," Rick's mother would say.

Rick has also had to navigate what to do about his kids as far as how to refer to him at home and to their friends. Rick decided to take a very pragmatic approach and tell them both that he was fine with whatever they chose to make life easier for them. So, Lisa tells her friends that Rick is her uncle, and at home, she refers to Rick as "Papa Rick."

I asked Rick if it would have been easier to take the more socially acceptable route of staying as a woman and having a male partner. "I've asked myself the very same question," Rick told me. "But being a woman was not who I was, no matter who I was attracted to. I couldn't be myself as Rebecca. In my mind and heart, I've always been Rick. Now, my body agrees with me."

I think many people would see Rick's change as needlessly complicated for himself and his family. I personally see Rick's life as rich and rewarding rather than complicated. But most of all, I see Rick's life to be one of personal honesty, integrity, and authenticity. Rick is many things, but he is a fraud no longer.

Find the Corners

Jack looked like a bouncer. His 6'2", 216 pound, beefy frame certainly lent itself to throwing obnoxious people out of a bar. The extensive tattoos going down his hairy arms and spiky tribal tattoo going up each side of his neck to his dark reddish hair certainly added to the general aura of menace. The fact that Jack wasn't shy about liberally throwing expletives and the occasional F-bomb into his general conversation meant that all he needed was a glare and snarl, and the most stalwart soul would think twice about crossing him.

In spite of all this, Jack was actually a really nice, pleasant guy. He had a smile that split his face in two and a quick, hearty laugh that started from his belly before bursting forth. The few creases at the corners of his eyes were made by smiles, not glares. Maybe it was his size, or maybe the "shoulders back, chest out" way that he carried himself, but Jack seemed older than a guy in his thirties.

Jack and I have always gotten along well for the four years he's been a patient. He came in for routine blood pressure checks and the occasional bronchitis or injury. As with all my patients, I was straightforward with Jack, laying everything on the table and saying things like they were. There was rarely a time when we didn't laugh about something or another at each of his visits.

I was therefore surprised when I walked into the exam room and found Jack pacing the floor, clearly distraught. "Doc, I need something to calm the fuck down," he said.

"Hey Jack, what's going on?" I asked, concerned.

He replied, "I'm anxious, depressed, and moody. I can't get comfortable, and I can't sit still. I just need something to get me through until I see my psychiatrist next Monday."

During the time I had been taking care of Jack, he had never mentioned depression as one of his issues, and he certainly didn't mention going to a psychiatrist. I asked Jack to explain further.

"The missus and I have been married for eight years. We got three kids to show for it. For the past year or two, I've been feeling this emotional distance from her. I love my wife, but I don't think I've been *in* love with her for a good while now.

"Do you remember at the last physical, when I told you I had erectile problems? Well, this was going on then, but I didn't really tell you. I just didn't really have interest in having sex with her, but I wanted to blame it on the performance, or maybe my smoking. But truth is, I didn't have feelings for her. Sex was like, a chore. Don't get me wrong, the sex itself is great. She's the best fucking lay I've ever had. None of my other girlfriends could compare to her. But after the sex, I just want to turn over. She wants to cuddle, and I don't at all. It's like after I cum, I don't want to have anything to do with her."

"So what's brought this all on?" I asked.

Jack explained, "When I meet someone, I give them my complete trust. But when they break that trust, I can't ever trust them again.

"I was looking for my phone last year, and I couldn't find it, so I got hers. When I looked through the texts, she was texting back and forth with this guy about all this shit. They were like flirting back and forth with each other. She told him that she didn't really love me anymore, but I provided for her, and she didn't want to leave that. I confronted her about the texts, and she said nothing happened between the two of them. They didn't have sex or anything. But I haven't been able to trust her since then.

"I left the house for a couple of days and spent some time with my wife's best friend. We hooked up a couple of times that weekend. Man, this bitch was crazy! She was like ready to leave her family and start a life with me if I would leave my wife and kids. I told her I'd think about it, but I didn't really mean to. It's like I love the thrill of the chase, but once I get a taste, I don't want it anymore. So now my wife won't talk to this friend of hers."

Clearly, Jack had some big blind spots in his life that needed to be addressed if he was ever going to find some peace and stability in his life. As I was thinking this, Jack continued to dig the hole deeper.

"I've done this a couple of times. There was this other girl, and I was, like, infatuated with her. I left the house for a couple of days then too, but then I got bored with her. When I got back home, my wife was doing all this stuff to get me to stay, telling me how she loved me and everything. It's like these women just throw themselves at me or something." I looked at Jack with an arched eyebrow, not trusting myself to say anything.

"There's a program called *Discovery* in Texas that I would like for you to consider going to. I think it would really help you figure some things out," I told him.

"I don't have that sort of money," he scoffed.

"I know it would take a sacrifice of time and money," I agreed. I gently nudged, "You know, cigarette prices have gone up again. If you could stop smoking or at least cut back, you could save that money and, over time, have enough to cover the cost of going to *Discovery*."

Jack said, "That's another problem I have. I just can't save any money. I just see something I like, and I get it. It really drives my wife crazy."

We talked more about his depression and anxiety as well as his other medical conditions. I encouraged him to follow up with his psychiatrist who he had recently been seeing. I know it was a big step for Jack, who was the quintessential "man's man," to admit he had a problem and seek the help of a psychiatrist. I congratulated him on his decision and assured him it was the right thing to do. We made an appointment for a one month follow up.

Jack showed up at the office as scheduled a month later. I smiled as I walked in. "How's it going, Jack? Are you taking the meds? Is it working?"

"Hey, Doc," Jack replied. "It's going OK I guess. Yeah, I'm taking the meds. I don't think they're working, because I don't feel any different. But the kids think they're working, so they must be doing something. They haven't been calling me 'Mr. Grumpy' lately. The kids have been nicer to me, maybe because I've been nicer to them."

"That's great, Jack! Things are heading in the right direction."

"I don't know, Doc. I still feel like my life is a mess."

"Have you given any more thought about going to *Discovery*?" I asked.

"I can't afford it," Jack scoffed. "I just went on a vacation and it was a disaster. The missus and kids and I went to an island. I did fine with the kids, but she and I were arguing all the time. I wanted to go fishing, but she was pestering me about spending more time with the kids. I'd take the kids out on the boat, and fifteen minutes later, they were bored and wanted to go back. We're on an island! There's nothing to do but swim and fish. And it's my vacation too, and I wanted to go fishing.

"When my wife and I were around each other, we hardly talked at all. She would be on her cell phone, and I would be on mine. It just seems like we were fighting all the time."

"Is there anything you can change or do differently?"

"I'd like to lose this gut, and I know I need to quit smoking. It's like everything's connected. It's like, *everything*, and I get overwhelmed."

"Do you know the Serenity Prayer that is frequently recited at AA meetings? Figure out the things you can change, and change them. Find the things you can't change, and let them go," I advised.

Jack brushed me off. "Yeah, yeah, I know it. It doesn't work for me."

I persisted, "Look, just find the things that you can change. What do you want to change?"

"I want to lose weight."

"OK," I replied. "Make a commitment to exercise three times a week and keep with it. The commitment is for you and no one else. You know you need to lose weight, so make yourself do it. It's something you have full control over, so no one is stopping you but you. And I think that when you're exercising, you'll find that you're more short of breath, and that will make you want to quit smoking so you can run better.

"Have you ever done a jigsaw puzzle? If you have a 5000-piece puzzle and dump it all down on the table, you'll look at it and say, 'That's impossible, I'll never be able to do that.' You won't even be able to get started, much less complete it."

"I always look for the corners," Jack interjected.

I smiled at Jack. "Exactly! I do too. I find the corners and put them in the right places. Then I find all the sides and snap them in place. Then when I've gotten the borders, I can see where the green pieces for the grass go and the blue pieces for the sky. I might not be able to put them all together, but at least I can separate them out into piles. It makes a very large puzzle a lot easier to manage."

Jack looked at me with understanding in his eyes. "That makes a lot of sense, Doc. I was looking at everything together, and it was so big, I couldn't handle it. If I can take things apart, maybe my life won't seem like such a mess."

"You got it, Jack," I congratulated. "Take the things you can change and change them. Once you've done that, maybe the things in your life you never thought could change will start falling into place. You start exercising, and that makes you want to quit smoking. You quit smoking, and that gives you more money. You have more money, and maybe your family won't be living from pay check to pay check all the time. Then maybe you and your wife will be fighting less. But, all of it starts with the first small step."

Jack took to heart everything I had to say. I gave him homework: He needed to come up with one or two things he could change and write down practical steps to get to that point. We were going to then talk about it at his next office visit in a month. Jack said, "You got a deal. Thanks!" He waved goodbye as he walked out of the office.

Laughter is the Best Medicine

"So you haven't had any other surgeries?"

"Other than my hernia surgery, no."

"And your circumcision," I said cheekily.

"That's because of my father's side."

"Why your father's side?"

"He was Jewish."

"What about you? Are you Jewish?"

"No."

"So what are you then?"

"Episcopalian. I'm an Anglican with Yiddish tendencies."

****

As a resident in Virginia, I got a phone call late at night.

"Mah daughta's ben vomicking, an' I can't get her ta stop," the woman said.

"You mean vomiting," I corrected her.

"Naw, I mean vomicking!" She replied.

"I'm sorry, ma'am, I don't know what that means."

"What, ya stupid? Vomicking is when it comes outta the nose too."

****

Stanley called the office for an emergency office visit. He had heart disease, with a triple bypass and a pacemaker. When he woke up that morning, his arms and legs were blue. Stanley was very concerned his heart was getting worse.

The staff told him to come right down, and I rushed him into the exam room. Other than his anxiety, he did not seem to be in acute distress. However, his arms were definitely blue. I did a complete heart and lung exam, which were normal. I then took a closer look at his arms. On a whim, I wiped his arm with an alcohol swab. The swab wiped off a strip of blue.

Stanley exclaimed, "Oh my God! I just bought new sheets!"

Mystery solved.

****

It was good to see Alex out of uniform. Usually, he came to his exam in his police officer garb, probably going to work or just getting off. This time, he was dressed in a New York Yankees shirt, jeans, and a ball cap.

He was clearly taking his blood pressure medicine because the reading my nurse got was normal. I chatted a bit with Alex and then got up to listen to his heart and lungs. When I put my stethoscope to his back, I did not hear a single thing. I turned it around and looked at it, wondering if it was broken somehow.

As I was examining my stethoscope, I noticed Alex trying to say something to me. I couldn't understand him until I took the stethoscope out of my ears.

"Doc, I'm working undercover right now. I have my bullet-proof vest underneath the shirt."

****

Several weeks earlier, I had sent my elderly patient Beatrice to physical therapy for neck pain, and now she was coming back for a follow up visit.

"So, is your neck pain any better?" I asked her.

"No, not really," she replied

"Well, I guess we can try something else then."

"No, I'd rather go back to physical therapy."

Puzzled, I asked her why she would want to go back to something that wasn't working. Apparently, instead of having Beatrice lie on the table to work on her neck, the physical therapist Dan sat cross legged on the floor mat and had Beatrice lie down with her head in his lap. The whole time, Beatrice stared up at him as he slowly worked on her neck.

I could see Beatrice reminisce about the whole situation as she was describing it to me. She ended the conversation with, "He's just dreamy!"

I told her if that made her happy at eighty-something, I would gladly renew her therapy sessions.

****

Ryoko is one of my Japanese-American patients. Although she has been in the U.S. most of her life and is married to an American serviceman, her Japanese accent is still so thick, understanding her can be challenging.

After one of our visits, Ryoko and I walked out of the exam room to the front desk. I was finishing writing up her note as she made a follow-up appointment.

"When would you like to come back, Ryoko?" Mike asked.

"Du Rye," Ryoko replied.

"Oh, well, I hope it's dry, but who can tell what the weather will be like," Mike said.

"No. Du Rye," Ryoko repeated.

Mike looked at her. "I'm not sure if it's going to be dry. Do you have a hard time driving in bad weather?"

"No, no! Du Rye! Du Rye!" Ryoko was getting flustered.

"I'm really sorry, Ryoko, but I just don't understand what you are trying to say," Mike apologized.

That's when I snapped out of my focus on her chart and realized what had been transpiring. "Mike, I think Ryoko wants an appointment in *July*."

"Yes! That's what I have been saying!" Ryoko exclaimed.

****

Tina and Diane are a lesbian couple who are my patients. That day, Tina had an appointment for a severe sore throat, and Diane came along for moral support. When I swabbed the back of Tina's throat, she immediately gagged and dry heaved. I barely finished the throat culture before Tina reflexively pushed my hand away.

As I was processing the swab, I asked her, "So I guess you're a gagger, huh?"

"Obviously," she replied.

"So I guess there are certain things you're not good at."

"No," Tina said.

"Like brushing your teeth," I continued.

"Yeah, she gags all the time when she brushes her teeth," Diane chimed in.

Tina looked at her partner and said wryly, "That's not what I was thinking."

****

The day before my medical student was supposed to come to the office, I was taking care of an older gentleman for his Medicare physical. I said to him, "It's too bad you didn't come one day later, you could have met my brand new medical student."

He looked up and said expectantly, "Tall, blonde, and Swede?"

I replied, "Well, his name is Brian Jones, and I don't know if he's tall, blond, and Swede. Would you like me to call you when I find out and let you know?"

He sputtered and said, "No, that's quite all right, Doctor."

When Brian showed up the next day and I told him the story, he grinned, saying, "Well, I'm none of those three." Brian is 5'5", with dark hair, and half-Chinese.

****

Priscilla was battling a bad cold, and to make sure she was getting better, I had her come back for a follow up visit. She showed up the next week with an older man sitting next to her who was clearly her husband.

I stood at the entrance to the waiting room and asked Priscilla's husband if she seemed to be doing better.

"Oh, she's doing fine," he assured me.

"No I'm not," Priscilla interjected. "I'm not feeling better. Don't listen to him. He has Alzheimer's."

RELATIONSHIPS

"In everyone's life, at some time, our inner fire goes out. It is then burst into flame by an encounter with another human being. We should all be thankful for those people who rekindle the inner spirit."

~Albert Schweitzer, 1952 Nobel Peace Prize recipient

Insomnia

Stephen called the office for a same-day appointment to deal with his insomnia and leg cramps. He and his wife Wendy have been patients at the office for several decades, long before I took over the practice from my step-father over ten years ago. They have always been supportive of me, the staff, and our medical mission trips, including donating money and goods for our fund raisers. I was more than happy to fit him into the morning schedule.

At almost 72, Stephen had been very healthy until a few years ago. Stephen's first sign of diabetes was loss of sensation in his feet. Neither one of us knew the extent of how bad it was until he went golfing one day and lost his golf tees. He spent the entire day walking the 18 holes, wondering where his golf tees disappeared to. Stephen did not find the tees until he got back home. When he pulled off his shoes, he found the bag of tees shoved into the bottom of his right shoe. He had lost so much sensation that he never felt the golf tees wearing away a huge ulcer into the bottom of his foot.

When Stephen got to my office, I was horrified at the mangled mess his foot had become. For several months, we were not sure if we would be able to save his leg or have to amputate from below the knee. Fortunately, after multiple specialists and daily wound care, his foot slowly healed. Stephen learned the hard way to check his feet daily.

Stephen did well for a while, controlling his diabetes and high blood pressure. Then, for the past two years, he's had one major issue after another. He developed acute appendicitis and was in the hospital for several days. During the post-op recovery, he became very short of breath. It seemed he had a blood clot travel to his lung. After many months of being on blood thinners and getting better, Stephen had episodes of severe hives, lip swelling, and fainting, which landed him back in the hospital. No cause of the hives was ever established. His arthritis, previously well-managed with anti-inflammatories, flared severely, leaving him in constant pain and practically crippled. Because of his pain, he went to an orthopedic surgeon, who suggested a total hip replacement. Stephen had an uneventful surgery, but the rehab was arduous.

Shortly after the surgery, he developed acute urinary retention, with an extremely distended, painful bladder. He had to go back to the emergency room, requiring placement of a foley catheter. After that, Stephen had gastrointestinal bleeding from the pain medicine for his arthritis, sending him back to the hospital for vomiting, dehydration, and fainting. Every time Stephen got over one thing, it seemed something else was right at his heels to cause him misery.

The day Stephen showed up at my office because of insomnia, he had gotten over all of his acute problems. His strength had returned. He and Wendy were able to go on a number of cruises and trips, their favorite way to spend their retirement. Physically, he felt more or less well. Emotionally, however, he was a wreck. It was like there was panic covered with the thinnest veneer of sanity.

The office visit started out innocuously enough. Stephen had struggled with insomnia for many years, and Tylenol PM or Ambien had always been enough to give him a good night's rest. But for several weeks, there was nothing he could do to get and stay asleep. The Ambien knocked him out, but at 3 AM, even faint sounds of traffic outside would wake him up and he couldn't go back to sleep. He had blinds and curtains, and he used a light-blocking eye patch. But even then, the most miniscule flash of light would wake him right up. Compounding the situation were leg cramps and stiffness at night, causing a great deal of pain.

As Stephen told me about his symptoms, his thin façade of calmness cracked, and he started crying. Grown men might get frustrated, angry, or even distraught about not being able to sleep, but not to the extent of grimacing weeping. I knew right then that Stephen had a much deeper problem than just insomnia. I basically told him as much. "What's really wrong?" I asked him.

"There are other things," he admitted. "I'm disappointed in myself, even though I know I'm doing good. I just don't want to disappoint Wendy. I want to be there for her, but I'm afraid I won't be."

Things became clearer to me. "Stephen, why don't you think you'll be there for Wendy?"

"I'm trying to do all the right things, taking all the right pills," he answered. "I feel like I'm insufficient. I don't want to live without Wendy. We picked out our gravestones and burial plots the other day. I had an OK time with the gravestone, but not the rest of it. I don't want to be emotional like this. I think I'm a fruit cake. This is not going to be good.

"I do OK when I'm busy. I used to like to read the newspaper and watch the news, but now a lot of world affairs bother me. Actually, everything bothers me, even the road noise, or the lights. It seems I don't want to hear any bad news.

"I think all of the medical problems over the past two years have done a job on me mentally. I don't have any real pain in my body. I feel good. But when I go to bed, I'm afraid that I won't be able to sleep, so I can't sleep."

During the entire conversation, Stephen would sit down for a bit, then get up and pace, and then sit back down. Throughout, he took tissue after tissue from the box I offered to wipe his eyes and blow his nose, and he kept on apologizing. "I'm sorry. I'm sorry." I had to tell him every time that there was nothing to be sorry about.

Sensing that Stephen needed something else, I asked him to get up. Being 6'4" to my 5'6", Stephen towered over me. To get to the same level as him, I had to stand on the exam table step. I called him over to me. He clearly did not know what I was intending, because he didn't come close enough, and then when he did, he turned with his back to me. I had to put my hands on his shoulders and turn him around. But when I leaned in to give him a hug, he would not accept it. He leaned away from me, would not put his arms up, and said, "I, I can't do this." He backed away and sat back down.

Clearly I had not calculated correctly and had made Stephen uncomfortable. He told me a story that explained why. "There are a couple of queer guys in our condo complex. They always seem to be at the pool when I go down there. One of them is fine. He says hello and I say hello back, and that's it. The other guy is always shaking my hand with both of his and holding it for a long time, and he's wanted to kiss me on the cheek. He always wants to know about me and what I'm doing. I don't kiss guys or hug them. I don't think he has anything for me, but it makes me uncomfortable with it all. I guess I wasn't raised that way."

We talked about cultural mores, and how some Europeans pecked each other on the cheek or mouth, and it wasn't a sexual thing at all. Still, Stephen was very reluctant about the whole thing. I needed to regroup and try to figure out how to help Stephen. I asked him, "Who in your life loves you?"

"Wendy."

"That's it?" Stephen nodded his head.

"There's no one else who loves you?"

"Right now? I don't think so. Wendy is the center of my world. She's everything. I don't want to disappoint her. I don't want to embarrass her. I wish I could start all over and be a younger person. I know I'm going to disappoint Wendy no matter what I do."

"Who in your life cares about you?"

"Wendy."

"That's it? Wendy's the only person in your life who cares about you?" Stephen nodded again.

"Are you able to accept the love and care that Wendy shows to you?"

"I think I am."

"If there were another person who wants to show love and care for you, are you willing to accept it?"

"I think so," he replied.

"Can I be on the list of people who care about you?"

"Yes," Stephen answered.

"Stephen, I care about you and love you. You and Wendy both are important to me. I want to do what I can to help you."

Stephen frowned as he paced back and forth. "I know your time is precious, and it bothers me that I'm taking so much of it."

I assured him, "If time is a gift, then I am more than happy to give you this time as a way to show I care. I'm really glad we have this time. In the decade I have known you, you have never dug as deep as you have today. I know it's not fun—"

"No, it's not," he interjected.

"—But it's necessary," I continued. "You can't keep on doing what you're doing. Your insomnia and muscle cramps, they're all from anxiety and probably some depression as well. You're so keyed up that the slightest thought or sound or light wakes you up. You're storing all the tension in your muscles, and you're tightening up, causing cramps."

"You're right, I know," he admitted. "I trust you. I can talk to you." He paused and said, "I don't love you." I assured him that was quite all right. He continued, "You've always taken good care of me and Wendy."

"I'm glad you think that. I have always considered it a humble honor to take care of you two. You two mean much more to me than just patients. The way I show care is by a hug, which is why I wanted to..."

Before I could continue, he said, "Let's give it a try." He quickly walked up to me and started to hold his arms out. I stepped onto the exam table, and this time, we gave each other a real, tight, long hug. It was almost fierce, the way Stephen was holding onto me. We held the hug for about twenty seconds until I felt Stephen loosen his grip. I know that the hug was a tremendous step for Stephen to take.

"I'm going to try to give hugs," he committed. Then he amended his statement, "I think I can give big hugs to women, but not men."

"That's a good first start," I encouraged.

"I'm going to talk to people more. I feel better when I talk to people. Do you think I need a psychiatrist or someone?" He asked.

"I don't think you need a psychiatrist quite yet," I replied. "But it wouldn't be a bad idea to consider a counselor or therapist. I can prescribe medicine if you feel like you're ready to take some. And you can always come in to talk to me, too. Like I said, I care about you, and I'm here for you."

"Thanks. I feel better after talking to you," Stephen said. Then he did something that took me my complete surprise. He rushed up to me without any prompting to give me another tight hug. This was coming from a man who called homosexuals "queer" and couldn't even talk about gymnasts in the Olympics pecking each other on the cheek. This hug was probably the most physical affection Stephen had shown another man. I could almost feel the walls around his heart breaking down.

Before we ended our hour-and-a-half visit, I challenged Stephen to write down on a list all the people he could think of who cared about him. "You should have at least two people on that list already, right? Wendy and me. But I know there are a lot of other people who should be on that list. Bring it in for your next office visit in a week. I want to see it."

Stephen agreed to do so and thanked me several more times before he headed out. When I started the morning, I was disappointed that before Stephen called, I only had five out of sixteen possible slots filled for the morning, and one patient didn't even show up. But by the end of the morning, I understood exactly why I was only supposed to see five patients. Stephen needed my help, and I could not have given him the time and energy that he desperately needed if I had been distracted by a heavy patient load. I guess the morning went just the way it was supposed to.

Doormat

"Gwen, you can't be a doormat forever." Gwendolyn sat across from me, dabbing her eyes.

"I know, Dr. Han, I know. But I just don't know what to do. Who's going to take care of Mother other than me? My sister sure won't. I planned for months to go on vacation with David. First, she said she would help with Mother. We bought the plane tickets and everything. And now, my sister says she can't do it, so I'm stuck at home with a ticket I can't use."

I responded, "So what would happen if you just left and told your sister her mother was at home, and she needed to take care of her like she promised?"

"I don't know! Sarah would likely leave Mother at home to die or something."

"I doubt she would die," I said gently. "We have emergency rooms. People are not dying on the side of the road or anything."

"I know. I just feel so guilty. I hate it that I let everyone walk all over me."

Truth is, Gwen became a doormat starting in her early childhood. Her uncle babysat her regularly when she was four years old. She couldn't understand at the time why her uncle would always insist that she take a shower before she left his house. He was her father's brother, though, and she trusted him. It did not seem strange to her at the time when he would join her in the shower.

Although Gwen could not verbalize it, her mind knew there was something seriously wrong about the situation. She had frequent nightmares about being in a metal box with pinging noises all around her. Only later on in life did she realize that she was reliving in her dreams being in the shower with water hitting the shower wall. This pattern went on for years until her grandmother found out about the situation and pulled Gwen out of the house. Instead of confronting the uncle, the family hid the crime. Gwen's mother and even her sister knew about the sexual abuse, but they never told Gwen's father. Her father died in old age, never knowing the atrocity his brother subjected Gwen to during her formative years.

As one might imagine, Gwen developed a terrible self image and lack of self esteem because of her sexual abuse. She had conflicted feelings for her family, whom she loved but held significant resentment towards as well. Lacking an environment of unconditional love at home, Gwen tried to fill that void with unhealthy lifestyle choices. She turned to alcohol at an early age to numb her pain. She had multiple casual sexual partners. She was willing to give away her body to feel like she was accepted, even if for a short time.

Because she was "selling herself" so cheap, her boyfriends ascribed just as little value to her as she did, and those relationships never lasted long or ended well. She got pregnant from one of those relationships, but because she did not think she could care for a child, she decided to get an abortion. Immediately afterwards, she regretted her action, and that guilt stayed with her for decades.

In an amazing gift of life, Gwen actually found the man of her dreams in her early twenties. Harold was handsome, loving, tender, and affectionate. He courted her and proposed, and she said yes. They got married and had a wonderful marriage for a while. Unfortunately, Gwen still had demons she had not exorcised. She ended up cheating on her husband. When Harold found out, it broke his heart, and it tore the marriage apart.

After the divorce, Gwen sought professional help. She went to a psychiatrist to help her figure out her self-destructive behavior. She couldn't believe it when the psychiatrist's advice was, "Just go to New York, have a fling, and get it out of your system." When Gwen told him that she didn't think this was what she needed, he told her, "Yeah. Life's a bitch and then you die." Gwen was let down by her family when she was young. She was let down by her boyfriends through her young adult life. Now, she was let down by the medical community when she needed help the most.

Gwen ended up picking herself up by her bootstraps and went on with her life. She did start dating again. Over time, she found a man whom she felt that she could spend the rest of her life with. She married Rich, and life was going well again. Until Rich took his own life by shooting himself. Life just would not give her a break.

I took over Gwen's care after my step-father left the practice to me. Over the years, Gwen and I worked together to find the right combination of medicines that would help her depression. Other than just robbing her of energy and enjoyment in life, her depression was causing physical issues. To deal with her negative feelings, she overate, particularly late at night. This caused her to gain weight. When I met her, she had already packed 230 lbs onto her 5'2" frame. Despite my efforts, she could not get a handle on her weight and increased to almost 270 lbs as time progressed. She told me once, "I feel like I'm losing my mind. I did good for a while, but I'm stuffing my face with anything I can get my hands on again."

Like one toppled domino setting off a chain reaction, Gwen's depression led to weight control problems, which then led to physical symptoms. Her blood pressure skyrocketed. Her arthritis worsened tremendously as her joints were forced to support her weight. She developed metabolic syndrome and pre-diabetes. Of course her poor health and obesity, in turn, worsened her self-image and her depression. It was a vicious cycle.

Several years ago, things got both better and worse for Gwen. At the time, she was dating a guy who was funny and could put up with her neuroses. But he was also a liar, a womanizer, and a drinker. He took her to a strip joint one night, and there, she met his buddy David. When Gwen got tired of her boyfriend's affairs, she dumped him and was set up by a friend to a guy at a bar. Lo and behold, it was David, her ex-boyfriend's buddy! Gwen and David hit it off, and they've supported each other through difficult times for the both of them over the past several years.

On the bad side, Gwen's mother's health deteriorated. When Gwen's father died, her mother took it very badly. Shortly afterwards, she began developing memory issues and dementia. She was in a nursing home for a while, but she was failing rapidly there. Seeing the lack of care that her mother was receiving, Gwen made the decision to pull her mother out of the facility and take care of her at home.

Caring for a family member with dementia is a full-time job. For a while, Gwen was consumed with caring for her mother. Every small detail that most people take for granted needed to be addressed and attended to. Gwen tried to do everything herself, but it was just too much to handle alone. She hired some helpers to care for her mother during the day, while she went there in the evening and slept through the night.

Over the years, the obligation of caring for her mother weighed heavily on Gwen. She received essentially no help from her sister or other family members. Her life was fractured. She was living part-time at David's house and part-time with her mother. She had conflicted feelings about keeping her mother alive and healthy for as long as possible and wishing she would just die and give Gwen her own life back.

Gwen felt like she had no time for anything. She wanted to join a gym and lose weight, but she didn't think she could afford the time and money. When she was with her mother at night, her mother didn't sleep well, so neither did she. Gwen was up twelve times a night checking on her mother. And when she was up at night, she tended to snack on junk food, which worsened her weight problem. This led to increased self loathing and guilt. Of course, she knew logically that it wasn't her mother's fault that she suffered with dementia. Her mother couldn't help asking the same question over and over every five minutes, nor could she help not being able to sleep at night. Still, Gwen couldn't help feeling resentment towards her mother for putting her in this position. This emotional conflict led to deepen her depression and anxiety.

This depression and anxiety manifested themselves as physical symptoms. Gwen came in once for an evaluation of practically daily chest pain. Because of the left-sided, constant chest pain and the history of high blood pressure, I did a full cardiac work up. Gwen was holding steady from a cardiac perspective, but the stress was clearly getting to her. Another time, she came in with severe headaches. The neurologic exam was normal, and I told her she was getting tension headaches from everything going on with her life.

Gwen knows she has some great difficulties. For her whole life, she has put up with everyone using her. She has never set a high value on her life and worth. She has tried to fill that void in her heart with all the wrong things: alcohol, empty sex, food. But over time Gwen has gained a much greater insight about her shortcomings. She also has a doctor who supports her and a boyfriend who cares for her. I am sure that Gwen will not stay a doormat forever. She is going to realize that she is a precious jewel with infinite worth.

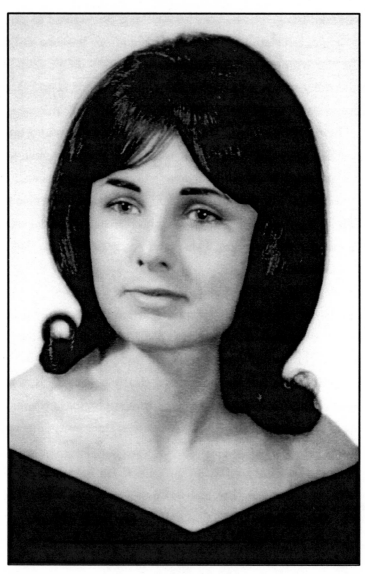

Gwen in 1966

Gwen in 2011

Being a Burden

Donalda called the office for a same-day appointment, stating that she was very stressed out. I completely understood her feelings. Ernest, her husband of over fifty years, was in failing health. In the previous two months, he had to be taken to the hospital numerous times. It all started with a simple slip that caused a severe ankle fracture. That led to a hospitalization of several days. Being the hospital exposed him to some bad bacteria, which caused significant *c. difficile* diarrhea. Ernie had to start broad-spectrum antibiotics for the infection. Because of immobility and decreased urination due to dehydration, Ernie then developed both a serious urinary tract infection and renal failure. While Ernie was in the ER, the foley catheter in his bladder did not drain any urine because his kidneys had completely shut down. Shortly after, Ernie had a very rapid irregular heart rhythm and low blood pressure. It seemed every organ was affected in some way. Ernie was placed in the ICU for intensive treatment by a number of specialists. When he finally improved enough to get out of the hospital, he was still too weak to care for himself. Because Donalda could not care for him, Ernie went to a skilled nursing facility. Clearly, all of this was a tremendous amount to take for a woman in her mid-eighties.

Donalda was sitting in her customary chair when I walked in. Her face was strained, like she was waiting for that proverbial next shoe to drop. I sat down across from her and heard her story. Even though I knew what was going on with Ernie, I let her tell the events at her own pace, because that was what she needed to do to get things off her chest. "I've been waking up in the middle of the night, and I can't go back to sleep. I just lie in bed awake all night long. Is there something light you can give me to help me sleep?" Donalda paused and admitted, "I was so out of it that I rear-ended someone the other day. I didn't even realize they had stopped. No one got hurt, but it did shake me up quite a bit."

"I'm glad you didn't get hurt, Donalda. You just had so much on your mind that you weren't paying attention to what was going on around you." Donalda nodded her head. "Do you have anyone you can talk to?" This time, Donalda shook her head.

"I don't feel like I have anybody. I do talk to the kids, but they seem to be so busy with their own lives."

"Is there someone else?" I asked.

"I have friends at the Senior Center who have told me to call them if I need something, but I haven't really done that."

"Why not, Donalda?"

Donalda sighed. "I've been so self-sufficient for so long that I hate imposing on anybody. I just figure I can handle it. But I'm getting to the point where I'm having trouble handling it. My cup was full, and now it's just running over. I'm realizing that I have a tough time communicating."

I looked Donalda in the eyes and held her gaze. "You know, Donalda, you are an amazing woman. You've accomplished so much in your life, most of it all on your own." Donalda nodded. "But now your greatest strength— self reliance and self sufficiency—has become your greatest weakness. You need to learn how to rely on others, ask for help, and admit vulnerability."

"So what do I do about it?" Donalda asked. She paused and came up with the answer to her own question. "I guess I need to find someone who I can talk to and have the person just listen."

"Can you think of someone in your life who can do that?"

"No, I can't," Donalda responded. "I don't know how to find someone or pick someone. My niece Susan is close to me. She's almost like my daughter. But she's going through a bad time herself right now with a pinched nerve. If I shared my worries, it would just add to her burden and pain. I think she's in enough pain as it is to worry about me as well."

I scooted a bit closer to Donalda. "Let me ask you something. Do you think it's important for people to feel like they're needed?"

"Yes, definitely," Donalda replied.

"Then do you think that asking Susan to listen to you and your concerns would show her that she's needed?" I asked.

Donalda said, "I don't feel that we could be any closer than we already are. There's been a lot of sexual abuse in the family, and we've talked a lot about it. She knows she's like a daughter to me."

"But do you think talking to Susan about your worries would increase or decrease her concern? Do you think she would rather be kept in the dark about how helpless you're feeling?"

Donalda lifted her hands up from her lap and put them back down. "I don't know," she replied.

"Well, Donalda, do you think there is greater fear in the known or the unknown?"

Donalda could see where I was headed. "It's worse to know something's wrong but not knowing what."

I felt like we were finally getting somewhere. "Donalda, I think you should honor the relationship you have with Susan and talk to her. Give her permission to know what's been going on and how you're feeling. It's clear that she loves you dearly and would not want you to be in the emotional state you're in. Removing yourself from Susan's life out of fear of bothering or burdening her is not helping anyone. It's just making things worse. Talking to her might help not just you alone. It might help both of you.

"I have homework for you, Donalda. I want you to call Susan, or better yet, go see her. I want you to spend ten minutes and talk. Susan should not talk herself, just listen. I think it will really help. Can you do that?"

"Yes, I think I can. Thank you for talking with me, Dr. Han."

I got up and we went to the front desk together. I prescribed a mild sleeping agent for her insomnia and asked that she come back in a week for a follow up. Donalda walked out of the office with her head held just a bit higher, her shoulders not as weighed down by the stresses life had placed on her. She now had other people to help bear her burden.

Donalda Matthews

Donalda and Ernie at their son's house, November 1982

Donalda and Ernie in their kitchen on Easter Sunday, April 7, 1985

Donalda and Ernie in 2013

Falling Apart

For a decade, I have been taking care of Sharon and her family. Throughout this time, the family has faced challenges with the blending—and clashes—of the different backgrounds they come from. While this was Sharon's first marriage, her husband, also my patient, was on his third marriage, was twenty-seven years older than her, and came from a completely different culture. Together they had two kids, and there were the children from the other marriages. Some of the children from the previous marriages were grown and independent, but the two teens lived with Sharon and ChungWoo.

It was a "triple whammy" of clashes: age, culture, and religion. Added to that was a blended family of stepchildren and half-siblings, all living under the same roof. The kids, themselves products of two cultures, wrestled with being Amer-Asian and learning how to combine the various aspects of their heritage.

To the credit of the family, everyone worked hard over the years to make things work out as much as possible. Sharon treated the older kids as if they were her own. In turn, the teens treated her as the mother figure, even if they didn't call her "mom." Sharon worked full time as a medical professional, while ChungWoo, semi-retired, did consulting work as an expert in his field.

All of the hard work, however, could not keep the family together. For several years, ChungWoo and Sharon saw me for individual appointments, detailing the struggles each had with the other. Much like the proverbial two-sided coin, I could see the different perspectives each was coming from on the same issue.

One good example was the topic of sleeping arrangements. During one of her appointments, Sharon shared one of her frustrations. "Did you know we haven't slept in the same bed ever since Tina was born almost two years ago? That's not what a marriage is supposed to be like."

When I saw ChungWoo for his own appointment, he mentioned the separate sleeping arrangements as well, but as evidence of consideration to his wife. Apparently, since the kids were born, he was in the habit of getting up at night to check on them. His wife was a light sleeper, and he didn't want to wake her up every night. So, he thought sleeping separately would actually be helpful to her. It was a lack of communication; they hadn't built those bridges of communication needed to understand each other's perspective.

Over time, the distance between them grew wider and wider. Little things that they previously were able to overlook in each other became burrs under the skin that caused constant irritation and resentment. That led to an emotional distance that was compounded by the different expectations of Sharon as a young American wife and ChungWoo as an older Asian man. Sharon had decreased motivation to clean the house or spend household money wisely. ChungWoo found it difficult to maintain his erections during their lovemaking because he was less and less emotionally engaged in the relationship. Both had higher blood pressure and stress levels that were getting difficult to control.

I counseled both of them, balancing the relationship I had with them as individual patients and keeping their personal stories confidential, but using that information to help bridge the gap between them. I was working towards getting the two of them back on the same page regarding their feelings and their marital relationship. My efforts, however, were not successful. Sharon could not learn how to forgive ChungWoo for his perceived slights to her. ChungWoo could not get over his conservative views on how a husband should treat his wife with emotional aloofness. Eventually, Sharon found her emotional support in the arms of another man.

When Sharon moved out of the house, things started getting ugly. ChungWoo used access to the children as a weapon against his wife, and he told her she wouldn't get anything since she was the one who was leaving. Sharon tried to enter into a different phase of her life but still be active in the lives of her children, whom she dearly loved. After a year of wrangling over custody and visitation rights, they came to a general understanding of the status of the kids. The divorce was finalized, ChungWoo stayed in the house, and Sharon continued to live with her boyfriend. The kids didn't like the fact that their parents had split up, but they rolled with the punches admirably.

Of course, life rarely gives long stretches of tranquility, with peace being the exception rather than the norm. After being with her boyfriend for two years, Sharon came to my office with bad news. She had been dealing with vaginal itching and burning for several weeks, and then she found out that her boyfriend had been unfaithful to her with his secretary, a mutual friend of theirs. To top it off, Sharon was taking roller-blading lessons and fell the day before, hitting her head and causing a mild concussion. She was all foggy-headed at work and couldn't concentrate, with occasional bouts of nausea, headaches, and vision changes. When she could think clearly, all she could focus on was her boyfriend's infidelity. She was a mess.

I examined her thoroughly, and fortunately, her concussion was not severe. I gave her pain medications and admonished her not to skate until she was completely better, reducing the chances of her falling and causing a severe "second concussion syndrome." Her vaginal infection was treatable, and so I gave her antibiotics for that. We actually spent the bulk of the office visit talking about her relationship with her boyfriend and whether or not she thought the relationship was salvageable. She still valued this relationship, and he promised that he wanted to work on it at the time he confessed his indiscretion. I suggested that she come back to the office for a re-check of her concussion in a week.

Only three days after I saw her, Sharon showed up at my Saturday morning walk-in clinic as my last patient, her eyes red and swollen. With no one else waiting in the office, I ushered her into the exam room immediately. She barely crossed the threshold of the door before her tears started flowing. She said, "Everything is falling apart!"

Sharon collapsed into the chair, her legs like jelly. She explained in halting sentences, "My boyfriend and I started a delivery service a year ago. We struggled at first, but we worked hard and landed a few great contracts. We were doing great. He and I were spending all of our free time together. For the first time in my life, I was happy.

"A few months ago, one of the couriers had to be let go. We couldn't afford to hire someone else, so Jake had to drive to Pennsylvania every day. He would drive all night and get home at 4 AM, and I would have to be up two hours later to go to work. We were like two ships passing in the night. It was during this time that Jake had the brief affair with the secretary.

"Jake said that he was not seeing her any more, and I believe him. Of course, she's here, and he's in Scranton, so I know there's nothing going on. It's still hard to trust though, so I'm working through that. But I know it's over.

"I thought things were going to calm down. Jake and I could work on our relationship, and we could make the business work out. But yesterday, we found out that one of our biggest contracts, worth $2 million, was just cancelled. We didn't know anything about it. We have fourteen families depending on us, not including our own. We just had to pay a lawyer $30,000 because we got sued, and we were just digging ourselves out of that one. Now what are we going to do?" Sharon buried her face into her hands and wept uncontrollably.

She continued, "I can't eat, I can't sleep, I can't keep anything down. I'm nauseous all the time. And I'm dealing with the concussion on top of it all. I can stay focused when there is something to do, but the moment I slow down, it all comes crashing in, and I fall apart. I can't stop crying."

"Is there anyone you can talk to?" I asked.

"There isn't anyone! My best friend at the job I was at before knew this contract was being terminated, and she didn't say anything. I can't trust her! I have a friend from high school, but she doesn't know anything about the business problems we've been having. And the only other friend I had was the woman we hired to be the company secretary, and she's the one who slept with Jake!"

"What about your parents or your family?"

"I don't want to talk to my family. I'm too embarrassed," Sharon said through her tears. "They just don't understand why I left ChungWoo. They don't know what it was like. They don't know why I'm with Jake. I don't want to be judged by them."

I looked around for some tissue to give to Sharon to clean herself up. There were none, so I ended up giving her a paper towel. As she wiped her tears and runny nose, I collected my thoughts and prayerfully considered what counsel to give her. It was clear that she was completely overwhelmed with everything going on in her life.

I asked, "Sharon, what can you *not* change about the situation?" I answered my own question. "You can't change the fact that Jake was unfaithful. You can't change that the company canceled your contract. Whatever you *can't change*, you should let go, or at least, set aside. So, what *can* you change? What are the next steps you need to take to make that change happen? Let's talk about that."

Sharon replied, "We've called all the drivers together for a meeting at 1:30. We're going to talk about what the next steps are for the company and who is willing to stick it through."

"What about your contract, is there some way you can fight it?" I asked.

"I spent most of yesterday collecting receipts. Our lawyer is looking at the contract to see if there is anything we can do."

"That's good," I told her. "Is there anything else that you can change right now?"

"Jake and I are going to try to talk through our relationship. He's coming back from Scranton right now."

"Those are great plans, and super next steps," I complimented. "Try to continue to focus on those next few steps you can do to change whatever you can change. That way, you don't get overwhelmed with all the things that are going on. Try talking to your high school friend. You haven't told her everything, but she sounds like she would be a good resource for you. I also want you to start this antidepressant, and let's plan to meet in a few days."

Sharon seemed encouraged by these words. I stood up first and she followed. I took a step closer to her and put my arms out for a hug. She gave me a crooked smile and accepted my embrace. I gave her a long hug, sending thoughts of comfort and concern to her.

"That's what I needed," she said as she let go of me. "I haven't had anyone to give me a hug since Jake has been gone all this time."

"Well whenever you need another, you just let me know," I replied. I expect I'll be giving her another hug when she comes in for her follow up visit.

All Shook Up

Mark was in his forties, but he really never went to the doctor. He was a lot like his dad, who didn't think a person should go to the doctor unless there was something wrong. Going to the doctor when you were well was just looking for trouble. After all, what if the doctor actually found something?

In addition, Mark had always been a man of very few words. A part of that stemmed from not wanting to be seen as a complainer. "Real" men were supposed to just tough things out. The other part was that Mark didn't know how to express his thoughts and emotions anyway—not to himself or to his wife and kids, much less to some complete stranger like a doctor. And because he worked for himself and had no insurance, it was easy to go from year to year without addressing the medical issues that were fraying the edges of his life. Even chronic sciatic back pain for over a decade was not enough for Mark to seek medical treatment.

Mark only ended up going to the doctor because he had to. His job as a landscaper and land clearer required that he have a commercial driver's license and medical clearance. Mark's brother finally coerced him to establish himself as a patient in my practice. Scott got along well with me when I took over the office from my step-father, so he thought Mark would be comfortable as well.

So here was Mark, sitting on the exam table, looking much like his older brother. Both were big men with broad shoulders and big guts.

Physically, they were clearly cut from the same mold. But where Scott was loquacious, Mark said as few words as he could get away with. Mark's physical was uneventful, but I did find high cholesterol on the blood work that needed to be addressed. I sent some medicine over to the pharmacy and scheduled a follow up visit.

Several months later, right before his visit, Mark's wife called to cancel the appointment. It seemed Mark never took the medicine I gave him. That set up a pattern for Mark's care. Because of his lack of insurance, he stretched out both medicines and follow up visits as long as possible. Still, Mark was a captive audience for at least once a year for his required driving test, so I fit in as much as I could on those visits. The rest of the time, he avoided me as much as possible.

Unfortunately, Mark's "modus operandi" of avoidance was not limited to medical care. I learned this when Mark's family started to come see me. When his wife Deb came in for her visit, she detailed how Mark refused to deal with anything. Their daughter was so depressed that she started drinking at an early age and cutting. In fact she attempted suicide twice by cutting herself. Instead of talking about the situation and helping his daughter, Mark avoided the house altogether by spending late hours at work. When he was at home, he refused to acknowledge how bad the situation was. That left Deb to have to worry about the entire family, and this level of stress was wreaking havoc with her irritable bowel syndrome and migraines. I could tell Deb was nearing the end of her rope, and she had no one to talk to about the terrible amount of stress going on at home. I prescribed her some medicine as well as counseling.

When Deb came back a few months later, she had positive news to share. Nicolette was doing better. Deb's IBS and migraines were greatly helped by the prescription medicines. And Deb and Mark actually went to a counselor. She told Mark to take more responsibility for his actions and for Deb to step back a bit and allow Mark to deal with more issues.

Thus, a pattern was set. Mark came in when he couldn't get any more medicine and needed refills. Deb showed up when the stress was getting so bad that her IBS or migraines flared. Through it all, they each struggled to break out of the life patterns that only allowed them to limp along, Deb as the Controller and Mark as the Avoider. There were times when Deb came really close to leaving Mark because she just didn't think he would ever change. They were both like cars driving on a dirt road so many times that ruts formed in the road. No matter what they tried, those ruts were so deep that they found it nearly impossible to break out of the damaging set of behaviors they had both formed. It was going to take something drastic to shake things up.

During one of Mark's visits, he happened to mention that his hands and legs had developed a bit of a fine tremor in them. He said he wasn't stressed, but I knew better. After all, the economy was bad, they had almost no money, Mark and Deb were fighting, and the kids were not doing great. So it was classic for Mark to bury his head in the sand and just pretend nothing was wrong. Clearly, his body was trying to tell him something. I told him just that and suggested he work on letting some of his emotions out instead of just keeping them all bottled up like a pressure cooker waiting to explode. He seemed calm enough in the office and wasn't shaking in front of me, so that was proof enough for me.

When Mark came back in several months later for his regular check up, Deb joined us. Deb knew her husband too well to trust him to tell me the whole story. "He's shaking constantly now," she informed me. "If he concentrates, he can make it stop. But if he's just sitting there, he just starts shaking. It's in his legs and stomach, and sometimes his arms. Our dog has to take medicine, and when I watch Mark trying to give it the pill, it looks like he's about to drop it any second."

I watched Mark as he sat there quietly. Sure enough, he had a very slight twitching in his fingers. I asked Mark to stop his shaking, and he did. Once he completely relaxed, the fine tremor came back. I performed a neurological examination on Mark, and he did very well. He did not have the "pill rolling" tremor that is classic for Parkinson Disease. And when he touched his finger to my finger and then to his nose, his actions were smooth and steady, stopping right at a point. So, his cerebellum was intact. I wasn't sure what was going on, but I thought it was possibly an essential tremor, a benign condition of shaking for no apparent reason. Just in case Mark did have some movement disorder, I gave him medication samples and told him to follow up in two weeks.

Two weeks went by, and I got a phone call from Mark. The medicine didn't help at all, and he didn't want to come in just to tell me that. I responded, "OK, Mark. You can come by and pick up some other samples. I understand you are paying out of pocket and do not want to pay for a doctor's visit needlessly, but I can't examine you over the phone. Give that medicine a try and then come in."

Mark came in as promised. Neither medicine was effective. He sat there with his hands and legs shaking gently. By then, the tremor had been going on for several months. "I'm all tensed up," Mark declared. "I can consciously relax, and the tremors stop for a while. But then they come back. It's not all the time, but it's happening more frequently."

I was at a loss for what to do, and I told Mark just that. But I didn't want Mark to go home without trying something else or having a game plan. "Mark, we've tried one class of medicine that didn't work. I'll give you two others. Try one and then the other. If they don't work either, then you have two choices. You can either live with your symptoms, or you can see a neurologist. I could also send you for other tests if you'd like."

"I can't afford other tests, and I definitely can't afford a neurologist," Mark replied. "I'll try the samples."

I didn't see Mark again for three months until he came in for his driving physical. He was shaking like usual, just like he was jittery. The medicines from the previous visit were doing nothing. "Could it still mostly be from stress and anxiety, Mark?" He denied the possibility. Of course I had other thoughts on that. Deb and I had discussed how she was disgusted with her marriage. She told Mark the marriage was over, and she was moving out. Because of patient confidentiality, I could not share what I knew, but I could definitely imagine this news could cause Mark to be jittery. "I'm out of options, Mark. There might not be any treatment for essential tremor. But my diagnosis could also be wrong. You really need to see a neurologist." Mark didn't want to go, again because of the money. I threw my hands up. "OK. But when you want that referral, let me know."

Over the next year, every time Mark came in or called, he asked if there was something that could be done for his shaking. His daughter thought it was a side effect of the cholesterol medicine, so he wanted to stop it. That didn't help. He wondered if it could be Lyme disease since he was in the woods all the time. That was negative. Meanwhile, his shaking was getting worse. It wasn't so bad when he was working and moving around, but when standing still, Mark shook enough that his shirt would quiver. That made Mark very self conscious when talking to people or being in social situations, so he avoided social interactions even more than before.

Mark got to the point where he had more than just shaking. Being a big guy with a big belly and a very physical job, Mark commonly had low back pain. But over the past year, it had been getting worse. It felt tight and stiff all the time. He started taking his wife's muscle relaxants which did help, but it always came back. And then Mark started finding that every so often, he would tell his leg to move, but it wouldn't, which caused him to stumble a bit. It was like there was a disconnect between his muscles and his brain. I was concerned that Mark might have a movement disorder, so I put him on Sinemet, the most common medication used to treat Parkinson.

When Mark came back a few months later, his tremor was no better despite the Sinemet. It might have even made him shake more. Mark wanted to stop the medicine. Deb, who came with him, said, "We need to do something. It's getting worse, and Mark won't say anything, but he's in pain all the time. Just walking hurts his back. He can barely get through the day. It just can't go on this way."

I sighed. "I know, Deb. But I've run out of ideas other than going to the neurologist. I've tried medicine after medicine, and nothing has helped. I know it's expensive to go, but Mark is losing money if he can't work. Maybe you qualify for assistance and can get a price break since you guys don't have insurance. You could try the UConn neurology program. It takes a while to get into, but they're probably less expensive than a private practice." Mark and Deb agreed to bite the bullet, and I saw them out.

Several months later Mark and Deb came back to the office. They finally got in to see the neurologist, and the diagnosis was not good. Mark had early-onset Parkinson Disease. Between my last appointment with them and the neurology evaluation, Mark's condition had accelerated like the proverbial snowball rolling downhill. His fine twitching was replaced by that classic rhythmic pill-rolling tremor. Mark lost the texture and small movements of his face. With his eyes staring straight ahead and his mouth partially open, Mark had the mask-like face so common in Parkinson patients. What was at first so difficult for me to diagnose was now evident even to a green medical student.

I talked to Mark and Deb at length about his diagnosis and how he was doing with it all. "What I don't understand is that I put you on three different medicines to treat Parkinson, and none of them worked. You even said your shaking got worse. That got me even more confused."

"They said I wasn't on it long enough," Mark replied. "I'm back on that Sinemet you gave me, and I'm shaking more actually. We're supposed to go back in a few weeks to see them again."

Deb chimed in. "He's gotten so much worse over the past two months. He's so stiff he has excruciating pain in his back. Mark has to stop and rest just walking from the car to the doorway."

"I'm off balance," Mark added. "I walk bent over, leading with my head. I'm constantly in danger of falling over. When I start walking, it's slow, but I'm leaning forward so much that by the end of the hallway, I'm practically running to keep from face planting." Mark got up and showed me. Mark's body was bent forty-five degrees, with his head way in front of his feet. He took short, shuffling steps, again so typical for Parkinson Disease. It was not hard to see how one misstep could send Mark toppling over.

"The doctor called Mark a Five Stepper." Deb explained, "He told us most people take two steps to turn around. Mark has to turn and turn and turn, and he's still not facing the other way. To get from the kitchen to the dining room, Mark has to grab onto the counter, the fridge, and the chair. He's always looking for the next thing to grab onto so he doesn't fall. And that's at home. He just can't do all the things he needs to do at work. A lot of our money comes from Mark selling firewood for the winter. We usually sell twenty cords in the fall. Mark will be lucky if he even gets in five." Deb arched her eyebrows. "With him like that, do you think I'd trust him with a chainsaw by himself in the woods?"

"The doctor also told me that I should go as Michael J. Fox for Halloween," Mark interjected. "But I'm a good bit bigger than he is." I thought the comment was darkly humorous. "And hey, we have a new granddaughter. We don't have to buy a rocker, because I can just shake her to sleep."

Deb continued, "We're thinking about filing for disability. Maybe if he gets on State, that will help with the medical bills. Do you know how much his medicines are costing? But no matter how much they are, Mark *has* to take them. And I don't even want to talk about the neurology bill. They charged us $300 for the last visit. Because I make $40,000 a year, we don't qualify for any sort of assistance. Our appointment is next week. And the woman at the front desk said if I did not hand her the money right then, there was no way we were going back to see the doctor. So that's where the next entire paycheck is going."

Deb continued, "We're getting a divorce. That way, they can't attach my paycheck. The bills are killing us. Nothing's going to change at home, of course. In fact, I'm rubbing his back at night because it's so tight. I help him dress because his shoulder is hurting so much he can barely get his shirt on. I'm shaving him because he can't stop his shaking to do it himself. It's comical when you think about it.

"It's not been easy, of course. You know Mark. He doesn't say much, but he's depressed about everything. And when I get home after a long day, I just want to sit on the couch and relax. But Mark is sitting there and he's shaking. I want to say, 'For God's sake stay still!' But he can't help it. We're at the dinner table, and the entire table is shaking when Mark's hands are on it. There are just a million things, but we're managing." Deb ended with a wry smile tinged with a bit of what could almost be considered fondness.

Listening to Deb's long accounting of the past two months made me consider what the past two years had brought the family. It was ironic, really. Previously, Deb threatened to divorce Mark. Well, now it was happening; Deb served him papers a week before. But the reason behind it was completely different from what they had originally envisioned. Sometimes, difficulties and challenges tear families apart. In this case, it brought Mark's family together. And it wasn't just help from Deb. The kids and in-laws pitched in to help Mark with responsibilities he couldn't handle by himself.

We ended the visit with a plan of action. If they were going to have to pay $300 up front, Mark and Deb needed to make the most of the upcoming neurologist visit. I told them to get detailed instructions not only for just the next step, but the next several steps. They had to be honest with the neurology office about their current financial situation. I hoped Mark could minimize the pricey specialist visit to once or twice a year and follow up with me for medication adjustments and refills.

For over a year, Mark had no answers for the cause of his condition. Now, he knew. Although it wasn't good news, at least now he had a starting point and a direction. And Mark was not going to travel this difficult road alone. Not only did he have me as his doctor to help, he also had his family to journey with him, one small, wobbly step at a time.

Mark and Deb

The Undertow

George was referred to my office from a patient who knew that we were an open and affirming medical practice, providing a nonjudgmental, welcoming atmosphere for gay and lesbian patients. George no longer felt comfortable at his previous doctor's office, so he asked a gay co-worker about where he could go for a physical and ended up with me.

George was taller than I at almost 6 feet, but fairly thin at only 147 lbs. He would have looked younger than a man in his forties, but long-standing smoking caused wrinkles around his eyes, aging him. George struck me as a very quiet individual. He showed very little emotion on his face, and he spoke with a very soft voice that required concentration and focus to hear. His blue-gray eyes were kind, if guarded. He reminded me of a dog in a kennel, wanting to love and trust but having been kicked around too much in the past.

Sitting on the exam table, George answered my questions about his medical history and life in general. I used the time to get to know him better and to let him know about my general personality and practice style. George's answers to my questions elucidated why he was so guarded. Raised in a very straight-laced, conservative, Catholic family in the 1960's, George had struggled with his sexuality since childhood. He knew he was attracted to the boys around him much more than the girls. This was in direct conflict with what he knew he was supposed to feel, but that didn't change anything.

In an effort to hide his true feelings, George played the "straight game" very well. He played sports, hung out with the guys, and dated girls. All through high school, he kept his secret feelings deeply buried.

In college, George explored his sexuality a bit, but he was definitely circumspect about it and still in the closet. When he met Tammy, he thought he had found the answers to his struggle. George's fraternity buddy was dating someone who knew Tammy, and they thought George and Tammy would be great together. George found Tammy's company to be pleasant. There was enough of a connection there, so they continued to hang out. Eventually, after a few years, they got married. Although there was love between them, any passion in the relationship was more one sided.

Through the first several years of their marriage, George worked hard to do what was expected of him. After all, that was the basis of the marriage from the start. George knew that he was expected to meet a girl, get married, and have kids. Well, he got the girl, and he got married. To make sure that everyone knew that he was not failing in the bedroom, George had not one, not two, but four kids.

George loved his children with all his heart, and they gave him great joy. But as he devoted his life to raising the kids, his relationship with Tammy grew more distant. Resentments set in, with conflicts on who should work, dealing with child care, dividing household expenses, and any number of other issues. Their sex life tapered off, as did the general intimacy they showed to each other. For the next ten years, they didn't have sex at all, living more like roommates than a married couple.

Each unresolved conflict and unexpressed frustration built up pressure in the relationship. It was the proverbial powder keg waiting for a spark. A relatively minor incident regarding taxes became an argument that blew up, with pent-up resentments exploding and harsh words spoken on both sides.

A week passed with no forgiveness or reconciliation on either side. Tammy looked at George and said, "Where does this leave us? Divorce?"

"Yes," George replied.

Tammy nodded. "Well, let me get a full-time job first."

George and Tammy started sleeping in separate areas of the house. George moved his belongings into the guest room. Tammy kept the master bedroom and claimed it as her own. The tension between them grew to such an extent that George could not stand to be in the same room with his wife for more than a couple of minutes. They ended up splitting their time with the kids. Although they all lived in the same house, George would "get the kids" for half of the week, and Tammy would see them the other half. Whichever person who didn't have the kids for that day was expected to stay in his or her room for the evening. The kids, ages 14 to 18, spent their teen years living in a literally divided house.

Typically, George arose and went to work before anyone else got up. On his days with the kids, by the time he arrived home from work, Tammy was already in her bedroom. George then fed the kids, made sure they did their homework, and got them to bed. On Tammy's days, he went directly to his room in the evening. If George stepped out onto the porch for a cigarette on an "off day" and saw the kids in the back yard, he would not approach them, and they would not say hello to him.

The kids knew which parent to ask for friends to come over or to go to parties, depending on what day of the week it was. Whichever parent had the "on day" took the kids to their various school and sports functions. When their son Jonathan had his baseball games, George cheered him on at first base, while Tammy went to the other side of the field at third base to show her support. After the game, they drove their separate cars back to the house.

Before the division, the family traditionally went to Tammy's parents' house in Pennsylvania, so George stopped going with them. For Christmas, George took the kids to his parents' house either Christmas Eve or Christmas Day, and Tammy got the other day. His oldest son's graduation was on an "off day," so Tammy sat with the kids during the ceremony, and George sat by himself. The kids came over to greet George while Tammy pointedly looked in the other direction.

After a while, George and Tammy could no longer talk to each other. Notes left on the kitchen counter were their only form of communication. The established living situation was toxic to everyone involved. Neither George nor Tammy could move forward with their lives. Mostly for financial reasons, they were stuck. Still, for five years life settled into an uneasy, dysfunctional pattern. Things would have continued if Tammy hadn't forced things into an even worse state. When George took the kids out of town on a vacation, Tammy broke into George's locked bedroom. There, she found materials that proved in no uncertain terms that George was gay.

When George got home, she confronted him with the information. He saw no reason to deny it. She also insisted that George inform the kids. George brought them all together and told them that he was still the same person, but that this is how he was. The two older kids were very supportive, while the two younger were more subdued. Still, overall, it went fairly well. George still spent time with the kids half the week, and his relationship with them did not falter.

At the time of his new-patient physical when I met him, George had just recently come out to his kids. He had had a boyfriend for a year and a half, and he was trying to figure out this next phase in his life. Maybe because of his smoking, or possibly from residual guilt about having a same-sex partner, George was having erectile dysfunction and increased blood pressure. I performed his physical exam, suggested some smoking cessation techniques, and gave him some Viagra. George did not want blood pressure medication, but he agreed to come back in a month for a re-check.

True to his word, George came back a month later. Unfortunately, his blood pressure was still very high. I discussed with George the importance of getting his blood pressure under control or risk having a massive heart attack or stroke. He agreed to go on blood pressure medicine at that point and said he would work on his smoking a bit more. I gave him medicine and saw him monthly, watching his blood pressure go from a very high 170/105 to a normal 130/80. Pleased with his progress, I gave George a three-month supply of his medicines and told him I would see him in the spring.

When George walked into the office for his follow up visit, it seemed like the body was moving, but the spirit was gone. George had no light in his eyes. One foot went in front of the other, more like a robot than a human being. He sat himself onto the exam table, not saying anything as I got myself situated.

"So how have you been, George?" I asked.

"Not that good," he responded in his characteristic soft voice, but now devoid of emotion. "My wife is taking my four kids from me. I also broke it off with my boyfriend. The relationship wasn't working out. I know it was the right thing to do, but I still feel for him."

"Oh George, I'm so sorry to hear that," I replied. "How have you been handling it all?"

"I've been smoking a lot more," he said matter-of-factly. "There's not much I *can* do."

"Well this would explain your blood pressure being a lot higher than it was the last time I saw you."

"Yeah, that would be it. I need more blood pressure medicine. But I guess I won't be needing any more Viagra any time soon."

George and I talked for a bit about his medical problems and the current situation with the custody battle for the kids. During the conversation, it seemed George's mouth was moving, but his heart was completely disengaged. After a while, I stopped talking and looked at George. He looked back at me, not saying anything either. "George, I have a mental image that I would like to share with you."

"Sure, go ahead," George said.

I continued, "Have you been to the beach and seen the warning signs that read, 'Dangerous Undertow'?" George nodded his head. "When I look at you, I see the image of a nice, calm, flat shore. Everything looks great, but if you go just under the surface, there is a rip current undertow that will sweep you right out to the ocean."

George smiled ruefully and said, "Yep, that's me."

"Well, this is something you're going to need to figure out if you're going to get to a better place for yourself. You can't go through your whole life wearing this mask like everything is going well when life is really eating you up inside."

"Yeah, I know," George acknowledged. "I've never been really good at dealing with my emotions." George did not want to go on medicines for his anxiety and depression, but he was willing to see a counselor. I gave George the name of a therapist who specialized in helping gay men, and I encouraged him to come back in a month for another visit.

"Ok, George, one last thing before we're done." I stood up and wrapped George in a tight hug. We both held that hug for what seemed like several minutes. George's countenance was visibly lightened when I let go. I patted him on the back and ushered him out.

When George returned in a month, I asked him about his current social situation. "Nothing's changed," was his reply. George did take one positive step though. He contacted Richard, the therapist, and had a few sessions with him. He was moving in the right direction of where he needed to be, but it was "baby steps," as he put it. I encouraged George to consider going to *Discovery*. I told him it would help him reconnect with his emotions and deal with them more constructively than burying them so deep he couldn't feel anything. Most importantly, I told George that *Discovery* would give him an opportunity to experience something that he might have never received before: unconditional love and trust. George was skeptical about the program, especially since I wouldn't tell him specifics of what to expect. Still, he said he would look into it.

The following month, George came back. He had considered but not committed to going to *Discovery*. He had concerns about sharing his story and being accepted as a gay man, especially since the program was in Texas, practically the buckle of the Bible Belt. I wanted to give George another resource. "I have a patient named Dean who has a very similar life story as yours, George. Dean was married and had two kids before he came out. Because of a couple of life situations, I recommended Dean attend *Discovery*. He just finished his third and last session, and he got a lot out of the program. Everyone in *D3* crafts a mission statement, and his is, '*to educate and support the gay community concerning issues related to HIV/AIDS and to let those that already have it know someone cares.*' Dean is a great guy, and he would absolutely know where you're coming from."

George looked at me with disbelief. "I thought I was the only one going through something like this."

"Oh no," I assured him. "I have a number of patients in your situation, at all different stages. You're definitely not alone in this." George seemed assured and relieved at this revelation. I gave George the contact information and left it up to him to touch base with Dean. I gave George another end-of-the-visit hug and encouraged him to follow up on the things we talked about.

George and I continued to have regular follow ups. He continued his sessions with the therapist, even if he didn't like the process. "He wants me to take out my anger on inanimate objects, and it makes me uncomfortable."

"Why is that?"

"I'm afraid of what I might do if I really got angry. But Richard says that there are no negative emotions, just emotions. I know I need to deal with it, but I don't like it.

"I have a hard time defining my feelings. I can give the effect of the feeling more than the feeling itself. For example, when Tammy walked into the kitchen as I was getting ready for work, I just got so uptight that I had to walk out. I wouldn't be able to tell you exactly how I felt at that time, just what it caused me to do."

"So you avoid and withdraw rather than facing the uncomfortable feelings you get," I concluded.

"Yes, that's it. I've also never been able to stand up to my wife. I've just always done what she's told me to do. Now, I'm supposed to ask her any time I want to have the kids. I had to ask her if I could have the kids for Father's Day."

"Wait, aren't you two still married? And you live in the same house? Don't you have just as much right to spend as much time with the kids as you want?" I asked quizzically.

"Yes, you're right," he replied sheepishly. "I just always have had a hard time standing up to Tammy. Even since college it's been like this. And now I just don't even want to talk to her. Richard told me I should tell Tammy that I'm serving her divorce papers. I just want a sheriff to show up at the door and hand her the papers."

"I think that's another instance of you avoiding the problem." I told him. "You're going to have to talk to her at some point, no matter what. I think it would be easier to do it now and work through some of those issues before the lawyers get involved."

George promised he would consider it, as well as work on his problem with conflict avoidance and passive–aggressiveness. As I gave George his customary goodbye hug, he said, "Thank you for caring." I told him it was an honor to take care of him and walk with him through this process.

George has a long way to go before he gets a handle on the various issues in his life. But at least he has resources now that he did not before. I still hope he'll consider going to *Discovery* some day. I know it would help him face his weaknesses, his disconnect between his head and his heart, and his running away from conflict. Most importantly, *Discovery* would give George a group of people who loved him unconditionally, and who couldn't use that?

Laughter is the Best Medicine

"What's that Dr. Han?" My nurse asked me as I was wrapping up a book to send in the mail.

"I'm sending out volume two of the book *The Art of Sex*," I told her.

"Really? They have a volume two?"

"Yes," I replied. "The first book was *The Art of Sex*. This one is *The Handbook on Treatment of Communicable Diseases*."

****

Don came in with shoulder and neck pain that had been going on for several weeks after a lot of yard work. His range of motion was good, and the neurologic exam was normal. All I found was some tight muscles around the area.

"I'll send over some anti-inflammatories for you, Don. But what would really help is a long massage from an attractive woman."

"Well what's my wife going to think about that?" Don asked.

I chuckled and said, "Actually, I *was* referring to your wife."

Don looked at me, his face reddening slightly. "Don't tell my wife I said that," he replied.

****

As a family doctor I have multiple patients in the same family. Examining one patient automatically brings to mind the other members of the family who also come to see me. Once when examining Marge, an elderly woman whom I had been caring for years, I offhandedly asked her how her husband was doing. I had unfortunately forgotten that he had recently died suddenly of a massive heart attack. She reminded me of the fact by saying, "I think he's doing much better, since he's in heaven now." Oh my God! I had completely forgotten he had died!

"Well," I told her, "it just goes to show you that I still think about him." This definitely was one instance of "open mouth and insert foot." Unfortunately, I did it again....

Marge continued to come see me, and on a subsequent office visit, I had a new first-year medical student with me. It was her first day in the office, and Marge was one of her first patients after several months of classwork. I introduced the two of them, and I told my medical student a bit about Marge's medical background. During my brief talk, I casually asked her, "So how's your husband Phillip, by the way?"

Marge gave me a flat look, and she reached out and gently took my hand. "You know," she said, "this is the *second* time you've asked me." Oh my God!! I just did it *again*. I just asked this poor woman *twice* how her dead husband was doing! And this time, I did it in front of my first year medical student. I wonder what she must have thought about her supposedly wiser and more experienced preceptor after he asked a poor woman about her husband who died suddenly from a heart attack.

It ended up working out well. My faux pas actually served to break the ice, and Marge and my medical student ended up becoming good friends over the three years the student was with me.

********   *Maureen Slattery*

Jeff was a relatively new patient to the office. I had only seen him a few times before. He had a previous history of erectile dysfunction, and he had already tried Viagra, Cialis, and Levitra, but none of them worked well. I decided to show him how to use a vacuum erection device to obtain an erection.

I brought in the demo unit of the model I was most familiar with, but when we tried it, it was broken and could not maintain a suction to produce an erection. After several attempts I gave up. But, Jeff was in luck, because a different model from another company had just arrived. I had not even taken it out of the box yet, but it was just a pump, so how hard could it be?

Jeff got lubed up, and we slipped the contraption over his flaccid penis. He held it close to him and pumped away, and lo and behold, it worked! In fact, it worked so well that he completely filled the chamber.

"OK, so how do I get this off?" He asked me. That's when I realized that I had no idea. This model did not have any button or knob like all the other units I had ever seen previously. I tried pumping it a few more times, thinking it had to release somehow, but that only made the situation worse. Then I tried twisting it, but that almost took off the poor man's member. "Ow, ow, ow!" He exclaimed.

Now I was really concerned. My poor patient had a penis pump stuck to his erection, and I had no idea how to get it off. Fortunately, after much work, Jeff was able to wiggle his finger in between his penis and the pump, thereby breaking the vacuum and allowing his penis to slip out.

When I gave the pump to my nurse Joan, she discovered the release mechanism in less than a minute.

****

Lance came in for a severe itchy rash in his armpits. It was spreading with red dots down his sides. When I took a look at it, I said, "It's a type of fungus, Lance. I'll write a prescription for you."

"What's it called?" Lance asked.

"Candida. It's quite common."

Lance exclaimed, "I can't believe it. She's torturing me even after our divorce. That's my ex-wife's name: C-A-N-D-I-D-A."

Lance spelled it perfectly.

****

Frank is one of my stereotypical middle-aged American patients—a guy who enjoys watching sports more than playing them. When he came in for his physical, I had to break some news to him.

"Frank, I'm afraid I have to tell you that you have Dunlops Disease."

"What's that, Doc?" Frank asked, concerned.

"Dunlops Disease is when your belly's "done lopped" over your belt," I informed him.

He laughed and said, "I guess you're right, Doc."

I told him, "Well, be glad you don't have DPS, the extreme form of Dunlops Disease. DPS stands for Disappearing Penis Syndrome.

SEARCHING FOR ANSWERS

"In oneself lies the whole world and if you know how to look and learn, the door is there and the key is in your hand. Nobody on earth can give you either the key or the door to open, except yourself."

~Jiddu Krishnamurti, philosopher and author of many books, including *The First and Last Freedom*

The Hidden Cost

I started taking care of John when I helped out at Palisades Family Practice for two years. John and I hit it off, and he planned his visits to coincide with my Thursday hours. John and I were both "straightforward, straight shooting" sorts of guys, and we seemed to laugh with each other at every visit. After my tenure at the office came to a close, John transferred his records to my main office and continued seeing me exclusively.

When we first met, John was a bit on the pudgy side, wearing 36" pants and overhanging even those. This did not help his diabetes or high cholesterol. He made a commitment to start exercising and took up racquetball. Over time, John went from 180 lbs to 164. He was able to stay off medicines and treat his diabetes with just diet and exercise. He did not come to the office very often, just for some regular diabetes checks and a few colds, arthritis pains, and self-limiting conditions. Overall, he was a very easy patient to take care of.

One of the appointments John kept each year was his annual physical. Along with the exam, I asked routine preventative questions. John did not smoke. He drank only socially and in moderate amounts. He and his wife were happily married, even if they were not physically intimate. "We're happy where we are," he told me. Since slimming down to a weight that was more appropriate, John seemed to be the model for a fit man in his 60's. In fact, John kept up his exercising after retirement and managed to get to 145 lbs. He was looking quite good.

About two months after his physical, John came back to the office. He had been feeling fatigued at the physical, but had not paid much attention to it. Since it was continuing, he came in for an evaluation. He had also been doing some work outside, and although he couldn't remember hitting his arm against anything, he had a big tender bruise on his upper arm. He was wondering if a recent change in his cholesterol medicine could have caused the symptoms. I did not recall easy bruising as a common side effect, but fatigue could definitely be caused by just about any medication. Since he already had a regular appointment for blood work scheduled for the following month, we decided to hold off changing his medicines or doing any further tests.

A month later, John showed up for his visit. He confessed he couldn't take the continuing muscle pain any more, so he stopped the cholesterol medicine a week previous. I told him it was quite all right, that I understood. I did his exam, which was normal, and the blood work done that day was also excellent. I told him to stay off the new cholesterol medicine, and things should improve.

Two months later, John was back in the office for a re-check. "I don't know what's going on, Dr. Han," he told me. "I have been feeling more and more tired. I sleep very well, but I get tired by mid morning. I feel like I can veg all day but not sleep. When I was working, I was on my feet for nine hours a day every day, and I never needed a sick day. Now, I can't do anything. And I'm losing weight, but I'm not going to the gym at all. I went from 144 to 137, and I'm not eating any less. And now I'm also getting pains in the back of my right knee."

Other than looking generally tired, John seemed healthy. However, I did a battery of tests and told him to come back in a week for a follow-up. That evening, the blood tests came back, and it seemed John had inflammation through his body because one of his blood results called the

ESR came back very elevated. I diagnosed Polymyalgia Rheumatica, an autoimmune condition that typically struck people in their sixties. I called John up and started him on high-dose prednisone, the standard treatment for the condition.

A week later, John told me he was feeling much better. Just a few hours after his first dose of prednisone, he had significant improvement of his fatigue. The pain in the backs of his legs and the rest of his joints almost disappeared. His weight stabilized. I was relieved that I found the right diagnosis and treatment for him. I told him to come back in a couple of weeks for an evaluation.

John showed up for his scheduled appointment. He was no longer having joint pains, but he was still feeling very tired, especially in the mornings. By the afternoons, he seemed to wake up more. More concerning to him, though, was the fact that he was getting a lot of diarrhea. He was wiping himself so often that his bottom was getting raw. This was also causing further weight loss, another six pounds since his last check.

His exam was normal except for his raw bottom that he had described earlier. Blood tests showed that his ESR had improved to 33, but still was not under 20, which is considered the upper limit of normal. Polymyalgia Rheumatica usually requires prednisone treatment for almost a year. I surmised that his illness was particularly stubborn to treatment. The diarrhea could be from the medicine I gave him to protect his bones against osteoporosis while he was on the prednisone. I was concerned, but it seemed John was on all the right medicine. I had him schedule another follow-up in three weeks.

John came back as scheduled. He had again lost weight, on average of more than a pound a week. The diarrhea had gotten worse. It came on so quickly that he actually had accidents if he was not within twenty feet of the bathroom. Frequently, five minutes after one attack of diarrhea, he would have another. Imodium did help, but only marginally. On top of all of this, John was exhausted all the time. He was sleeping from 10 PM to 8:30 AM. After getting up, shaving, and having breakfast, he had to rest for another hour. He did much better in the afternoon, but it seemed the entire morning was a waste.

I was very concerned with John's condition. His illness was going far beyond the normal course of Polymyalgia Rheumatica. I offered him a referral to a rheumatologist for a second opinion, and he said he would consider it. I made an appointment for a close follow-up in a week.

John ended up not being able to wait a whole week. The diarrhea had gotten so bad that he left early from his vacation and came back for an evaluation at the Express Care and then my office. In the past, John had not been interested in getting a colonoscopy or seeing a gastroenterologist. After struggling with his illness so much, he agreed to an evaluation.

Our office scheduled an urgent appointment with a gastroenterologist for that same day. The GI doctor thought the diarrhea was most likely from an infectious cause and sent cultures. Since John had not had his screening colonoscopy, the doctor scheduled this as well. The colonoscopy did not look all that bad, but every biopsy came back showing an acute cytomegalovirus (CMV) infection.

With this diagnosis, the GI doctor sent John to an infectious disease specialist. From the time I sent John to the GI doctor to when he was seen by the ID doctor, John had lost another 20 pounds and was now a frail 117 pounds. The ID doctor went through all of the medical records and labs to date. He started John on antiviral medication for CMV. Because CMV infection is most frequently seen in people with a decreased immune system, the doctor did a host of other tests. For completeness sake, he tested for HIV, which came back positive. Worse yet, John's CD4 count had already dropped to an alarming 47. A CD4 count below 250 tipped him into the diagnosis of frank AIDS.

I got the call from the ID doctor on the day it was diagnosed. When he told me the results, I was shocked. "Did John tell you where he might have gotten it from?" I asked.

"I didn't feel like asking," the doctor confessed.

"What did his wife say when you told them?"

"She wasn't with him today," he replied. "John is the only one who knows. We're going to start him on triple therapy for his HIV, along with the antiviral for the CMV. I was going to have you follow up with him."

"I'll see John right away," I assured him.

John came tottering into the office the next day, and he looked just terrible. He had gone from a spry 150 lbs to barely 115. John looked like he had aged fifty years in a matter of a month. His skin was hanging on a frame of bones, and he was painful to watch as he shuffled down the hall to the exam room.

John let out a sigh as he sank into the chair, while I pulled up the stool and sat facing him. I did not say anything for a bit, trying to take stock of John's emotional state. John waited quietly, letting me break the silence. "I'm really sorry to hear about your diagnosis, John." He breathed out and nodded.

"Have you told your wife?" John shook his head no. "How do you think she's going to take it?" I asked.

"She's going to take it very hard," John said simply.

"When do you think you might have been exposed to HIV?" I asked.

"Maybe five to eight years ago."

"HIV is usually only transmitted through sharing needles or sex," I told him. "Was it drugs or sex?"

"It was sex."

John was answering my questions, but giving me only exactly what I asked. I persisted, "Was it a person you knew or didn't know?"

"I didn't know."

"Did you pay for sex?" I asked.

"Yes."

"How long did it go on?"

"A few months."

"Did you use condoms?"

"I believe so."

I thought that was a fairly noncommittal answer. "So after a few months, you stopped."

"I couldn't afford it any more," John replied.

"That was a fairly ironic answer," I said, but gently. I thought about the hidden cost, how the tryst cost John so much more than money. Because of a poor decision and being in the wrong place at the wrong time with the wrong person, John was not going to enjoy the retirement for which he had worked his entire life.

Because of our many years together and the bond of trust we had built, John continued to unfold his story. He and his wife were nearing forty years of marriage. The sex at first was good although not very frequent. After having two kids, they were not interested in having more. John's appetite for sex was always more than his wife's, whose preferred method of birth control was abstinence. Still, John respected his wife's wishes and did not push too hard for sex. The time between their lovemaking grew longer and longer, until eventually they stopped having sex altogether. They were still deeply in love with each other and did everything together, just not the sex.

After almost a decade of abstinence, John had a resurgence of interest in sex. He did not feel comfortable pressuring his wife for sex, so he decided to pay for it. After a couple of times, John found it drained his pocketbook while not giving him lasting fulfillment. He cut off ties, again contenting himself with his platonic though not loveless relationship with his wife. He could not have imagined that his short period of experimentation would lead to the complete unraveling of his life eight years later.

"How are you going to tell your wife?" I asked John.

He paused. "I'm going to say, 'The expensive medicine I have to start taking is for HIV.'"

"Well, that's definitely one way to do it," I said. "I don't think there's a perfect way. No matter what, it's going to be devastating news. She's known for a while that you have been sick. Just find a time to sit her down and be honest. There's bound to be a lot of grief and anger and fear. If there's anything I can do, let me know."

John and I talked a bit further about increasing his caloric intake and getting as much weight back on as possible. I tweaked his medication and suggested that he come back in a week or so for a follow-up. I gently put my arm around his stooped shoulder as he shuffled out.

John couldn't make it back to the office. He continued to grow weaker and lose weight despite the Ensure, HIV medicine, and antiviral CMV medicine. Because he was looking dehydrated and dizzy, his wife took him back to the GI doctor. He was found to have a low blood pressure and fast heart rate. The GI doctor made the decision to admit him to the hospital to stabilize his condition.

When John was admitted to the hospital, I called his wife. She confirmed that he told her about the HIV but that no one else in the family knew. Both kids were flying in, but she was not planning on telling them more than "your father has a serious viral infection." I could tell she was barely holding on to her composure and sanity. I gently encouraged her to seek some advice from her doctor and possibly a counselor. She needed someone she could freely express herself to and vent and scream if necessary. This was not something that she should try to handle all on her own.

Every few days, I called John's wife at home to get an update on his condition, which worsened. In spite of high doses of medicine, the CMV spread to his lungs and caused a viral pneumonia. John had to be put on a ventilator at increasingly high levels of oxygen. A feeding tube was placed to give him nutrition. He became agitated and had to be sedated so he did not fight the ventilator. John required so much fluid and IV medicine that a PICC line was placed in a large vein, but it clotted.

Two weeks into his hospital course, John's wife told me that the ID doctor told the kids the whole truth. "They took it fairly well," she said. "At least now, I don't have to spend all my energy trying to come up with more lies." I told her that it was a really good thing that they knew, and she had a lot of better things to do with her energy than hiding the truth. I encouraged her to spend as much time with John and the kids as she could, but she needed to save some energy for herself as well. She couldn't use up all of her reserves, because she was going to need those reserves in the future.

Unfortunately, John's condition never improved. The amount of oxygen he required doubled and then tripled. His organs began to fail one at a time. A month after John was admitted, he passed away. As a consolation, John died peacefully with his family by his side. I called John's wife one last time to offer my condolences. John was finally at peace, and some day, his family might get to certain level of peace themselves regarding the loss of a loving husband and devoted father.

A Difficult Diagnosis

I was in the middle of seeing a patient when there was a knock on the door and my nurse entered. "Dr. Han, Dr. Potter is on the phone and wanted to speak to you about a mutual patient." I always answer phone calls from physicians immediately, so I excused myself from the room and picked up the phone.

"Hi Minh, this is Bob. You sent Bruce Levesque to me to treat his iritis. We've tried multiple medicines for the itchiness, redness, and pain in his eyes, none of them seemed to work. So I decided to do a couple of tests. Now, I'm stuck with the results and what to do with them. His RPR was over 4000."

RPR is a screening test for syphilis, and I had never heard of a number so high. I told Dr. Potter as much. "Bob, this isn't conclusive for syphilis, but there is definitely concern. You can do the follow-up tests and treat him, or you can send him to me. If you do diagnose him, then you're also obligated to report the incident to the health department and have them follow up as well."

"Can you do it then, Minh?" Dr. Potter asked. "It's been a long time since I've ordered any tests or treatment for syphilis." I told him I would be glad to see Mr. Levesque back in my office.

A few days later, Bruce came in for his appointment. While we reviewed his labs and the next step, Bruce's demeanor seemed very subdued. "The guy I've been with for the past year was just diagnosed with HIV," Bruce confessed.

"Oh, Bruce, I'm so sorry," I replied. "Is there any chance you might have contracted it?"

"We've always been safe," he assured me. "But I know things can happen. We should check and make sure. My friend is actually taking the news really well. But he's always been that sort of person. I'm really more anxiety-ridden about my possible syphilis than he is."

I assured Bruce that we would add the HIV to the panel of tests I was ordering. I asked Bruce if he had noticed any rashes or lesions, and he told me there was one under his scrotum that had been there off and on for a while, and it was tender to the touch. I examined the area and cultured it. The area was sensitive to my swab, and I told Bruce that was actually a good sign. Syphilitic ulcers were usually painless. I put the specimen with the blood tube and told Bruce I would call him with the results as soon as they came in.

I am sure the following few days were painfully slow as Bruce waited for the test results. They did finally come in, and I called him. The news was mixed. Thankfully, the HIV test came back negative. However, I could not tell for sure that Bruce did not have HIV because the incubation period could be as long as three to six months. If he had contracted the virus in the past six months, he might actually have HIV even though the test was negative. Bruce had a Ph.D. and was very intelligent. Although he did not know medicine, he understood my explanation perfectly.

Furthermore, the confirmation test for syphilis came back positive. It looked like Bruce indeed had syphilis. That meant I had to get the health department involved. They would interview him, determine all of his sexual contacts, and follow him to make sure he received proper treatment. At the least, Bruce was facing a very large shot of penicillin with a very large needle. To add insult to injury, the medicine was also very expensive at $150 a shot. I informed Bruce of all of these things and laid out the treatment plan. He seemed resigned and said he would pick the medicine up before his appointment.

A few days before his appointment, I received a call from the health department. The nurse assigned to his case told me that if Bruce could determine that he had contracted syphilis within the past year, he would only need one shot of penicillin. If not, he would need three shots spaced a week apart. Furthermore, the nurse was concerned that the syphilis had migrated into his nervous system, causing neuro-syphilis. This might explain his eye problems, with the syphilis travelling down his optic nerve to cause inflammation in his eye. It would also explain why the RPR was so incredibly high. To rule out the possibility that it had spread to the brain, Bruce needed a lumbar puncture. If this was positive, and there was syphilis in his nervous system, Bruce would have to be admitted to the hospital for a week-long treatment of IV antibiotics.

When Bruce came in for his visit, there was tension written all over his face. When he spoke, he was barely audible. "I talked to the woman at the health department. They called me yesterday. I have to go for a spinal tap, right?" I confirmed what he had heard. "Is there something you can give me? I couldn't get through my day yesterday when I heard." Bruce's lips trembled and his voice cracked as he tried to finish his sentence.

I looked at him, and instead of answering, I said, "Stand up." I stood up as well, and as we faced each other, I wrapped my arms around him and held him tight. Bruce's chin went into the crook of my neck, and his body wracked with sobs. For several long minutes, Bruce wept on my shoulder, while I closed my eyes and held him tight, not saying a word. I knew that no words would express the depth of my concern and care as much as my hug could communicate. As time passed, Bruce's sobs grew less frantic, and they faded into hiccups and deep breaths. I felt his arms loosen from around my neck, and we separated. "I'm so scared, Doctor," Bruce said.

I dismissively replied, "You don't have anything to be scared about." Right after I said it, I realized that I was not acknowledging and respecting Bruce's feelings. I was minimizing his fears instead of validating his feelings. I quickly corrected myself and said, "What are you scared about?"

"If I'm positive, they're going to find out."

Again, I jumped to conclusions and thought that Bruce didn't want his colleagues nearby to learn about his diagnosis if he was treated at the hospital in his town. "You can get your treatment done in another hospital if you don't want to use St. Marys," I told him.

"No, that's not it. I haven't told my sister or the rest of my family." His voice was distraught. "If I have to go to the hospital, they'll find out. And yes, I'm scared of the spinal tap as well. I heard I have to lie flat on my back for an hour after the procedure, and the headaches can be bad."

I encouraged Bruce not to get too caught up with the "what ifs" since we didn't know if there was any neuro-syphilis yet. We would cross that bridge if we needed to, but worrying about the possibilities was not going to help the situation.

Bruce added, "My friend got tested, and he's positive for syphilis as well. He's getting his shot from his doctor."

"That's a lot of bad news for your friend to take all at once. Is he doing OK?" I asked.

"He's actually doing fine," Bruce replied. "We were talking about this the other day. I'm much more stressed out than he is, and he's the one with the bigger problems. But he's always been able to deal with life better than I have."

"Well, we better get this penicillin into you, Bruce." Bruce sighed as he turned around and dropped his pants, bending over the exam table. As I gave him the shot, he started crying again, his shoulders shaking with his sobs. I got done quickly, and he pulled his pants up, still crying. "Take as much time as you need to get yourself together, Bruce," I told him.

"Thank you for your concern, doctor," he said. I told Bruce that it was my honor to take care of him, and that we would figure this all out together. He could take as long as he needed to recompose himself before walking out to the front desk. I sent him out with the lumbar puncture requisition and the hope that things would get better than they had been.

Holding Water in a Clenched Fist

When Mona came in as a new patient to the office, I had a hard time believing she was almost fifty. She was smartly dressed in business attire, accentuating her tall, slim figure. Her hair curved elegantly around her oval face, with its almond eyes and petite, slightly upturned nose. Her taut skin belonged on a woman easily a decade younger. Her dark complexion clearly had African roots but also hinted at a mixed heritage, melding the best of several nationalities. In short, I found her strikingly beautiful.

Mona told me she picked the office out of the benefits package offered by her new job with a nearby university. Mona clearly had held professional positions for most of her adult life. That explained why she spoke in the same way she carried herself, with poise and grace. She approached our visit with deference but not subservience. This woman knew the extent of her worth.

Mona had lived in Connecticut many years ago but most recently was in New York. She had just moved back and needed a primary care physician to address her medical issues. She had high blood pressure and thyroid problems, but her most pressing concerns were anxiety and poor sleep. Her previous physician had given her Xanax and Ambien, which she had been on for years. Mona got to the point where she could not even consider sleeping without popping some sort of pill.

I could tell that Mona was not in the least amenable to stopping her habit-forming medications. In fact, since she had been on those medicines for years, I was fairly certain that she had already developed a physical dependence to the chemicals. Mona's statement, "I definitely need them to sleep" proved my point. Additionally, her anxiety was giving her heart palpitations and affecting her blood pressure, which was quite high. I decided to tackle her issues by increasing her blood pressure medicine and adding a non-habit-forming prescription for her anxiety. To prepare her to consider weaning off those other drugs, I gently advised her that any chemical that made her feel like she could not function without it warranted some close scrutiny. She agreed to try the new medicines and return for a follow-up visit.

Over the next several years, Mona continued to come to the office for her regular checks. It seemed to me there was very little change in her general health. Her blood pressures were generally controlled except for times of anxiety, which was a constant struggle. Mona also had persistent sleep issues. She tried several medicines, all with lackluster results. At times, she had problems shutting down her brain. Other times, she fell asleep fine, but she could not stay asleep. After four hours, she would wake up and spend the rest of the night tossing and turning. She saw a psychiatrist for a while, but the medicines he tried on her didn't help, and she didn't feel like he was spending enough time with her. She then switched to a counselor and tried cognitive behavioral therapy, while I took over her medication management.

One day, Mona came in for a visit, and I could tell she was not her usual self. She was a bit disheveled, and there were stress lines by her eyes that I had not noticed before. Even her speech, usually so confident and commanding, was subdued and halting.

Mona looked at me quickly and then looked away. She took a deep breath and said, "I didn't tell you this before, but I lost my job. I'm feeling very down, depressed, and hopeless. I have all these things to do in the house, but I just can't do any of them. I resent all my chores."

"I'm really sorry to hear that Mona," I replied. "When did this happen?"

"More than six months ago," Mona said. I was surprised, because Mona had been in the office the previous month for worsening insomnia, but she never mentioned anything about losing her job. She continued, "I thought I would have been back in the work force long before now, but I'm not. I have a Type-A personality, and I went from being a workaholic to having nothing to do. I'm turning into a vegetable!

"This has really been affecting my sleep as well. I just can't get a good night's sleep, no matter what I do. I tried some of that trazodone you gave me last time, but it gave me a bad reaction. I had nausea and vomiting, and I was so dizzy that I fell two weeks ago and hit my head. That scared me so much that I threw them all away."

I told her, "It was a good idea you stopped the trazodone. You can try the other medicines you have, but I honestly don't think it's more medicine that you need. I recently went to a program in Austin called *Discovery* that I think would be really good for you. But I know you're out of work, so it might not be financially possible for you right now."

"No," Mona assured me, "I have been saving up, so I have the money. I just need to work because I feel useless otherwise. What's this program about, and why do you think it would be good for me?"

"Well, Mona, I can answer your question, but it will mean I have to share with you some assessments I have of you first. I'm not trying to offend you, but you have to know what the problem is before you can fix it. Are you willing to hear what I have to say?" Mona nodded. "OK, first, I think you have some control issues. In fact, you're kind of a control freak. You have to have everything just right, or you get all out of sorts. Am I off base?"

"Oh no," Mona said, laughing. "You got it all right."

"There's a mental image I get when I look at you, Mona. I see a woman who is trying to hold water in a clenched fist." I put my hand out in a ball and flexed every muscle in my arm until it was shaking. "Look at my hand. I'm working and working, but how much water am I going to hold in my hand for all the work that I'm doing?"

"Not much," Mona conceded.

"Now look at this," I said. I relaxed my arm and put my hands together, curved into a bowl. "Now, I'm doing no work at all, but if you poured water into my hands, it would fill my hands to overflowing. Mona, I think this world has so much joy to give you, but with all of your misguided hard work, you're squeezing all the joy right out of your life. If you could learn to let go of that fist, that need for control, you'll find that you're life will be fuller as a result."

"I know you're right, Doctor. But I'm not sure I know how to do that."

I said, "You're doing some right things already. You're still seeing your counselor, and you're taking your medicine. *Discovery* doesn't take the place of those things. It just gives you another set of tools to help you along the road to greater joy and less anxiety." I gave Mona the web address for *Discovery* as well as some medicine for her depression.

At her follow up visit a month later, I asked how she was doing. "It's all about the same," Mona replied. "I did take a look at that site like you asked. It sounds like it would be perfect for me. I need all those things they talked about. I was surprised at how cheap it was. I thought it was going to be much more than that.

"There was only one thing. I read on the site that they assign you a roommate for the weekend?" I nodded. "I don't think I can handle that," Mona said. "Can't I just pay for my own room? I don't care about the extra cost. I just have to know there's somewhere I can get away to be by myself.

I'm too old to have to deal with strangers in my room as I'm working on all of this stuff."

I told her, "It's not that bad, really. And part of *Discovery* is about getting you out of your comfort zone, showing you that you can do things you didn't think was possible before. I think it goes back to that control issue. Trust me, it will work out. Maybe you'll find that the person becomes a good friend; I've seen that happen. Or maybe for you it will be a test to show you that you can handle it."

Mona looked skeptical. "I don't know. That part is the only thing that is keeping me from going. Everything else sounds great. I'm going to have to think about it more I guess."

"*Discovery* will be ready for you when you are ready for it," I assured her. "It happens just about every month, so if the next month doesn't work for you, maybe another one will."

Mona missed her next appointment, so it was over five months before I saw her again. This time, it was a new complaint. Mona had two weeks of daily burning upper abdominal pain. It was so severe at times it doubled her over. Pepto bismol and Zantac didn't help, and she wasn't sure if it was serious or if there was something she could do.

I did a complete work up, and my conclusion was heart burn and gastritis. Mona still had as much stress and anxiety as ever, and she still was not dealing with it as well as she could. Her body was trying to get her attention. Mona's anxiety was literally eating her up inside. I gave her a potent acid reducer for the problem and told her to follow up again if she still had problems.

She must have gotten better with the meds, because Mona didn't come back for several months, and only because her blood pressure medicine ran out and I wouldn't give her more until she came back in. Even though she had found a new job, all of Mona's problems were still the same, including her anxiety and insomnia. She was still seeing the counselor and struggling with being a perfectionist. The topic of *Discovery* again came up during the office visit, and Mona still could not get over the fact that she would not have her own room. "I just need to know I'm going to have a place to myself and be able to get away," she told me.

I responded, "Mona, how long have we talked about this? You've been taking your medicine, seeing the counselor, and visiting with me. But you still have problems. You have gone to the *Discovery* web site, and you think it would be a good thing for you. You know you have some serious control and perfectionist issues. It causes you anxiety and loss of sleep. Just how many nights of sleep have you lost in total since we started talking about this? Even if you didn't get a wink of sleep for the entire weekend, how is that different from almost any other night? Aren't you willing to give up two nights of sleep to save all the countless others?"

Mona looked at me and replied, "You know, you're right. Now that you put it that way, I guess I've been pretty silly, huh? It's only for two nights anyway, so I don't know why I'm making such a big deal out of it. OK, I'll sign up. Thanks for talking with me and giving me a different perspective."

I knew it was going to be a difficult decision for her to let go of just a bit of that control and face rooming with a person she had not previously met. But I knew that if she took that leap of faith, she would not regret it. I walked Mona out, hoping that she would consider my words and find her way to *Discovery*.

Mona 2014

Big News

I was surprised to see Nikhil and Lakshmi back in the office at my Saturday clinic. They had been in just the week before, everything was going well, and I told the couple to follow up for their low Vitamin D in three months. Lakshmi sat on the exam table while Nikhil stood by her side. I asked them what I could do for them as I settled into the stool and rested my back against the wall. "We have big news," Nikhil said. "Lakshmi is pregnant."

"Congratulations! That's incredibly exciting news!" I beamed. Nikhil and Lakshmi looked back at me with subdued faces. "Oh," I said. "This wasn't a planned pregnancy. Were you on birth control or using condoms or anything?"

"We didn't use a condom. We weren't planning on getting pregnant until next year," Nikhil said.

"Nikhil, when it comes to pregnancy, if you are trying to get pregnant, you don't use birth control. If you are not planning to get pregnant, you have to take steps not to get pregnant."

I turned to Lakshmi and addressed her. "Are you planning to carry the child, or are you looking to get an abortion?"

Lakshmi would not answer my question but instead looked to her husband. Nikhil answered, "That is why we are here, to get your advice. Lakshmi does not want to have the child."

"If you are looking for abortion services, there is a Planned Parenthood on Main Street. They can provide those services for you. It's not something I do," I told them.

I paused to gather my thoughts. I looked at Lakshmi and continued, "This is your body and your decision. I just ask that you carefully consider what each decision might mean. I know it is a very tough choice, no matter what you decide. I just want to give you as much information as possible."

"That is why we are here," Nikhil said. "To get your advice."

At the same time, Lakshmi asked, "Is there going to be more risk for me in the future?"

I responded, "Are you asking me if there will be a higher risk for you or if it will be more difficult for you to have a child in the future if you have an abortion now?" Lakshmi nodded. I pursed my lips and put my fingers together over them. "I think the risk is greater, but only slightly greater. It's not tremendously greater, but it's not nothing either.

"At this point, you would likely get a chemical abortion, since you are only a couple of weeks pregnant. Planned Parenthood would give you medicine to induce a period, and you will pass the fetus. You likely will not need a surgical abortion like a D&C, where they open up your cervix and scrape out the lining of your uterus. If you were much further along and needed that, then I would say the risk would be a good deal greater."

"So I will have a regular period?" Lakshmi asked.

"No," I clarified. "This will be much heavier than a regular period. The lining of your uterus has been growing for almost a month and a half, and there's the fetus in there as well, so this will be a much greater flow. You will have significant stomach cramps after you take the medicine."

"So is it going to affect my ability to have children in the future?"

"I don't know, Lakshmi," I said. "My crystal ball is broken right now. I can't tell the future. I will tell you this: There are many women who have had abortions and then later had children without problems. But I know of a number of women who had an abortion and then struggle for years afterwards to have kids."

"She knows a couple of women like that," Nikhil said.

I responded, "I just don't want you to come back to me three years from now saying, 'You should have never allowed us to have an abortion, because now we can't have kids.' The fact of the matter is that I just don't know.

"It's not just the physical aspect of an abortion that affects women, it's the emotional component as well. There are some women who not only have no problems with having an abortion, they will use it as a form of 'birth control.' They don't take any precautions and have five or six abortions. Personally, I think that is wrong and completely irresponsible. And then there are women I have talked to who regret the abortion they had more than twenty years ago. It's just something you should consider as you think about your options. Were you planning to have kids at some point?"

"Next year," Nikhil replied. "Lakshmi wants to go to school and get her degree first. I told her she could still do that with a child."

Lakshmi looked at her husband and muttered, "But it would be much more difficult."

I replied, "I agree that it would be more challenging, Lakshmi, but women are doing that all the time now. Especially with the Internet and online courses, there is a lot you can do without having to leave your house." Lakshmi seemed uncomfortable speaking to me directly, so I turned to Nikhil and asked, "What degree is your wife trying to finish? A master's, or a bachelor's?"

"A bachelor's in engineering. But she's just starting," he clarified.

"So that doesn't make sense to me," I responded. "What difference is a year going to make? You can't finish a bachelor's in a year anyway. Even if you started right away, you would only be done with a year of schooling before you plan on getting pregnant. You would still be stuck in the middle of school with a child. Now, I could understand if you said that you were planning to wait five years after you finish your degree to have a child, but a year is no time at all.

"And if you were to wait for five years, you would be in your early thirties. I do not know how many children you plan to have, but the longer you wait for your first child, the older you will be for your last one. And pregnancy after the age of thirty-five is considered higher risk, where the chances of Down Syndrome go up."

"We had thought about that too," Nikhil confessed. "Is it harder to have a child when you are older?"

"For some women, yes," I responded. "In general, the younger you are, the easier your body will be able to handle the stresses of pregnancy. Of course, I'm not talking about being twelve years old. But Lakshmi, you're in your twenties right now, which is a very appropriate age to have a child.

"The thing is, life is like a long corridor filled with doors. When you open a door and walk through, it closes behind you and other doors come into view. Life might take you back to that point again, but usually, you can't ever go back. No matter what you decide, there are some doors that will close for you and others that will open. I want you to make the right decision for yourself.

"Of course, it's not just you who are affected by this, Lakshmi. Your husband is involved as well. How do you feel about it, Nikhil? Do you want to have the baby or not?"

"My wife does not want to have it, and I will do what she wants," Nikhil replied diplomatically.

As I was speaking, Lakshmi's clasped hands started moving back and forth over each other, like the motion for washing. I could see the turmoil of her heart translated in the movements of her hands. When her husband deferred his wants to her, she wiped away tears from her eyes.

I got up and handed her a tissue, which she accepted wordlessly. "I know this is an incredibly tough decision for you, Lakshmi. I am here to support you in whatever decision you make. I do not do abortions in my office or give medicines to induce abortions, but I can give you information about Planned Parenthood. I have taken care of pregnant women and have delivered many babies. I could prescribe prenatal vitamins for you and take care of you while you wait for an appointment with an obstetrician. Being a family doctor, it is a joy to me to take care of children. I would be honored to take care of your first child, whether you choose to keep your pregnancy or wait for three years.

"It's my job to give you as much information as I can so that you can make the decision that is right for you. I realize that it will be more difficult for you to have a child now and go to school. I would not want you to look at your child every day and think your life could have been so much better if you got your degree in engineering instead of becoming a mother. But honestly, it's almost unheard of that that happens, and those are the women who should never have been mothers to begin with. Usually, what I hear is that life is difficult, but the mother would never have it any other way."

Nikhil looked at me but said to his wife, "So it sounds like Dr. Han wants you to have the baby." There was a hint of hope in his voice.

I considered my words and said very carefully, "I am not here to make your decision for you, Lakshmi. It's a very personal decision, as it is for any woman. I can understand why some women choose to have an abortion. If you were a victim of a rape or some other sexual assault, I could see how you would not want to keep the child. But you are married. You're in great physical health. Your husband loves you and is able to provide for the family. The child was conceived in love, and it would come into a stable home. If I were in your position, I would have the baby. I just want you to understand that it is what I would do personally, and it does not affect how I would take care of you. I will support whatever decision you make.

"I know you wanted to wait a year to get pregnant, but sometimes life doesn't give you what you think or want. All I know is that this is a life-changing event for the two of you, and I am ready to stand by your side, no matter what. Look, this is Saturday, so I suggest going home and taking some time to think about things. A few days will not make a difference either way. Just let me know what you decide and how I can help."

I got up from the stool. As Nikhil thanked me for my time, Lakshmi would not look up from the floor as she stepped off the exam table. She walked woodenly to the door. I intercepted her and said, "Hold on." I held my arms out. Lakshmi allowed me to put my arms around her, and her head slumped to my chest. I felt like I was hugging a statue. "No, no. This won't do," I told her. "I want a real hug." I gently pulled Lakshmi's arms from her sides and leaned in. This time, she did give me a timid hug. I thought this was a big step for her. Indian women are extremely modest and never show public affection, especially not with other men, and most especially not with their husband looking on. But, I was sure that both of them knew my heart and my care for them.

I encouraged them to keep me posted on their decision as I led them out of the room. Nikhil thanked me again for my time as he put his arm around Lakshmi and the two of them walked out of the office.

Frogger

Adrian came in for a preventative physical having heard about the practice from a friend. Although it was true that he had not had a physical exam in quite a while, it was not only his body that needed attention. Adrian got married at the young age of nineteen. His wife was then deployed for a three-year stint at Sheppard Air Force Base, so Adrian followed her from Connecticut to Texas. Not even a year after coming back to Connecticut, Adrian's wife left him for someone else. Adrian was reeling from the sudden change, and in an effort to make sense of life, he got into a relationship with another woman shortly after his separation. Ironically, that relationship took him back to Texas but only lasted for less than a year. A relationship that started well turned sour, and they were fighting all the time. Adrian found that he was just floating along without any set plan for his life, so he broke up with his girlfriend and returned to Connecticut. As part of the process of getting his life in better order, Adrian asked folks for suggestions on a doctor, and he ended up in my office.

I walked into the exam room, taking note of the young man sitting in front of me. Adrian had close-cropped hair and beard, both reddish-blond, framing an oval face. He shook my extended hand warmly and said hello. I sat down and listened as he told me his story. He finished by saying, "My life is kind of a mess."

"It sounds like you've already had a difficult life for your young years," I commiserated.

"It was difficult even before that," Adrian conceded. "My mother has bipolar disorder, and my father was emotionally absent. From day one, as a kid, you see things and think they are normal, that this is what everyone must go through, but it's not. My parents were fighting all the time. There was always yelling going on. Finally, when I was four, my parents got divorced. Me, my two brothers, and my sister, we all stayed with Mom. I remember when I was four or five, I would play outside from eight AM until dark. Then Mom would leave the four of us at home all alone, no baby sitter or anything, while she was somewhere else all night. My oldest brother was only ten. I didn't think it was strange then, but now I know that it was really wrong for her to do that."

Adrian switched topics in mid-thought, like he didn't want to talk about his past anymore. "I want to be screened for ADD. Focusing on any sort of task takes a lot of energy. I find myself drifting off mentally during class. And then I get these intrusive thoughts during conversations. I just don't know how to focus on something. You know, even the thought of staying in one place for any length of time is stressful to me. Maybe that's why I kept on moving back and forth from Texas to Connecticut."

"So does anything help?" I asked.

"Exercise does help a lot," Adrian replied. "I have anxiety too. I've gone to the hospital before because of chest pain and heart racing, and it turned out to be anxiety. I get social anxiety, and I use alcohol to make myself feel better."

"How much do you drink?"

"I usually have two to three drinks a night, but many, many more on weekends." As with many people, Adrian was self medicating with alcohol. Adrian continued, "I think I might be depressed. Things I used to love to do don't excite me anymore. Nothing feels like it has anything to it anymore. Everything feels empty."

I said, "Well, let's do your exam, and we'll see what else I can put together for you." Other than being overweight, Adrian's exam was normal. I did a whole set of lab work, including testosterone and thyroid tests to make sure Adrian did not have an organic cause for his depression and anxiety. I encouraged Adrian to quit drinking, or at least cut way back. He did not want to be on any medications yet, but I asked him to consider it at some point. I also gave him some screening forms for both depression and ADD. We made plans to meet again in a month.

At the month follow-up visit, Adrian was not doing much better. He still was not that motivated. He had not resumed any of his old hobbies or found new ones. He brought the screening forms back, and both were mostly filled out with X's in the "often" or "very often" columns. He had significant symptoms of depression, and he also had many attention deficit categories checked off. At the bottom of the page, Adrian indicated that several days out of the week, he thought that he would be better dead or hurting himself in some way. When I asked him specifically about this issue, he said that he did not have any active thoughts of suicide, but if a brick were to fall on his head, that wouldn't bother him too much.

Nevertheless, there were some definite improvements from the last month. Adrian really took to heart my suggestion to cut down on alcohol, and he was now only having one or two drinks a week. He was also now willing to consider therapy.

I took a good long look at Adrian, and he kept my gaze. "You need wisdom," I told him.

Adrian nodded his head. "Yeah, I do."

"You're lacking the skills to move ahead in life. You need wisdom and those skills. Have you ever played the video game Frogger?" I asked.

"Yeah, I have."

"You know how you have to move that frog through those lanes of traffic and then across the river? If you stand in one place, then the car in your lane will run you over. But if you move ahead too quickly, the truck in the next lane will run you over. What you have to do is wait for just the right timing and move ahead into the clear area in front of you." Adrian nodded his understanding. "It seems you're sitting at the Pass line, watching the cars zoom by, too paralyzed to move ahead because you're afraid you're going to be squished.

"All the while, there's a timer counting down, and if you don't make it across in the allotted time, you die. You're just like that poor frog, Adrian. You're sitting in one place in your life, not moving, while your life ticks away a second at a time. But I know moving ahead takes skills and knowhow not to get run over."

Adrian said, "Hey, that's pretty good, Doc. Did you read that somewhere, or did you just make that all up?"

"I just made that all up," I confessed. "But it did sound really good, didn't it?" Adrian and I laughed together.

"Do you have anyone to talk to, Adrian?"

"I have a lot of close friends I can talk to," Adrian said immediately. Then he paused and clarified, "Anxiety has caused me to put up a wall, though. Most of the time, I find myself just keeping it in because I don't want to push them away. I worry about what people will think when I share things, so it makes it hard to get past that. And who wants a guy who is a downer all the time? I do talk to my mother, though. She has a long history with mental illness, so I feel like I can tell her things."

"I'm glad you have your mother to talk to, Adrian," I said. "Still, I'm sure there are things on your heart that need to be shared that you can't share with your mother. That's where a therapist comes in. And of course I hope you feel like you can tell me anything. There is no judgment from me.

"I'd also like for you to consider some medication for your issues. I'll be honest with you, it seems you have a good deal of both depression as well as what looks like ADD. I'm not sure if it's ADD or a lot of anxiety, though. I think the first thing to do is to treat the depression and anxiety, and if you still have ADD symptoms, we can take it from there."

Adrian responded, "I don't want to be dependent on anything like meds."

I could understand Adrian's concern because of his history with drinking. I assured him, "Well, for starters, I'll give you medicine that is not habit forming. So you can't become physically dependent on the medicine. The other thing is that taking medicine is like needing to wear glasses. You don't *have* to wear glasses to survive, but life is much easier and richer with them than without." Adrian agreed to give the medicine a try, to look for a therapist, and to come back to the office in a month after he did those things.

It took Adrian two months to get back to the office, but he was looking good. He was still on his medicine, and he was barely drinking alcohol at all. He was also looking much more fit and trim, owing to his regular work outs at the gym. His depression was fifty percent better, but he still had a lot of anxiety, especially in social situations. Since he had not yet found a therapist, and I had only a few patients scheduled for the day, I asked more about his family situation.

Adrian detailed a long line of mental illness, dysfunctional family dynamics, and codependency, starting with his grandparents. They were the physical and emotional hub of a broken wheel, lurching crookedly along the road of life. They used their financial means to constantly bail their kids and grandkids out of one mess or another, thereby enabling and continuing destructive behavior. Adrian heard his grandfather say all the time, "Now, this is the last time I'm going to do this." But there was always a next time.

His mother learned those dysfunctional patterns from her parents and used them on her own kids. Adrian vividly remembers his mother always screaming and yelling, telling the children how terrible their father was and all the things wrong with him. And because their father would not stoop to the same level of criticism, the only input the children got was the negativity their mother fed them, and they believed her. In order to be near his kids, Adrian's father lived just a few doors down from the house for ten years. When Adrian was fifteen, his father moved several hours away. Adrian's oldest brother held deep resentments towards their father for abandoning them, and he would not speak to his father for over a decade. It wasn't until Adrian was much older that he understood his father had to move away to protect himself and his own sanity.

Adrian and his siblings had no role model of structure and solid parenting from their mother, so they fell into many of the same traps. His sister struggled with bipolar disorder and substance abuse. His brothers went in and out of jail, one fathering a child with a heroin addict. Street gang members revolved through the house and were basically running the show. Police raids occurred, and Adrian would wake up to a flashlight shining in his face and an officer asking him what he was doing there. "Uh, I live here," Adrian would say. Eventually, it was impossible to live in the house, and the family ended up in a homeless shelter for more than six months.

Adrian thinks it was because of a lack of good upbringing, or maybe always wanting to take the easy way out, that led him to get married prematurely. Following his wife down to Texas was certainly easier than thinking about getting a job or going to college. Each subsequent step of choosing the easy road led him right over the cliff. When he finally crashed at the bottom, he made a decision to change his life. He moved back to

Connecticut, got his own apartment, worked a steady job, and learned how to live with much, much less.

Adrian concluded, "I'm an adult now and I can't keep falling back on things that seemed easy. Don't get me wrong. It's still a constant battle. There are days when I wake up, and I just don't want to go to work. I don't want to exercise. But when I do those things, I feel better at the end of the day. I just have to remember that the next time I'm feeling like giving up. I'm switching to doing the hard stuff first, so I can get the stuff that's even better later."

Catching a Break

Barry was the last person I expected to see crying like a hurt little boy when I walked into the exam room. Barry carried over 380 lbs on his six-foot frame. Sitting atop a thick neck was his big bald head and a face with a goatee and three-day shadow. Tattoos went down his broad shoulders and hairy arms— each bigger than my thigh—down his side, and covering his legs. Sure, he had a good bit of fat on him, but that fat was overlying a hefty amount of muscle as well. I was sure if he wanted to land a punch, it would knock anyone flat to the ground. Barry looked like a Harley-riding biker who could be the head of a motorcycle gang. Yet here he was in my office, sitting in the chair with his head hung low, his eyes bloodshot from crying.

I had been taking care of Barry for several years, and in spite of his gruff looks, I knew him to be kind, gentle, and soft-spoken. He came in a few times each year for a refill of blood pressure medicine and the occasional bronchitis. During his visits, we also talked about the daily stresses he had as a self-employed contractor without insurance for his family. When the economy was good, Barry enjoyed the good life with a bunch of big-boy toys like his motorcycles, dirt bikes, and a camper.

Unfortunately, he unwisely skipped out on paying his income taxes, thinking he could take care of them some other time. And then the perfect storm occurred with the economy collapsing and the IRS catching up with him. Suddenly, Barry had Uncle Sam breathing down his neck and no jobs to pay the bills. He went from a pretty good lifestyle to not knowing where the next meal was coming from. In spite of all of these things, Barry seemed to keep his chin up and at least a half smile on his face. That is, until this office visit.

I pulled up my stool right next to him and asked what was going on. Barry looked up, wiping his eyes. "I should have come in a lot sooner. Everything's terrible."

"Like what?" I asked.

"Home and work," Barry said simply. I motioned him to continue. "Work is killing me. I couldn't make ends meet just doing remodeling. So, I took a job as a foreman. I'm getting older, you know? I can't be swinging a hammer forever. But the economy is hurting the company just as much as it did me, so instead of being a foreman, I'm sent out to jobs all the time, and the pace is grueling. I get there early in the morning, and I don't get done until 8 PM. In fact, just waiting for my appointment in the waiting room, I got several texts about emergency calls that I have to make after I'm done.

"I'm not going to be done until 9 or later tonight. And I'm breaking down in the middle of a job site in a customer's house, crying for no reason. Today my boss asked me to do something, and I told him, 'Get someone else to do the fucking job.' He's a friend, and I've known him for ten years, but he's still my boss, and I can't be saying things like that. I knew I needed to come in.

"On top of that, home has its own problems. My wife and I have been dealing with my son's teenage issues. He's had a lot of depression and anxiety. We found him cutting. We brought him to the hospital, and at first they said they wanted to keep him for five days, which we thought was a good idea. But then they said he should be discharged. I got him set up with a therapist at the hospital and took him there. When they were talking to him, I started to break down and cry. My son said he didn't want to talk anymore because he didn't want to see me get upset like that. My own son's got all these problems, and he's worried about his dad and trying to protect me!" Again, Barry's blue eyes welled up with tears, soaking through his tissue.

Barry folded and refolded the tissue, trying to find one last dry spot to use. I reached over and handed him the entire box. Sheet after sheet came out as Barry tried to compose himself but failed. "Who do you have to talk to about these things?" I asked him.

"No one," Barry said. "My daughter tries to talk to me, but kids shouldn't have to give advice to their parents. I know she worries about me, but she has her own concerns, and I don't feel right telling her things."

"What about friends?"

Barry responded, "I have friends, but I don't tell them anything either. They're the ones who come to me. I've always been the strong one. I'm the one who gives the customer extra services to keep him happy. Or I'm giving a friend a job out of my own pocket that I can't really afford just so they can put food on their tables. I don't go to others about my problems. That's just not me. Sitting with you here is the most I've ever talked to anyone about my problems."

"I think that's a big part of the problem, Barry," I told him. "You have always had to play the strong one, the one with the answers, the provider for your family. You play the role so well that you don't know how to do anything different. And now, the external things that have given you a sense of purpose are falling apart, and you can't figure out what's left. And you're so unused to asking for help that you don't know where to turn."

Barry nodded. He held his hands out, outlining the shape of a square. "It's like I have this box, and people keep on dumping stuff into my box. And now it's full. It's more than full. And I don't know how to dump it out." Barry took his hand and turned it upside down. "I need some way to dump out this box. Maybe that will give me another five years."

I shook my head. "Barry, you don't just need to dump out your box, you need a whole new container. The problem is that the box you had before worked great for you back then, but it doesn't work for you anymore. Even if you dump the box out, it's just a temporary fix, and then it gets filled back up again, and you're right back where you started." I then switched visual images and held my hands out with my fingers outstretched. "When you were a little kid, you could use your fingers to do all your counting. And I'm sure it worked great. But what happened when you ran out of fingers? Your life is too complicated to try to count on just your fingers. It's time to try something different.

"Is there something in your life you can change to help make things better?" I asked.

This time, it was Barry who shook his head. "No, I can't think of anything, or I would have done it already. I used to have me-time. I spent all day riding the ATV or the dirt bike. People think you just sit on it, but it's a major workout. I was standing up and moving through the trails. It was fun, and it was a great form of exercise. But when the IRS came, I had to sell everything. I don't have any of the bikes or toys like I used to. Now, all I have is my Xbox. So what do I do? I sit on my ass and play my Xbox. And because I'm at home and bored, I eat. All the time. I've gained over a hundred pounds in the past year. Of course that makes me feel worse about myself. And because I don't feel good about myself, I don't really feel like getting it on with my wife, which of course doesn't help things at home either. So it's just this vicious circle I can't stop."

"Can't you find anything that you or your family can do for fun?" I asked.

"Yeah, we do," Barry said. "We have to do something on one of the weekend days, or else everyone gets stir crazy. But the money is so incredibly tight that we have to do something on the cheap. When I make a couple of extra bucks, I give it to my wife, and she stashes it away. We were going to go on a cruise just to get away. But then she had to get a new car because hers crapped out, so now we have nothing again. It's like I just can't seem to catch a break!

"And another thing. It's good we do things as a family. I get it. But I don't ever get time just for me. I used to have an entire day all by myself or just with my buddies, but now I'm always being a dad or a husband, and I don't ever just get to be me. I don't even know who I am anymore."

I took my hands from under my chin and said, "I really wish you could get to Texas to go to *Discovery*."

Barry and I had talked about *Discovery* in the past, but it didn't seem like it could work out for him because of his job and his need to pay the bills. In fact, Barry's response to my comment was, "Who's going to pay the bills for the week? And I can't even think about paying for the tuition, hotel, and flight. That's like a thousand dollars right?"

"No, Barry, it's not a thousand dollars," I corrected. "I totally understand your need to work, but you are not any good at work right now anyway. And if you talk to your boss the way you just did, you might have even more problems with work. You talked about not having time for yourself, and I think that's exactly what you need. If you're not healthy for yourself, how can you be healthy for anyone else? You need to find out who you are, not what other people expect of you."

I paused and looked at Barry, while he stared back at me. His eyes were still red, but he wasn't crying anymore. I put my hands together in front of my mouth and deliberated. "Excuse me one second." I stood up and walked out of the exam room.

A minute later I returned and sat back down. Barry followed me with his eyes but did not say anything. Breaking the silence, I said, "I think there is a time in everyone's life when they need a little grace at just the right moment. When's the last time somebody did something for you that was unexpected, giving you a gift out of the blue?"

Barry sighed. "I can't even tell you. I'm always the one doing things for everyone else. I'm the one who's always giving. I don't know when I last got something."

"Well, I think it's time you got something." I handed Barry the voucher that I had gone to retrieve. "This coupon is for two people to a nearby water park. That should give you a weekend with your family for a fraction of the usual cost."

Barry took the voucher with a bit of disbelief on his face. "I don't know what to say except thank you. This is exactly the sort of stuff I and my son like to do. I know we're going to have a great time. And don't take this the wrong way, but now I know I have to go." I knew exactly what Barry was talking about. He had gotten so depressed that he didn't have any motivation to do anything. Now he had an opportunity and couldn't use the lack of money as an excuse not to do it.

I wasn't done yet. "Barry, can you get time off next month to go to *Discovery*?"

"I'd love to go to *Discovery* some time, doctor, but I won't have the money to get to *Discovery* next month. I could start saving up a little bit at a time and maybe have enough some day."

"I don't think you have 'some day,' Barry. And I'm not talking about the money. I'm just talking about the time. Can you talk to your boss about getting off that time?"

"Yeah, I think so," Barry replied.

"Well, if you think you can do that, then I have something else to offer you. I will ask the *Discovery* office to see if they can extend a scholarship for both your tuition and your hotel costs. You could go to *Discovery* for free. This is what you need right now. And, I know that when you're in a better place in your life, you'll be able to put that money back into the scholarship fund. That way, someone else who might need it can use it. It's all a part of paying it forward."

Barry's mouth worked before he said anything. Finally, he said, "I can't believe it. I can't remember when anyone has done something like this for me. I absolutely can put that money back when I get the chance. I know this is just what I need. But I don't have the money for the flight."

"Let me take a look into that as well, Barry," I said. "What you have to do is talk to your wife and your boss. Sign up and fill out your application. At the end, click Pay Later and fill out the scholarship application. I'll call the office tomorrow and finalize plans.

"OK, one more thing." I stood up and motioned for him to do the same. I held my arms out. Standing on my toes, I put my arms around his expansive girth as Barry cried into my shoulder.

"Sorry I'm getting your shirt all wet," Barry hiccupped.

"Hey, it's a great honor," I murmured without letting go. I just let my love for Barry flow through that hug. I didn't release my grip until I felt his tears fade away. I walked Barry out to the front, where he gave me another big hug and shook my hand.

"Thank you so much. I feel like I have hope for the first time in so long," Barry said.

Later on that night, I got an e-mail confirming that Barry had signed up for the next *Discovery* session.

Laughter is the Best Medicine

The nurse at Avalon Nursing Home called me. "Dr. Han, we were bathing your patient Mr. Wright, and we found a mass in his stomach. Could you come by some time and take a look at it?" I told her I would come at my earliest convenience.

When I arrived, the patient was lying in bed. I greeted him with a warm smile. "Hi Marvin! How are you doing? The nurses asked me to come by and examine your stomach. It seems you might have something in there. Would you mind if I took a quick look?"

I lifted up his gown and put my hands on his stomach to examine him. The moment I touched him, he wailed, "Oooooo!"

I snatched my hands away, startled. "I'm sorry, Marvin! Did I hurt you?"

"No," he said, "but your hands are FREEZING!"

****

One of the most onerous tasks for a medical student is the job of retracting during a long surgical procedure. You stand there for hours, holding the retractor, while the attending ignores you completely, talking instead to the surgical resident.

In one such case, I was retracting on one side of the patient, while the attending and chief resident were on the other side. It was a thyroidectomy, so the surgical field was very small, and I couldn't see anything. Their quiet chatter washed over me as time slipped away. I found myself drifting off, and I fought it with all my muster. Sleep eventually won out, and I had a split second of nodding off. I relaxed my grip on the retractor and started to tilt to the side. Just as I was about to fall off the stool, I startled myself awake and jerked upright, shaking the entire table.

That caused the two doctors on the other side to stop and look up at me. The chief resident turned to the attending and said wryly, "Our medical student is having seizures." *Oh my God, I've just failed my surgery rotation*, I thought to myself.

The resident chuckled when he saw the shocked whites of my eyes above my surgical mask. "Don't worry," he said. "It's happened to all of us."

****

A young man came to see me about bumps around his anus that he noticed while bathing. Upon examination, the bumps had the characteristic appearance of condyloma accuminatum, genital warts. I informed him of my findings and I asked him about his previous sexual history.

"Well, I'm currently seeing someone, but I'm his first," my patient informed me.

"What about anyone before?" I asked.

"Well, I did have a boyfriend for almost a year, but he was the only other one. We did have sex, but not anally. He told me that he had hemorrhoids and didn't want to worsen them. I never saw them, but he told me they looked like Willy Wonka Nerds."

I had to tell my patient that I didn't think those were hemorrhoids.

****

My pharmaceutical rep Beth was six months pregnant and came in with her ultrasound images. The fetus was on profile, and you could clearly see the curved body, with its thumb going to its mouth. The other thing you could see was the umbilical cord snaking up quite a ways from the body.

I took the picture and showed it to my nurse Melissa. I pointed to the umbilical cord with raised eyebrows and a knowing look. Melissa looked at the picture and said, "Oh. *Oh!*"

I gave the picture back to Beth and showed her what I was pointing at. Beth laughed and said, "Takes after Jim."

I had to point out to Melissa, "That's the umbilical cord. If it were anything else, it would be like a foot long."

Beth had a baby girl.

****

One very useful thing pharmaceutical companies pay for are prescription pads. The disadvantage, however, is that every fourth or fifth sheet in the pad is a drug ad. I find it very annoying to be writing several scripts and then get "hit" with an ad as I'm in a rhythm. So, I tend to go through each new pad and take out every ad sheet before using the pad.

One time, I somehow missed a pad. So during an office visit, as I was writing some scripts for a patient, I came across an ad. I decided to take the time and rip out the rest of the ads right then. As I flipped through the pad and methodically tore out each ad, a sizable pile of sheets accumulated on the counter.

With growing alarm, the patient exclaimed, "Are all those prescriptions for me?"

****

Mai was a Vietnamese patient in her early 60's who had recently been coming to the office. She had high blood pressure and diabetes, mostly from her extreme obesity.

She was as frustrated with her weight as I was. "No matter what I do, I can't seem to lose weight. I hardly eat anything, and I exercise two hours a day."

"Well what are you doing for exercise?" I asked her.

"I use the *Jiggler*," she replied.

"The *Jiggler*?" I asked quizzically.

"Yes. It's something I saw advertised on TV. You strap it around your waist, and the machine jiggles your fat around, breaking it up. It's guaranteed to make you lose weight! I use the *Jiggler* for two hours while I watch TV in the evenings," she replied happily.

I was dumbfounded how people could fall for such gimmicks and bald-faced lies. "No, Mai, it doesn't work that way. *You* have to move your arms and legs around. You can't burn calories any other way."

Mai accepted my advice and left the office. Several months later, she came in for a follow up, but her weight was no better than before. "Mai, you haven't lost any weight. What are you doing for exercise?"

"Oh, Doctor, I took your advice, and I stopped using the *Jiggler*. I'm using a different machine instead."

"Really? What machine is that?"

"You told me I had to move my arms and legs, so I got a machine that shakes my legs around as I'm watching TV."

I gave up.

****

I walked into the exam room for a new-patient physical. Karl was sitting on the exam table with his shirt off. The first thing I noticed was just how incredibly hairy he was. From his koala-ear hair tufts, to the mat of long dark hair on his chest and back, and the thick layer of hair on his forearms that would stymie a mosquito, this guy was just covered with hair! Karl was a genetic throw back to a Neanderthal or even Cro-Magnon man.

Of course, being respectful, I did not mention anything about his fur carpet. We did the exam, and the last part was the hernia check. Karl stood up and dropped his pants. Right at his crotch was a perfectly shaved triangle of bare skin. He looked like a "hair negative" of a normal person.

After the exam, as Karl was buttoning up his shirt, I said, "So Karl, I have to ask, if you're so hairy and don't shave anywhere else, why do you shave your pubes that way?"

Karl looked at me and said with a completely straight face, "If I shave then my girlfriend gives me head. If I don't, then she doesn't."

No need to say more.

CONFRONTATION

"Criticism, like rain, should be gentle enough to nourish a man's growth without destroying his roots."

~Frank A. Clark, writer of "The Country Parson"

Untrustworthy

Maria Vasquez, a young mother of two toddlers, came in to see me about weight loss. She definitely needed it, since she was 5'6" and 270 lbs. I gave her counseling on diet and exercise because she was doing neither. She insisted on some sort of diet medicine as well. I encouraged her not to rely on medicines and chemicals, because lifestyle changes were the best option for weight loss. Still, she persisted, so I relented and wrote a prescription for Xenical, the prescription strength of the over-the-counter medicine Alli. I concluded the office visit by giving her handouts on meal plans, calorie counting, and exercise routines, and I asked her to come back in a month.

The next month, Maria showed up for her follow up visit. She really didn't lose any weight. When I asked about her exercise, she had a lot of excuses and not a lot of successes. Regarding her diet, she said she was trying, but she couldn't really say how. When I asked what specifically she was eating, she told me two things, one that did not surprise me, and one that shocked me.

"I eat emotionally," she confessed. "I eat when I'm happy, and I eat when I'm sad. I eat when I'm bored, or when my husband and I fight."

I told her this was very common, both for women as well as men. Eating releases hormones and endorphins, so eating helps calm emotions. Also, when a person eats, they don't have to focus on the things that are bothering them, so it pushes things out of their mind for a while. Unfortunately, the moment they stop eating, those negative thoughts come back again. It starts a terrible cycle. The person is fat, and that makes him guilty. To assuage that guilt temporarily, he eats. This leads him to get even fatter, which then makes him feel more guilty. This leads to more eating, and so forth.

What Maria said next revealed the extent of her addiction. "I drink two two-liters of Pepsi a day." One 8-oz serving of Pepsi is 140 calories, and a two-liter has 8 servings, equaling over 1100 calories. Multiplied by two, that was 2200 calories, or the equivalent of 150 teaspoons of sugar, that Maria was consuming in soda a day. The caloric intake from the Pepsi alone was more calories than an average person should ingest for the entire day. Since one pound of fat is equal to 3500 calories, Maria was drinking enough Pepsi to make 230 lbs of fat a year. No wonder she wasn't losing weight!

I counseled Maria extensively on the excessive sugar and caffeine intake from the Pepsi consumption and how that was sabotaging her ability to lose weight. She needed to drastically reduce her Pepsi consumption, or better yet, stop altogether. When I asked her to consider switching to diet, she scrunched her face up and said, "I don't like the taste." When I revisited the topic of exercise, she sighed and said, "I know, but I just don't have the time." Clearly, Maria was lacking motivation to change her lifestyle habits to get her to her goal of losing weight. I did what I could and asked her to follow up with me in one month.

Maria missed her one month appointment, but she did eventually return a few months later. She had lost a few pounds, but it was negligible. Still, I congratulated her on the weight loss she did achieve. After all, it was better than *gaining* weight. What frustrated me was that the first thing Maria said to me was, "I want you to refer me for a stomach stapling."

"Why do you want a stomach stapling?" I asked.

"Because I just *can't* do it!" She retorted. "Even my husband has given up on me. I found a really great treadmill on sale. I wanted to get it, but he wouldn't let me. He said that we already had a bunch of exercise stuff at the house that I wasn't using, and he wasn't going to waste his money on getting me anything else."

I looked at Maria and said pointedly, "That's because you're untrustworthy."

Maria stared back at me with shock. "That was mean, Dr. Han!"

"I'm not trying to be mean," I replied. "I'm just being honest. You have constantly said things to me and to your husband that you have not followed through on. You've promised things that you have not kept. Your husband has no reason to trust that you're going to do what you say you will. And why would you need another machine if you have so many at home now that you're not using?"

"I would have used it!" Maria interjected.

I replied, "Prove to your husband that you can follow through on what you say you're going to do, and build his trust in you. He has no reason to believe you right now. You know that I care about you and your health, or I wouldn't have taken all this time to counsel you or tell you things that you might not *want* to hear but you *needed* to hear. That's why I said you were untrustworthy.

"Furthermore, I don't think stomach stapling is the right thing for you. A lap band, stomach stapling, or a gastric bypass takes an incredible amount of commitment and will power. If not, you will either eat right through your banding, or you will get very sick. A prerequisite for any bariatric surgery is extensive counseling, so you know exactly what you're getting yourself into.

"The thing is, your problem is not your weight. Your problem goes much deeper than that, and your weight is only one manifestation. I see a woman who lacks self-confidence, self-esteem, and self-love. If you don't fix that part of your life, no diet plan or stomach stapling is going to work.

You've turned to sugar and caffeine to numb the feelings you have inside, but you and I both know it's not going to work. The last time, I asked you to quit drinking soda. How did that go?"

Maria replied, "I cut back. I'm only drinking five cans of Pepsi a day now. But I have to drink at least three Cuban espressos to get me through the day." I helped Maria do the math, and I pointed out that five cans of Pepsi still added to a 2 liter a day. And the espressos more than made up for the difference in caffeine intake. Clearly, there was still a lot more work to be done.

"It's a start, Maria, but you have a long way to go. I honestly think you need to figure out why you have such a bad relationship with food. Maybe that will help with a lot of other areas in your life, including your relationship with your husband," I said.

"I know, I feel so bad. I know my husband works really hard to provide for me and the boys, and I'm just wasting his money on food." She confessed, "I think we spend $200 or $300 a week on food, and most of it is junk. He's at work all day, and I get bored and lonely, so I eat."

"I think you can find a much better use of your money than all the food that you shouldn't be buying in the first place. Something better than yet another exercise machine that you do not have the discipline to do anyway."

Maria left the office with a follow up visit. She had a combination of a thoughtful look on her face and a lighter, more hopeful countenance.

Calling the Police

At Bernice's physical, she confessed that she wasn't taking care of herself very well. Physically speaking, she was fine. It was with all those other ways that there were problems. Bernice grew up too quickly, getting involved with boys in her early teens. Eventually the inevitable happened and one of her boyfriends got her pregnant. Her boyfriend was not interested in being a part of his son's life, and Bernice did not have much in the way of family to help. As a single mother, she had to work, go to school, and take care of her young son. There didn't seem to be enough minutes in the day to have any time for herself.

I did her exam, which was normal, as I expected. I then encouraged Bernice to find time at least once a week to focus on herself. She needed to take care of herself so that she would be healthy and be able to take care of her son. I asked her to come up with a list of ten things that she could do that would not take money but would still help her to recharge her batteries.

When Bernice came back for the follow up, I asked her if she came up with her list. "I can go for walks, read, exercise," she replied.

"Well, that's a good start, Bernice. Keep on trying to find things to do that can help you keep your sanity even when you're crazy busy. There are so many things you can do that do not cost a penny. Call a friend for a chat, or listen to your favorite song. It has to be your list though, not mine."

Bernice said, "I have this low level depression and a lot of anxiety. Just dealing with my son's father increases my anxiety. I feel like this is holding me back."

I talked to Bernice a bit more and thought she was more than a little depressed. I gave her a prescription for Prozac to help with the depression as well as the anxiety. I also suggested that she choose something she could do for relaxation and consistently do it.

When Bernice returned for the next visit a month later, she told me she never took the Prozac and was still having mood issues. "I feel like I have a hormonal imbalance because there is hair growing on my chin, and my body hurts all the time. Aleve hasn't helped all that much. I'm tossing and turning at night, and I always want to crack all my joints. And I'm going to go on birth control. I want to make sure that medicine you gave me won't affect my birth control."

I examined Bernice. "I don't think you have a hormonal imbalance," I told her. "Your muscles are just very tight from all the anxiety that you carry. And it's honestly not uncommon for black women to have a couple of hairs on their chin. Actually, it's not uncommon for most races. It's nothing to worry about. I did all your blood work at your physical a few months ago, and it was all normal.

"You just have a lot going on. Try taking your medicine like I prescribed, and find some ways to deal with this anxiety you have. I know you don't have a lot of time, but counseling might be really good for you."

Bernice was very noncommittal about the suggestions I gave her, but she agreed to come back for another follow up.

Bernice did come back, and when I walked into the exam room, she was sitting on the table, looking straight ahead, with her hands folded together. Her stillness was not one of calm, but rather of a spring just on the verge of snapping. In a soft, flat voice, she said, "I'm really, really anxious right now.

I'm having dreams and waking up at night. I lost 5 lbs last week. I can't concentrate on my school work. My jaw is hurting because I'm clenching it all the time. I'm shaking and sweating. I'll wake up with my heart pounding in my chest, and I can't go back to sleep."

"What's going on?" I asked Bernice with concern.

She replied, "I'm afraid of what I'm going to do to my son's father. I'm trying to stay out of trouble but it's hard."

"What do you mean by that?"

"He owes me money. I just want to find him."

"And what are you going to do when you find him?" I asked.

Bernice hesitated. "I want to find him to talk to him, but in the past it hasn't always gone so well. I know I just need to leave him alone. I have no desire to eat. I feel weak. I know that how I'm feeling right now is not going to end well."

My concern for Bernice and her predicament was growing. "So are you planning to hurt him in some way if you find him?"

Bernice looked away towards the wall. "I'm not planning to hurt him in some way, but it's possible."

"Were you going to bring some sort of weapon with you when you go out looking for your ex-boyfriend?"

"I wouldn't bring a weapon with me, but I don't feel like I can control myself right now." Bernice continued, "I went to his house this morning before coming to your office. I wanted my money he owed me. He yelled out that he'd be right out and for me to wait. Then he ditched me by going out the side door while I was waiting at the front door."

At this point, I had some serious concerns about Bernice's safety as well as what might happen if she and her ex-boyfriend were to get into an altercation. Anything could happen in the heat of the moment, and it could be something they would regret forever.

"Bernice, as your doctor, my job is to keep you both healthy and safe. I am really worried about you and what might happen to you or to your ex-boyfriend. If one of my patients makes statements about possibly hurting themselves or hurting other people, I have to report it to the police.

"And I'm not just worried about him, you know. I'm concerned that if you find your ex-boyfriend and you lose your cool, he might do the same thing. Terrible tragedies happen in the heat of the moment, and you can never undo what's been done."

Bernice's countenance got even colder, if that were possible. "I understand that that's what you have to do, but if I wanted to do something, I would have. I wouldn't be here to try to talk to you."

I tried to assure her, "I will do everything that I can to help. I don't think you're in imminent danger of doing something, or I would keep you here against your will. But I would like for you to stay here. That way, I can be the mediator between you and the police."

Bernice looked away again and said, "I'm good."

I wanted to get a definite yes or no, so I pressed her. "I know you're good, Bernice, but I want to know if you would be willing to stay until the police arrive."

She shook her head. "I could have called him myself, but I came here."

"And you did the right thing," I told her.

"But it doesn't seem like that right now, so you just do what you gotta do." Bernice folded her arms in front of her, tapping her fingers.

I asked, "What about the medicine? You could continue the Prozac, or I could change it to something else like Paxil if you're having side effects or something. "

Bernice shook her head again. "I'm all right."

"So you're not going to take anything?" Bernice shook her head.

"Where are you going to from here?" I persisted.

"They can find me at my house." Bernice was clearly itching to go.

"I'm trying to help you. I understand how you might feel this is a betrayal, but I'm doing what I think is best for you and him. I want to be here for you. If you go home, are you going to stay there?" Bernice nodded. "And do you have any intention of hurting yourself?" She shook her head. "Are you *sure* you won't stay here? It would go much better for you if you did." She refused again.

I paused a moment to collect my thoughts and see if there was any other way I could help this woman. "Are we done?" She asked. I couldn't think of anything, so I said yes. Bernice walked so quickly down the hall and out the door that she probably didn't even hear my secretary call her name.

I sighed and let her go. After I got done with the last two patients for the morning, I stayed at the office while the rest of the staff went for lunch. I called the town police department and explained to the dispatcher what had transpired. She said she would send an officer my way.

Not even three minutes later, a young officer came in and introduced himself. He asked me to give my story again, which I did. I reiterated to him that I did not think Bernice was in imminent danger to herself or to her ex-boyfriend, but I thought it would be wise for someone to talk to her. He agreed and said they would send someone out to her house to check up on her.

I might not ever see Bernice again as a patient. She might see that trust bond as broken and never come back. Bernice might not think so, but I feel like I did the right thing. If I hadn't and something did happen to either one of them, I would feel terrible forever. As much as it saddens me to lose a patient, I would gladly give up that patient if I can save a life.

Respect

Lester was a patient I inherited from my step-father when I took over the medical practice over ten years ago. At first impression, I thought he was a nice enough guy. I took care of his daughter for a time, as well as his son-in-law and a fair number of the son-in-law's family. Lester seemed like the "salt of the earth," not very well educated, but straight forward and affable. He seemed to be content with his lot in life as a lower-middle-class individual. Every three months, Lester would come in for his blood pressure check, routine blood work, and refill of his medications.

At every annual physical, I would counsel Lester on his smoking and drinking. They were two vices to which he was not willing to give up, no matter what I said. What I was not aware of was how addicted to these substances Lester had become. They formed the warp and weft of his daily life. Although he did tell me that he smoked about a pack a day and he drank some, he was fairly evasive about exactly how much he drank. Since the social history and lifestyle risk factors were only a small part of the physical, I gave them the attention I could. I still had to accomplish dealing with his chronic medical problems, preventative maintenance, annual shots, referrals to specialists, and a host of other labs and tests, all squeezed into a half-hour time slot.

Gradually, Lester's drinking in particular became the poison that was turning Dr. Jekyll into Mr. Hyde. He began spacing his appointments further apart or missing his appointments altogether. When he did come in,

Lester was surlier. He was more indifferent about his medical conditions. He didn't want me even to mention smoking or drinking. He was dismissive of my concerns for his health and the consequences of his worsening conditions.

When I encouraged him to keep his regular three-month appointments, he got resistant. "I'm doing *fine*. If there's something wrong with me, I'll come in. I don't want to pay for no God-damned visit." I tried to tell him that he had both Medicare and a supplemental that would take care of his co-insurance. It did not affect his premium, and in fact, if I could keep him healthy, it might improve his overall cost. Lester would hear none of it. I finally gave up and told him to follow up when he wanted. However, based on the long-established office policy, we could only fill his prescriptions if he came in at least every six months.

For two or three years, I saw relatively little of Lester, maybe only about two or three times a year. He came in when he absolutely had to, or when he had some acute problem that needed to be addressed. And although he was not concerned about missing an appointment with no phone call or explanation, Lester wanted an office visit the very day he would call for an acute problem.

Because Lester was no longer pleasant to be around, I did my job dealing with his medical problems as fast as I could and got him out of the office. He seemed to be an energy drain, and any good mood I had before I walked into the exam room with him evaporated more quickly than a drop of water in Death Valley. It got to the point where I dreaded seeing him on the daily schedule, because I knew I had to prepare for some sort of fight over one thing or another.

Lester called the office one day and once again insisted we had to see him *right away*. As it turned out, we had an open spot in the schedule and squeezed him in. When I walked into the room, I met Lester's wife for the first time. She had a look of concern on her face as she shook my hand gently. In contrast, Lester was sitting on the exam table beside her, looking stone faced as usual. I made the conscious decision to keep the smile on my face and lightness in my voice as I asked, "So what brings you to the office?"

"I haven't eaten for four days, and I want you to give me a pill to eat more," Lester replied brusquely.

"Lester, I need more information. What else is going on?" After a number of open-ended and leading questions, sometimes like pulling eye teeth, I got a clearer picture of his symptoms. Lester had no appetite for four days. Every time he tried to eat, it would come right back up, undigested. He had no fever or chills and no constipation but did have diarrhea all the time. He was feeling dizzy and wobbly. I then found out that Lester had been having a "big chest pain" when he coughed, radiating to his back. As I asked more about the cough, I discovered Lester had apparently been coughing so hard that he was vomiting.

His physical exam was equally troubling. His blood pressure was low at 90/50. He had a heart murmur, which I couldn't recall if he had before. He was not breathing well, the air barely moving through his lungs with each breath. His liver was very large, a sign of significant liver disease, likely from his alcohol intake.

Clearly, there was a lot going on with Lester, not just the fact that he wasn't eating. And there was no simple "pill" that would fix his problem. I told him, "I'm very concerned about all of the things going on. You have a higher risk of lung cancer from your coughing, difficulty breathing, and smoking history. You could very well have a stomach cancer that is blocking the passage of food. That could be why you keep on vomiting. And then there is a chance of liver cancer, with your drinking and the large liver. We need to send you for a number of tests to look into these things."

Lester leaned away from me and crossed his arms in front of him, a classic posture of stubbornness and rejection. He narrowed his ice blue eyes and sneered, "I'm not going to no doctors. I'm not going for no tests. I just want a pill to get my appetite back."

"Lester, I have no idea what's going on. There isn't any pill that can fix your problem, not unless we know what we're facing. If you can't eat, you should at least drink Ensure. You're going to need the energy."

"I'm not drinking no Ensure neither." Lester was digging his heels in.

I sighed. "OK, well, that's up to you. It's your body. Let's get some blood work at least." Lester refused the blood work as well, but his wife convinced him, and only because my nurse was going to be able to draw the blood right in the office. Lester stomped out of the room to the front of the office, and I walked into the adjoining exam room to see the next patient.

Later on that night, I got an emergency call from the lab with a critical result. Lester's sodium level was dangerously low at 116. My nurse called him first thing in the morning to inform him of the result and my recommendation. He needed either to go to the ER or to come back to the office for a re-check of his sodium level. Lester's wife answered the phone, and Amber relayed the message to her. "Oh, I don't think he will want to come, he's lying down." Amber told her that this was an urgent matter, that Lester could have a heart attack or possibly die if he didn't address this issue immediately.

A little later on in the day, I saw that Amber had written Lester's name on the appointment board. I guess Lester changed his mind. Or, more likely, his wife coerced him to change his mind. Actually, the most likely explanation was that Lester was trying to avoid the ER like the Plague, so my office was a lesser evil. So, for the second time in two days, I had a man in front of me with whom I did not particularly enjoy interacting.

"All right Lester, your sodium level was very low, and we need to recheck it today. Have you been able to keep anything down?"

"I ate some stir fry today and kept it down."

"I'm glad for that. How about going for those tests?"

"I *told* you, I'm not going for no tests!"

His wife interjected, "What about his sodium level, Doctor? Is there something we can do?"

His wife's question gave me the excuse to pull away from the glare that was forming on my face. "Your husband can try half-strength Gatorade," I responded.

"I'm not drinking no Gatorade," Lester interjected. His wife glanced at him from the corner of her eye and motioned to me that she would try to get him to drink it.

I looked back at Lester. "I gave you the option of going to the ER or coming here. Why would you come here if you're not going to follow the suggestions I give you?"

"Because I thought you would give me a pill to make me eat better!" He said.

Once again, I explained that I could not be expected to fix his problem if I didn't know what was going on. The entire time I was speaking, Lester held that arrogant, obstinate posture of keeping his arms crossed over his chest and looking at me from the side of his eyes.

I was past the point of exasperation. I said, "Do either of you have any last questions, because I have one last thing to say." I took a deep breath, put my hands together in front of my mouth, and collected my thoughts. "Lester, I feel like we have gone above and beyond due diligence to give you stellar care. I have given you all the medical advice that I can give. At this point, you should seek my advice only when you are willing to accept it and follow through. I'll tell you straight out. You have been nothing but stubborn and crotchety, and you've refused care. Most offices would have fired you from the practice by now."

"If you want to fire me, then fire me. I could care less," Lester snapped.

I wonder if my facial expression conveyed the incredulity that I felt. Lester's wife looked back at me apologetically. I got up from my chair and walked to the door. "You know, Lester, the only reason I'm not firing you today is for your wife's sake. You can do whatever you want, it's your body. But the thing that disappoints me the most is the level of disrespect you have shown me today. If you want your blood drawn by Amber today, that's fine. If not, that's OK too." I walked into the next exam room, not even caring what Lester decided.

Lester must have gotten his blood drawn, because I got the results the next morning. His sodium levels were even worse at 113. I had Amber call the house and tell Lester to go to the ER to get IV fluids. His wife answered the phone and told Amber that she understood, but she doubted she could convince him to go to the ER.

While Amber was on the phone, she could hear Lester in the background, saying, "I'm not going to no God-damn emergency room. I'm fine where I am." Amber finished her conversation and told me what the wife said. I asked her to document everything to show how we were doing our due diligence. If Lester were to actually kick the bucket, we would be protected from litigation.

Apparently, Lester went to the ER. In the middle of the day, the ER doctor called the office. Lester's sodium level had improved from 113 to 123. That was low but not low enough to keep him in the hospital. However, he was having cardiac rhythm problems which were not there before. I informed him of Lester's penchant to refuse care, but I promised I would send his medical records over.

Lester ended up spending almost three days in the hospital. They would have kept him longer, but he refused to stay. During the hospital admission, they found that Lester had been drinking a six-pack of beer by mid-morning and at least another six-pack through the day. Without the alcohol flushing out his electrolytes, his sodium level rose nicely. The doctors told Lester that he needed to stop drinking, or this was going to happen again, but of course he refused. He also didn't want anything else done and clamored to leave. The doctors finally threw up their hands. They "tanked him up" enough to go home, and he was released under the promise that he would follow up in my office the next day.

Lester and his wife came back to the office for the follow up. He was actually looking much better. Instead of addressing him, I spoke to his wife. "The doctors asked him to cut down on his drinking. Did he do that?"

As his wife was shaking her head, Lester said, "I told them I wouldn't." He also refused the supplemental cardiac work up that was ordered at the hospital. I replied that it was within his right to refuse treatment, but it would be his responsibility if there were negative consequences from his decisions.

I looked Lester straight in the eyes and said, "Lester, you have been rude and disrespectful to the office in general and to me in particular." I held my fingers up close together. "I came this close to firing you from the practice the last time, but I didn't for your wife's sake. However, if you persist, I *will* discharge you from this practice."

Amazingly, Lester responded, "I apologize. I did not mean to be rude."

"I really appreciate that apology, Lester," I said. "That means a lot to me. Your communication needs to change if you expect our doctor-patient relationship to work. I want to take care of you, and I want you to be healthy. But we have to work together on this, or it will not work out."

"OK, I apologize," he said again. "I'll do that."

"That's all I ask." I opened the door and let Lester and his wife walk out first, while I followed behind them. The office visit ended in a much more positive note than previous sessions. Lester still was making poor life choices, and I knew that at some point, those choices would come up to bite him in his behind. But I was satisfied with the level of care I gave him. If anything happened, it would not be because I did not do everything I could to the best of my ability.

As a physician, I have a certain set of specialized skills. I work hand in hand with my patients to bring them to a greater level of health. It's not about making anyone do anything. Rather, it's about giving a person all the information necessary to help him or her make the most informed decision, even if it's not the decision I would personally make.

But being a doctor is more than a job, it is a life calling. I take that calling very seriously, and I am always humbled by the fact that people would trust their lives and those of their loved ones into my care. Because of this, I deserve and demand a certain level of respect. In turn, I treat each of my patients with the same level of respect. If a person cannot follow basic rules of propriety, they have no business in my office. It's pretty rare that I have had to fire patients from the practice for inappropriate behavior. When that does occur though, I am never sad to see them go. I challenge those patients to find another physician who will give them the same level of care I provide.

Not Always Easy

I have sometimes said living my Mission is easy because people come to see and pay me to help them. Well, that's actually not always true. In fact, my staff have frequently heard me say, "Please, God, let this be an easily lucrative day." One day, God had to deny that prayer in order to answer the other.

My very first patient bright and early Friday at 8 AM was scheduled for a physical. That plan had to be immediately scrapped. Before I could even start the history taking, Annie told me that she had been severely depressed over the past month. It had gotten to the point where she could not even get out of bed many days, and she had to call in sick so many times that she was in danger of losing her job. When I asked her to fill out the depression screening form, Annie circled the most severe numbers all the way down the list, including the question of, "Do you think you would be better off dead or have plans to hurt yourself." When I urged her to explain her response to that question, she told me that just about every day, she wished she would just never wake up in the morning.

To deal with this terrible depression, Annie confessed she numbed herself by drinking at least a pint of liquor three to four times a week. In my experience, people who drink frequently grossly understate the amount of their drinking. So, in my mind, she was quite possibly drinking half a quart of liquor nearly every day. She confided in me that she felt guilty and shameful about her drinking. Annie would sneak into the liquor store and buy her alcohol without looking at anyone, drive home, and lock herself in her bedroom to drink.

The situation was even worse because Annie was also a single mother of three kids from eight to seventeen years old. Clearly, they were not getting the care they needed if their mother was so depressed that she couldn't get out of bed, and when she did, she would go buy booze to numb her pain. When I brought up the need for her to get help, she said that she would love to, but she couldn't miss any more work or they would fire her, and she didn't have the money to pay for counseling. She also had state Medicaid insurance, which meant access for psychiatric services was severely limited. When I suggested an inpatient treatment program, she told me there was no way, because there would be no one to take care of the kids. She was an only child, brought up by her grandparents, who were both deceased. The father of the children was essentially out of the picture.

I excused myself from the room and called the information hotline, looking for any source of help for this woman. After half an hour of careful searching, I could not come up with any program for a person on Medicaid to get inpatient care and still be able to care for her children. That left me with only one option: the Department of Children and Families. I spoke to the social worker and presented Annie's case. Together, we again reviewed all the options and could not come up with anything. The only recourse was to get DCF involved to make sure the children had their basic needs cared for while the mother dealt with her health issues. My question to the social worker: How do I present this to the patient without her feeling like I was "turning her in" and destroying the trust relationship we had with each other?

With a burdened heart, I walked back into the exam room. I gave Annie all the numbers of the inpatient treatment facilities, and I reiterated to her the need for her to be healthy so she could take care of her kids. I told her I could see that her kids were the love of her life, and she did everything for the sake of her children. I shared with her the analogy that the social worker gave me. When you're in an airplane, the flight attendant always tells you to put the oxygen mask on yourself first before putting it on your child. If you are not healthy, you can't help your children or anyone else. I pointed out to Annie that she was clearly not healthy and not in a place to care for her children. I brought up the topic of DCF getting involved to assist her in the care of her children, *not take over or take her kids away from her*. Through this whole conversation, the tears that had started before were now pouring nonstop down her face. She was terrified at the idea of losing her family and that she had made a horrible mistake by telling me what was going on.

The two of us walked from the exam room into the office. Annie sat in front of me, her face twisted in anguish, as I called DCF to officially report the case. I made it very clear that she was in my presence during the call, and she was voluntarily asking for help. I asked that the record reflect her cooperation to give her just a bit more peace of mind. The DCF worker took all the information down and said someone would call her on Monday. When I put the phone down, I walked around the desk and held Annie close as she sobbed into my shoulder. As best as I could, I assured her that she had made the right decision to get help for herself so she would be healthy for her children. I committed to doing whatever I could to get her into a better place in her life.

In all, that 15 minute scheduled appointment took over an hour and a half. I never quite got a handle on my day, missing a good bit of lunch to catch up with the morning appointments. I had to apologize to every single patient for running so far behind. Even the next morning, when calling a patient to report lab results, his wife told me that he was still grumbling about how long I had made him wait the day before. And to top it all off, because Annie had Medicaid, that meant I essentially was not going to be paid for any of that time.

So, God did not answer my prayer for an easily lucrative day. But my mission is not to have easily lucrative days. My Mission is to help people find greater physical, emotional, and spiritual health. That, I did. It wasn't easy, but we are not promised easy Missions. Few things of true value in life tend to come easily.

Banging My Head Against the Wall

Benny came to the office because his mother basically made him. She was concerned that he was very depressed and was thinking about suicide on a regular basis. She had mentioned Benny to me at one of her own previous office visits and asked me if I knew any psychiatrists who would see Benny as soon as possible. I told her that it usually took months unless a patient was in the ER with an acute suicidal crisis. I also told her I would be happy to evaluate Benny and at least get the ball rolling and get him started on some treatment. I suggested that we start with a physical. That way, we could get blood work as well as let Benny get to know me before discussing more difficult issues.

There was trouble the moment Benny walked up to the front window. When he was given the new patient sheet to fill out, he put in the bare minimum of name, date of birth, and address. Mike called him over and said, "I need you to fill out the primary insured information."

Benny cocked his head and shot up his hand with the insurance card in it, as if to say, "I gave you the stinking card already."

Mike saw his look and said, "The card has the name and ID number, but we need to have your address, date of birth, and social security if you have it. There are also the other sections. Does your family have any medical problems? Do you take any medicines? And there's a whole section here on smoking and alcohol. I need you to circle something on each of these lines."

Benny rolled his eyes, flicked the sheet out of Mike's hands, and flopped down into the chair. Several minutes later, he came back with the sheet. He wrote "nothing" all the way down the sheet except for allergies, where he wrote "filling out forms makes me apathetic."

I glanced at the intake sheet. I took a deep breath, plastered a smile on my face, and opened the door. "Hi! I'm Dr. Han. It's good to meet you." I held out my hand, and Benny shook it noncommittally. I tried to break the ice and make some small talk. "What has been going on with you?" I asked.

"I've been living at Occupy Hartford for the past three and a half weeks, and before that, I was at Occupy Wall Street for a week."

"That's pretty interesting," I commented. "So what has it been like?"

"I'm really frustrated. The world is a freakin' terrible place." Benny sighed. "Oh, my mother wanted me to tell you that all I want to do is sleep and there is no joy in my life." Benny said it like he didn't believe a word of it, but he was doing what he was told to do, so there it was. But as he continued, I could tell there was definitely something wrong. "I got so frustrated the other day that I was banging my head against the wall. I did it so hard that I got discombobulated."

"So other than the world, what has you so frustrated?"

"My main problem is with my ex-girlfriend."

Benny didn't elaborate further, so I tried a different track. "Benny, what do you want to get out of life?"

He replied, "I want to make the world a better place. Not just a little better but substantially better."

"I think that's very noble, Benny," I complimented. "What do you think you need to do to make it happen?"

"I don't know. I just know I'm fucking depressed. What I need are some uppers and downers. When I'm lethargic and need a boost, I can take a pill to do it for me. And I want some benzo's because I know they work for me. I don't want something that I have to take every day."

I replied, "I'll try to figure out what the best thing for you would be. So do you smoke?" Benny nodded. "What about alcohol?"

"Yeah, but not excessively," he replied.

"Any recreational drugs? Pot?"

"Yeah, I smoke that a couple of times a week."

I decided to gloss over the fact that Benny had circled "never" for all three substance uses. "What about sexual activity?" Benny affirmed he was sexually active and not always safe about it.

"OK, let's move to your exam," I said. Things were normal until I had Benny lie down for the abdominal exam. When I lifted up his shirt, I found long pale scars crisscrossing his abdomen. "What's this from?" I asked.

"Oh, I did that a couple of years ago. I wanted to show this girlfriend how she was making me feel inside." I didn't say anything, but alarm bells were going off in my head. Benny continued, "I've been cutting more on my wrists lately. Once they went kind of deep, and I got scared." Benny pulled up his shirt sleeve and there were signs of self-inflicted scars on his forearm as well as an elaborate design etched into his wrist with a deep red line going across his tendons and artery.

I continued with the exam and got to the hernia check. Benny would not let me perform the exam. "I'm not that worried about it," he said. When I suggested STD checks because of his sexual behaviors, he refused those as well. Again, he said, "I'm not really worried about it."

I got done with the exam and asked Benny to go to the front of the office and have one of the nurses draw his blood. Benny asked me, "What about getting a pill?"

"I do not have enough information to prescribe anything at this point. You were scheduled for a physical today, and I think you should come back for a visit specifically to discuss these issues in greater depth. You should also consider going to a psychiatrist."

Benny dismissed my words with a wave of his hand. "I've been to many before, and they don't listen to me."

I knew Benny was going to be a tough nut to crack. I wanted to find a way to help Benny with some deep psychological issues. Clearly, Benny had his own agenda for this visit, namely, getting Xanax. I needed to bring our individual objectives closer together. I told Benny, "It's clear to me that you have a really big heart. You want to make a tremendous difference in the world, and that's not something most people would strive for. But I want to tell you something that is *not* meant to be an antagonistic comment. You lack a certain amount of insight about yourself. You should consider trusting people who might have a bit more experience and knowledge than you do."

Benny's reply was, "Who would have more knowledge about myself than me?"

"I think a professional could help you figure out why you're so depressed and maybe help you stop cutting. I'm concerned about your health, and I want the best for you, Benny. But you have to be willing to consider that there is a perspective that might be different from your own that is a more viable option than what you're doing right now. Through this visit, there are a number of things that I have encouraged you to consider, and you're not willing."

"What, because I won't let you touch my junk?" Benny retorted.

I shook my head slightly in resignation. "No, that's not it."

"Well what about giving me a pill? That's what I need."

Benny had all the signs of classic borderline personality disorder. This was not something that a pill could fix. I was also not about to give him Xanax or any other mood-altering controlled substance with his history of drug use and unabashed lying. Although his depression needed to be treated, it was not something I could dive into at the moment, since it needed to be as part of a comprehensive package of care for him.

I knew Benny was not ready to accept any further input from me at this juncture, so it was time to close the visit. "I don't have enough information right now to prescribe anything for you. I think it would help if you made a follow-up appointment to further discuss your psychiatric issues in detail, since this visit was not scheduled as a psychiatric visit. If you're having active thoughts of suicide, you should call 911. I would like to again encourage you to consider going to a psychiatrist, even if you don't think they've helped you before." I opened the door and motioned Benny to the checkout counter.

At the checkout counter, my nurse saw the lab slip for Benny's blood work and said, "If you have a seat in the lab, we'll draw your blood."

"I don't think so," Benny said.

"OK, well, Dr. Han would like to see you back in a couple of weeks. What day would be good for you?"

"I'm not making an appointment."

My nurse asked him again and he refused a second time. Benny then walked out the door.

Because I was concerned of Benny's volatile behavior and his suicidal thoughts, I called his mother a few days later. "Mandy, you know I can't legally divulge any private information about the visit I had with Benny. But, if you have any concerns as to his personal welfare, or if he gives any indication of active suicidal thoughts, you have an obligation to call 911."

"I was wondering about his visit," Mandy admitted. "I thought he was going to get a physical. Benny said you didn't order any blood for him."

"Oh no, that's not true," I corrected.

"So, you did get blood?"

"No, we didn't, but not because I didn't order it."

Comprehension seeped into Mandy's voice. "He refused it. That little shit!"

"Benny wouldn't make a follow-up visit either. We have the lab slip, which we can fax to any drawing station he wants."

Mandy said, "I'll get him to do it. He wants to fly to California, but he doesn't have the money for it. I'll tell him I won't buy it unless he gets this done."

"I just want the best for Benny," I assured her. "We're here if you need us, but if Benny seems suicidal, you should get him help immediately."

"What do I do, call the police and have them take him to the ER?" Mandy asked.

"That's exactly what happens," I said. "Benny honestly needs some significant help. I will do what I can, but he needs to trust me. It would also help if I could talk to you more openly. If you have him sign a medical release form, I can talk with you but still keep his confidence when appropriate."

Mandy said she would get him to do that as well. She thanked me for my time and for taking care of Benny. Only time will tell if Benny will get to the point of accepting the help he needs to be in a better place in his life.

Pressure Cooker

For over a decade, I have been taking care of Jane, a beautiful mother of two wonderful daughters, now in their teens. About six years ago, her husband Donny started acting strangely. At the prompting of his wife, he came in to talk to me about his symptoms. His thoughts were racing, and he had the unshakable feeling that his wife was having an affair, even though she had never done anything to make him suspicious. His temper was getting worse, and he was fighting with everyone at work, including his boss. He felt like everyone was against him.

After a long interview and several screening tests, I diagnosed Donny with schizoaffective disorder and gave him medicine. Unfortunately, before the medicine could take effect, his illness caused him to mistrust me as well, and he stopped his medicine, refusing to come in for follow-ups.

Over the next several years, Donny's condition grew more severe. He called every one of his friends one by one and told each of them how stupid and worthless they were. He burned every bridge and has not had any friends for a long time. He stopped working, and he blamed everyone else for his unemployment. For a time, he was belligerent and nearly violent to Jane and the kids. Jane spent many months with house and car keys always in her hands, just in case she had to gather the kids up quickly to make a run for safety.

Everyone in the family was suffering. The girls were embarrassed to bring friends over, because they never knew what their father would say. He would talk to himself and not even know he was doing it. Jane couldn't mention the possibility of Donny finding a job because he would blow up at her. Donny had had a worker's comp case in litigation for four years, and then he suddenly decided that his lawyer was "incompetent" and summarily fired him. Jane did not want the kids to see their parents fight, so the only time to talk to Donny was after the kids went off to school and before Jane went to work. But she didn't want to go to work upset, so she would not bring anything up, and usually just say "bye" as she was heading out the door.

What at first seemed like a light at the end of a tunnel turned out to be a train. Donny had agreed to see a psychiatrist a few years ago, and he went back on a very low dose of his psychiatric medicine. The only reason he did so was because he was told it was a sleeping medicine. Instead of using this opportunity to really help Donny with his illness, the psychiatrist was content to see him for two minutes twice a year and simply refill his medicine without changes. While the medicine controlled Donny's most violent tendencies, it was not enough to adequately treat his condition. This caused Jane to feel really stuck in the situation because Donny was not sick enough to warrant getting further professional help, but he was not well enough to hold a job or have meaningful interactions with his family.

Over the course of six years, Donny's illness took a terrible toll on Jane's physical health. I treated her for chest pains and heart racing, severe acid reflux, protracted bronchitis episodes, high blood pressure, neck pain, sciatica, and finally the autoimmune disease ulcerative colitis. I told her several times that the majority of her symptoms were either caused by or exacerbated by her current situation with her husband. Usually, I dealt with just her physical issues. On one particular office visit, I decided it was time to dig a bit deeper.

"How are things really going Jane?" I asked. Jane gave an "OK" glib response at first, but I wouldn't let her get away with it. "Jane, you say everything is OK, but inside you're like a pressure cooker. That pressure is building up, and for any pressure cooker, if there is no release valve, that cooker is going to explode. You look like you're pretty close to that point."

"I know," Jane replied, wringing her hands. "I just don't know what to do. He's stable right now. At least I'm not afraid of what he's going to do anymore like when he was not taking any medicine. He's not good to me and the girls, but they would miss him if he were not there."

"What about asking him to leave?" I asked.

"How am I going to do that? He would just refuse to go. I told him once that I was going to file for divorce, thinking that would change things somehow. He said, 'Fine, go ahead and try that,' like he didn't have a care about it at all. I think he thinks he's going to get the house and the kids. What he said just made me so mad! And a part of me still loves him. What if I kicked him out and something happened to him? He can't take care of himself."

"Jane," I replied, "in this country, you don't see people dying on the side of the road. If Donny needs help, *someone*, either the state or the police, will see he gets help. And maybe if Donny actually had to live on his own, he would realize he can't do it by himself and consider seeking treatment for his problem."

Jane's eyes welled up with tears. "I don't know. Maybe it would be good to get a divorce. It would sure help my money situation. He hasn't worked for four years. I'm paying for his car, his gas, and all his food. My older daughter is going to college, and I can't afford Catholic school for Michelle, so she's going to have to switch to the public high school in the fall. She's already scared about that. I'm working two jobs, and I just can't make ends meet. Without him there, I might be able to save up a little bit of money."

I told her, "No matter what, you can't continue the way it is. Something just has to change. You are enabling him to do nothing but stay at home and complain. The reason Donny hasn't been mean to you is because he is getting everything he could want. Who knows what would happen if you didn't cater to his every whim? And if he gets violent, you have every right to call the police and tell them you fear for the safety of you and the kids. They'll definitely do something about it."

I reminded Jane of the incident of a man in a nearby town with bipolar disorder who barricaded himself in the house with his family held hostage under gunpoint. The police finally had to shoot and kill him to protect the lives of the rest of the family. I continued, "I immediately thought this was you and Donny when I heard the news, Jane. And if you're not careful, it really *could* be you. You have to do something to protect yourself and the kids."

"I know, Doctor, I know." Jane continually dabbed her eyes with the Kleenex. "I tell myself every morning, 'I'm going to do something about this,' and then I don't. I just think maybe it will get better somehow, but it never does. Now look at me. I didn't want to go to work upset with my mascara all smeared."

I responded, "Jane, you know that the reason you come here is because I know both you and Donny. You know I care about you and how you are doing, physically and emotionally." I smiled at her. "And you know that when needed, I will gently and lovingly kick you in the butt." Jane laughed and nodded her head.

I told Jane it seemed clear to me that she was living in a codependent relationship. I printed out an article on codependency and gave it to her. I also recommended she look into counseling for herself since she did not have anyone to talk to about her problems. I assured her she could make an appointment with me just to talk about how things were going and how she was feeling.

There was one more thing for me to do. I told her, "All right. There is just one last thing, but you have to stand up for it." I put my arms out and wrapped my arms around her as she sobbed into my shoulder. I did not say a word, instead letting my hug express my love and concern for her. Once or twice, she loosened her grip as to let go, but I wouldn't let her. I just held on until I felt she had no doubt that she was precious and worthy of love. My hug had to fill a soul that had lacked a loving touch for more than six years. The moment was so touching that my medical student who was present for the visit started crying herself.

As we walked out of the exam room, I encouraged Jane not to slip back into her old self-destructive patterns. I wanted her to take one small step to change the situation she was in. She wouldn't promise me that she would do it, but she did say that she really needed to and she would think about it. Ultimately, that's all I can do. My job is not to make people do anything. My job—my Mission—is to give people the tools to improve their life situation. It is up to them to use those tools when the time is right. If I can do that, then I consider that a success.

Jane

Laughter is the Best Medicine

I had been taking care of Mr. Truyen Tran for a decade, watching the old man continue to decline from his emphysema and multiple other medical problems. He was admitted to the hospital more and more frequently until finally, the family decided that they would no longer take him to the hospital and cause him further suffering.

Mr. Tran's son came in to the office one day for his appointment, and I asked him how his dad was doing. "Oh, Dad's doing much better," he replied.

"Hey, that's great!" I said. "When is he coming back in to see me?"

"Dad's not coming back in," Tuan half chuckled. "He died. That's why he's doing much better. He's not in pain anymore."

I complimented Tuan on how well he was taking everything.

****

Johnny came in with a fever, coughing, and feeling terrible. Nevertheless, he still retained his sense of humor. "So, am I going to live, Doc?"

"Well, this is a very rare form of the flu," I replied. "It's a cross between the swine flu and the avian flu. It only happens when pigs fly."

****

Charlie said, "You need to get everything done in the next couple of months because I'm retiring and going on Medicare."

"How long have you been with the company?" I asked.

"Forty-nine years," Charlie replied.

"Forty-nine years! How about sticking it out for fifty?"

"I'm sixty-eight already Doc, and I won't hit the fifty year mark until next October. I'd shoot myself before then."

"But wouldn't they give you something really nice if you make it to fifty years? Like a watch or something?" I asked.

"No, they give you the same thing."

"What are they going to give you?"

"A gun."

I looked at Charlie in shock. "A gun? You're kidding, right?"

"No," he said.

"Charlie, who do you work for?"

Charlie said, "Colt Manufacturing."

****

During medical school, I served as a Vietnamese-English translator for the hospital. One late night, I was called to come in to help translate for a woman in labor. "Push! Push!" I told her in Vietnamese.

Hearing what I was saying, the nurse tried to imitate my word for push. When she said it both the patient and I burst out laughing. "What's so funny?" The nurse asked.

"Well," I told her, "You didn't say *push*. You said *cockroach*."

****

Barbara is a pharmaceutical rep who calls on the office. As is true with most of the drug reps, she is a pretty woman, 5'10" with blue eyes and long blonde hair, as well as legs that go a mile. In fact, she has referred to herself as "Barbie Barbara."

One morning, Barbara came to the front window to get a signature for samples, and noticing that we seemed to be dragging, she offered to get us some coffee down the street. We gratefully accepted the offer, and she took our coffee orders. "OK, I'll be back in 15 minutes," she said.

Fifteen minutes went by, and no Barbara. Half an hour, and still no Barbara. More importantly, no coffee. We were all wondering what happened, but we were too busy to give it much thought.

Almost an hour later, we got a call from Barbara. "I'm so sorry, but I'll have to get you coffee some other day. I'll make it up to you, I promise. I had a wardrobe malfunction."

Barbara proceeded to explain that she had parked her car across the street in a parking lot surrounded by a low guard rail. In an attempt to save time, instead of going around to the opening, she decided to step over the guard rail to get to her car. Unfortunately, she neglected to take into account that she was wearing a very stylish tight-fitting skirt that day. When Barbara lifted her leg to straddle the rail, her skirt split from top to bottom. Because she did not have a change of clothes with her, she had to drive all the way back home to get another outfit.

She made it up to us by bringing us cookies later in the afternoon.

****

The chief complaint at the top of the chart for Carlos' visit was "sore throat." When I asked Carlos about his symptoms, he said, "It's not really sore. It doesn't hurt at all. I've been feeling this tickle in the back of my throat, and I have to clear my throat all the time. So I took a look in my mouth. You know that dangly thing in the back of your throat?"

"It's called the uvula," I told him.

"Yeah, the uvula. Well, when I looked in my throat, there was something growing out of my uvula."

I said, "OK, let's take a look." Carlos opened his mouth and I took a peek. Sure enough, jutting from the side of Carlos' uvula was a cauliflower-like mass. It was big enough to almost touch the back of his tongue and epiglottis. "So Carlos, it looks like you do have something back there. It's probably irritating the back of your throat and causing you to cough. It looks like a genital wart, but I would have to take it out to send it for testing to be sure."

Carlos looked at me blankly. "A genital wart? How would I get a genital wart back there?"

I stared back at him without saying anything.

****

One of Raymond's ways of showing his appreciation for the office is to buy us huge bags of lifesavers. He told me once, "I gotta heck of a sweet tooth, even when I was young. Now, I'm old, and all my teeth are long gone, but I still have a sweet tooth. I guess they're now more like 'sweet dentures.'"

AGAINST THE ODDS

"Our greatest glory is not in never failing, but in rising up every time we fail."

~Ralph Waldo Emerson, American essayist, lecturer, and poet

Sudden Death

Eddie Courtright was a handsome man, at 6', with medium length sandy blond hair, blue eyes, and a neatly trimmed mustache above a straight-teeth smile. No one, least of all Eddie himself, would imagine that he would suffer sudden cardiac death at the young age of 38.

Eddie had just moved to a new condo complex in 1993. When he went out to the mailbox, a woman caught his eye. He decided to go introduce himself, and he and Debra exchanged information. Their friendship grew into a romance, and after four years, Eddie got married at the age of 37.

The couple had a year together as just the two of them until Shane was born in January 2000. The delivery was complicated by an emergency Cesarean section, and Deb's recuperation took a little longer than expected. For three months, Deb stayed at home with Shane, while Eddie worked to provide for the family. By April, Shane was three months old and Deb got the green light to start driving. Eddie was at a new job and working lots of hours. Things seemed to be going great. Then, Eddie started getting heartburn symptoms. He was eating Rolaids like candy, but the discomfort kept on getting worse and worse. Eddie also had sharp pains, like a pencil was being driven into his wrist.

Eddie had no idea what was going on. Over-the-counter medicines were not helping, so he went to the ER for an evaluation. The tests were inconclusive but seemed to indicate Eddie had some cardiac abnormalities. Eddie was told to make a follow up appointment with a cardiologist at his earliest convenience. The next day, Eddie went to the cardiologist and had an in-office stress test. The test was quite abnormal, so the doctor told Eddie to go to St. Francis Hospital immediately for an urgent cardiac catheterization.

Before Eddie left the cardiology office, the doctor detailed the plan of action. Eddie would likely need to get a stent placed. The interventional radiologist would thread a catheter from his groin to his heart and into the blocked vessel. There, he would pass a balloon through the narrowed opening and expand the balloon. A wire mesh on the outside would then attach itself to the walls of the artery, thereby restoring normal blood flow. That was the plan, anyway.

When the doctor went in, he found a very large blockage of the main coronary artery that he was not able to bypass. Meanwhile, Eddie was developing cardiac distress on the cath table. The doctor had to change the procedure to an emergency open heart surgery. Once they cracked open Eddie's chest, they found many more blockages than they had anticipated. Eddie ended up having veins taken out of his legs for a quadruple bypass.

Eddie's operation went well, and after a couple of weeks, he returned home to recuperate. The doctors were not concerned because Eddie was young and thought he would do fine. Eddie took his medicine and did his exercises, but even after several weeks, he didn't improve. Eddie remained very weak, got short of breath easily, and had recurrent chest pains. One night, as Deb was nursing Shane, Eddie called out. Deb ran into the room and found Eddie clutching his chest, his face ashen. She immediately called 911, and the ambulance took Eddie back to St. Francis Hospital.

Tests revealed that all of the vein grafts had collapsed, and blood could not get through to Eddie's heart muscle. After stabilizing Eddie over two days, he was again prepped for surgery at six AM. The doctors told Deb this was a much more complicated procedure than the first surgery and that it could take eight hours. By four PM, when Deb expected that Eddie would have been done, she hadn't heard anything. Six PM came and went without any news.

At nine PM, five hours after everything should have been finished, the surgeon called Deb as she paced anxiously in the waiting room. "We had some complications," he told her.

Apparently, the surgery was much more complicated than anyone could have anticipated. Eddie's original bypass grafts failed because his veins had extensive disease. The surgeons then had to harvest several arteries for a revision of the bypasses. At five PM the team finished and closed him up. Minutes after, Eddie suffered severe cardiac compromise and his heart stopped. The team immediately placed electrical paddles on his chest and restarted his heart. His heart beat a couple of times and stopped again. This time, when the doctors used the paddles, it did not work, and Eddie remained flat lined.

Most surgeons would have stopped and admit defeat. However, Dr. Chawla, the head of the team, was not about to give up on his patient. Dr. Chawla reopened Eddie's sternum, spread his ribs apart, and manually pumped Eddie's heart. Dr. Chawla continued to cradle Eddie's heart in his hands and pump until the physical massage caused the cardiac muscle fibers to contract automatically again. At nine PM, the team was able to close Eddie back up and take him to the Cardiac ICU.

It was at the time when Eddie had clinically died that he had an out-of-body experience. He described it like this: "I saw a bright light. When I looked to the right and left of me I saw two creatures. They reminded me of those gargoyle bookends I used to have on the book shelf when I was a kid. The three of us, with the gargoyles on each side of me, were looking down to a lighted area. There seemed to be a light on something, but it was out of focus. Everything lasted no more than a minute or two."

When Eddie was going through his surgery, a great deal of fluid had built up in his lungs, and this likely caused his heart to stop. Even after Dr. Chawla was able to restart Eddie's heart, his lungs still were severely injured. Eddie's entire pulmonary system was compromised. Eddie's carbon dioxide level was completely saturated. Over the next twenty-four hours, that carbon dioxide level slowly went to 80%, then to 60%, and eventually to normal. Later on, a chest tube was placed between two of his ribs, and in just a few hours, over three liters of fluid was drained from his lungs.

Every one of Eddie's organ systems was affected. Two days after arriving in the ICU, Eddie developed a fever of 105. An infectious disease specialist was added to the team, and he pumped Eddie full of antibiotics. A few days after that, the doctors found Eddie could not move anything on his left side. Eddie could shake his head and motion with his right hand, but it was like his left side did not exist. A neurologist was called in and surmised that Eddie had a stroke from the prolonged lack of oxygen to his brain during the surgery and cardiac arrest.

Eddie developed "ICU psychosis" from the inability to have a normal sleep cycle and the multitude of treatments he was receiving. He believed the nurses giving him IV medicines were the mafia slipping him drugs. Eddie remembered all the McDonalds kiosks in the hospital, and his addled brain interpreted that as Ronald McDonald was after him. At one point, Eddie panicked and ripped out his ventilator tube, severely injuring his vocal cords in the process. Another time, he yanked out his feeding tube. The doctor was going to sew the feeding tube directly into Eddie's nose so he would not be able to pull it out. Instead, Deb convinced them to use arm restraints. Eventually, Eddie required antipsychotic medications to keep him calm enough for the staff to care for him.

Against all odds, Eddie started to improve. He was eventually weaned off the ventilator, and his voice returned. His infections cleared, and he even regained some use of his left side. In all, Eddie was in the ICU for a month. After the ICU, Eddie was moved to an inpatient rehab center for another month. There, he had a whole other set of challenges, including developing hundreds of severely painful blood clots in his legs that were moving to his lungs. Eddie had to go back to the hospital once again to get a Greenfield filter placed in his inferior vena cava. The Greenfield filter would keep blood clots from going to his lungs and causing a pulmonary embolus.

On July 15, 2000, Eddie came home. When he went to the hospital in April, he was 200 lbs. He now weighed 98 lbs. Eddie looked like a man in his eighties. He was forbidden to lift anything over four pounds. He could not lift up Shane or even change his diaper. However, with the tireless help of his wife and the visiting nurses, Eddie slowly got strength back.

Eddie's body was not the only thing that was injured through this ordeal. Eddie was suffering with post-surgery depression. For a long period of time, he feared that each day would be his last day to live. He was crying all the time. Every time he looked at his son, it was worse. Eddie figured he would never get to see Shane grow up.

The first six months after the surgery were very frightening for Eddie and Deb both. Every chest pain could have been a major issue. Eddie had a lot of fears about the future, how short his would be and what would happen to his family afterwards. That anxiety manifested itself as chest pain, which further confused the picture. Eddie decided to go to therapy. The counseling helped Eddie deal with his anxiety and gave him a safe place to voice his fears. The relationship lasted three years and greatly helped Eddie recover emotionally.

Time continued to march on, and Eddie spent it with Deb, Shane, and his family. He still needed a great deal of physical and emotional healing though. He required the placement of yet another stent. He got bouts of pneumonia several times, some of them severe. His exercise tolerance was still low. But, Eddie did get to watch Shane grow up, something he could not have imagined would happen.

Two years after the cardiac surgery, Eddie turned forty, and Deb decided to throw him a surprise party. She rented out an entire lodge and had food catered. Eddie was driven to the lodge by a close friend, and when he walked in, there were more than 125 people waiting for him, cheering. Deb invited all the staff and physicians involved in Eddie's care, and many of them came. The charge nurse for Eddie's floor as well as many of the floor nurses came to the party to see the man who had died and been brought back to life. There was a great deal of laughing and crying that night for everyone.

After Eddie turned forty, he started developing an interest in church. The weekly sermons gave him faith, helping him understand why he went through what he went through. The church was also a social outlet, a place of community gathering and fellowship. Eddie's spiritual seeking helped him find possible answers to why he was still around, why his life was spared.

In May 2004, I met Eddie while visiting at his church. As I was talking to my patient who had invited me to the church, I mentioned that I was putting together a medical mission trip to Thailand in July. Greg said he couldn't go, but his friend Eddie might have an interest. When I told Eddie about the trip, he was very excited. He asked me if it was OK for a person with heart problems to go. Based on previous trips, I did not think the trip would be overly taxing. Of course, I did not know the extent of Eddie's heart disease, or I would have more carefully considered those long airport walks and the many hills in Thailand. Blissfully ignorant of Eddie's condition, I told him if he was cleared to go by his physicians, I would be happy to look after him medically.

Over the next two weeks Eddie contacted his physicians, who gave him a cautious green light. Then came the task of expediting a passport, while I added Eddie's name to the group of plane tickets. Eddie prepared his clothes and travel gear to travel to the opposite side of the world. He helped break down medicines and pack the ten duffel bags with donated clothes, toys, and toiletries. When the scheduled date came, Eddie and the rest of our small team said our goodbyes to our families and boarded the plane.

Through all of this, Deb was battling her own doubts and fears. When Eddie brought up the idea of going to Thailand, Deb knew that he needed the opportunity to push himself and explore, both physically and spiritually. He might not ever have the opportunity to do something like that again. They both knew there was a lot of risk, but Eddie was very excited about the trip. Deb had to let him go. It was a part of her own healing process to trust things would work out.

I roomed with Eddie through the trip. Every day, we went to a different village treating patients. While I examined patients, Eddie separated and counted the medicine with other team members. There was also time to distribute donated items, play with the kids, and visit with the villagers. It was amazing how much a smile and a touch cut across all cultures and language barriers.

One would think that working in such close quarters would immediately bring us all together. But, I was actually so busy seeing one patient after another as well as serving as the team leader that I had very little time to get to know Eddie on a personal basis. It took a game of charades late one night to break down any remaining barriers. While Mike, his son Egan, and I kept our laughter to a dull roar, Eddie valiantly attempted to pantomime "the virgin birth." From that moment Eddie's friendship with the three of us blossomed. To this day, the topic of Eddie curving his hands in a pregnant gesture and swinging his arms from below his knees causes peals of laughter.

Ever since that Thailand trip, the Courtrights have become close friends. We have shared Eddie's moments of great progress and health as well as setbacks that threatened his life. In 2010, when the family was on vacation in Ogunquit, Maine, Eddie had a major cardiac episode. If it were not for the amazingly rapid response of the EMS and the stellar care of the medical staff, Eddie would not have survived. A year later, for Eddie's 50th birthday, the Courtrights went back to Ogunquit to see the paramedics who helped save Eddie's life.

I asked Eddie what he has learned through all of the struggles he has gone through. He said, "I'm grateful to have these last thirteen years where I'm at now. I shouldn't be here. I appreciate every waking moment that I've had. We have a very good life I think; we're very fortunate people. I know what's important: good friends, family, and patience."

Deb chimed in, "Eddie has had to work hard at that patience thing. He used to be very impatient, but he's had to learn patience. Eddie used to want it fixed and fixed yesterday. In the past, he was a more scheduled person, but now he looks at things in a more laid-back way."

Eddie finished, "You see what your priorities are. Those little things that used to matter so much don't really matter. And I'm blessed to have Deb. There would be no way I would be here without her."

And I am blessed to have Eddie and the Courtrights in my own life.

Eddie with Shane, July 2003 at the Maine potato festival

Eddie in front of Wat Pra Kaew in Bangkok, Thailand

Eddie and me riding an elephant in Chiang Mai, Thailand

Eddie, Deb, and Shane Courtright in 2011

Eddie and the EMT team who saved his life in Ogunquit, Maine.
Left to Right: Ofc. Brett Owens, EMT Jessica Christian, FF Dave Moore,
Sgt. Matthew Buttrick, and EMT Jeff Smith

Unforeseen Circumstances

Sherlymary Santiago responded to our job posting for a medical assistant. At nineteen, she was young, especially as a mother of a one-year-old son. She seemed to be well spoken and earnest. It was clear she needed a job, and the office was short staffed. We also figured she would do better on the computer than the last employee, who was very nice to patients but not at all electronically proficient.

Sherly integrated herself into the office workflows. She mainly did front desk jobs like checking patients out and taking money. Since she was trained as a medical assistant, she could also draw blood, get vital signs, and set up EKG's. I frequently called on her clinical skills as well as her ability to speak Spanish. Although she had her weak points—and who doesn't—Sherly still was a valuable asset to the office. Since it was just I as the physician and three and a half staff, every person played a vital role, and the office was more like a small family. Like any family, there were times when we all got along, and other times when we had bad days or had conflicts that needed to be resolved. By and large, the office functioned smoothly.

Those dynamics changed when about a year into her time at the office, Sherly informed us that she was pregnant with her second child. We were surprised and concerned on many levels. We worried for Sherly, who was already struggling to support herself, her son, and her boyfriend, who did not work more than a few odd jobs here and there. How was she going to be able to take care of an infant as well as keep financially afloat? On a selfish level, we were also concerned about the office and how to get everything done with one less person to help with the work load. The paper work, prior authorizations, medication refills, and a million other things that had to be done were piling up. But we did it. The office hired a temporary staff person, while Sherly had her baby and took maternity leave.

Because of tight finances, Sherly did not take the full six weeks of allowed maternity leave. Although the leave was available, she was not getting paid while she stayed home. Only about three weeks into her leave, she was carting Jeremy into the office. Keeping him by her side, she did paper work for a couple of hours a day. Her boyfriend did not have any sort of steady income, so the money she brought in was essential to put food on the table.

As Jeremy got older, he stayed at home with his brother and father, while Sherly worked more full-time hours. But now, with two sons, Sherly's attention was divided between her work and her home. As any parent of an infant knows, emergencies happen when one least expects or desires. Sherly was chronically late to work, sometimes rushing in more than half an hour late. Since she sat at the front desk checking patients in and out, when she was not there, the rest of the staff had to scramble and fill in the gap. Sherly also often had family complications in the middle of the day as well, where she would have to leave early. She worked hard while she was in the office, but she missed many work hours and barely kept her full-time status and therefore her benefits.

Shortly after Jeremy started crawling, Sherly began having her own medical issues. She had a dull, nagging headache almost every morning. Her joints were aching one by one. Not confined to any one place, the strange joint pains would move all over her body. She was more tired than usual, even for a mother of two. She was thirsty all the time, and she then needed to go to the bathroom. Overweight and with a strong family history of diabetes, she was understandably concerned.

As is typical of many young adults, Sherly did not have a primary care doctor. She saw how the office operated and the fact that I served as the physician for the entire staff, so she asked if I would consider taking her on as a patient. I, of course, was honored to do so. Over the next several months, she booked appointments for herself as a patient. The symptoms were so vague and encompassing that it was difficult to pin down one diagnosis that could explain everything. She had signs and lab results that seemed to indicate that she had some sort of auto-immune disorder. Based on that, I tried giving Sherly prednisone to see how she would respond.

Although Sherly did at first respond somewhat to the prednisone, the pain control was minimal, and the labs were still elevated. I felt like I had met my match as a primary care doctor, so I sent her to a rheumatologist. The first several that we tried were not accepting her state Medicaid insurance, and so she had to be seen at the clinic affiliated with the teaching hospital.

Unfortunately, Sherly's experience there was less than ideal. She did not feel they spent any time with her, and they did no better a job at diagnosing or treating her symptoms than I had. I have to admit, I felt good and bad about that. I felt bad for Sherly, that she was not getting the relief that she needed. Still, I felt slightly vindicated that although I could not figure out what was wrong with Sherly, neither could the specialists. Sherly got so little help from the clinic that she dropped them entirely and continued her treatment with me instead.

Throughout all of this, Sherly had to come to the office every day to do her job. She continued to come in late, and she continued to miss work. Like many places, our company provided paid time off rather than separate sick time and vacation time. Sherly had used up all of her PTO because of illness and had no vacation time left. To make up for the time and keep up a paycheck, Sherly "borrowed" her future vacation time for pay. When the rest of the staff took a week to go on a medical mission trip, Sherly stayed behind to answer the phones.

One day, in the midst of a combination of a crazy work day and multiple interruptions from her mother who was taking care of the kids, Sherly said in exasperation, "This is *it*! I am not having any more kids. I can't handle these two." However, not even a month or two later, Sherly missed her period. Sure enough, she was pregnant yet again. We were all shocked. I even reminded her what she had said just a few short weeks previously.

"What happened? Did the condom break or something?" I asked.

"We don't use condoms," Sherly confessed. "Scott doesn't like the feel of them."

Sherly came from a Catholic background, and she had no intention of doing anything other than carrying, having, and raising the child. I have to admit, I was not very happy with Scott. He found it so easy to stay home, get his girlfriend pregnant, and not even try to find an honest, steady job to provide for the three children he sired. At the same time, I felt so sorry for Sherly, that the burden of being the mother as well as the sole provider fell squarely on her shoulders. It was so much for any twenty-two year old to handle.

Again, Sherly had to take maternity leave, but this time was even shorter than the last. The family basically had no money. Sherly started at the office as a struggling mother of one child. Now, her work as a mother had tripled. And to top it all off, she developed a whole new set of medical problems.

Shortly after Bryson's birth, Sherly developed severe lower abdominal pains, diarrhea, fatigue, cramping in her fingers, and worsening headaches.

Again, I was stumped. I could not figure out what was going on with her. My best guess was gastritis and inflammatory bowel disease, like Crohn's. I started her on prednisone again and added Nexium. When the treatments did not help, I recommended that she see a gastroenterologist. Once more, because of her state insurance, Sherly had a hard time finding someone who would accept her case. She finally got the colonoscopy and endoscopy, which showed abnormal cells underlying her gastritis. The cells were typical of pre-cancerous lesions in older individuals, not in the stomach of a woman barely in her twenties. Clearly, there was something going on that needed close attention.

In the meantime, Sherly tried to continue her job as a medical assistant in my office. I found myself wearing multiple hats as her boss, her doctor, and her friend. Sometimes, the responsibilities of one clashed with those of the others. Although Sherly was trying to do her job, she was falling woefully short. She commonly trudged in more than half an hour late. When she was in the office, she was barely functional, and a number of very important patient issues got scrambled because she was not performing up to par. Often, she said she was feeling so bad that she just had to go home early, leaving the office in a lurch.

The other staff were grumbling about how I as her boss and Mike as the office manager were being way too lenient and not calling her on the carpet. Mike tried to mitigate the situation by officially changing her schedule to start a full two hours later than everyone else. Sherly was given every latitude, but she still could not keep up her responsibilities. Mike had to write her up officially for failing to inform him when she would be late or not be able to come in. At the last write up, he gave her an ultimatum: she needed to tell him if she would be missing work, or she would lose her job.

About a week before Christmas, Sherly again failed to show up for work and did not inform anyone that she would not be making it. Mike asked every member of the office if Sherly had called; she had not. Mike waited through the whole morning and still did not hear anything. The time had come to make a decision. Mike had to submit employee hours to the central office for payroll. Sherly had overdrawn her PTO, and she was not entitled to the full paycheck if the office was going to let her go. Mike came to me and asked my opinion, and I said it had to be done. Mike sent paperwork to the central office to terminate Sherly's employment, crying the whole time.

Late in the afternoon, Sherly did call the office. She apologized for not calling, but her mother had died the previous day. When Mike told her he was really sorry to hear that but asked her why she had not called the office much earlier to let someone know, she had no answer. Mike had to tell her that the paperwork had already gone through for her termination. Sherly said that she understood, and they both cried. So, as it turned out, right before Christmas, Sherly lost her mother as well as her job.

Life was not done with giving Sherly bad news. She continued to struggle with her health. Her abdominal pain and fatigue worsened. She was barely functional through the day. When Sherly went back for a repeat endoscopy, the pathology was much worse than before. She now had frank gastric cancer, something that was virtually unheard of in a twenty-four year old. Sherly's case was so uncommon that numerous multispecialty conferences were held to discuss her treatment strategy. In the end, she had almost her entire stomach removed and endured several rounds of chemo.

One of the things that I have most admired about Sherly was that she was able to separate the professional need to terminate her employment from the other aspects of her relationship with the office as a patient and a friend. Sherly still came to the office as a patient even after she was fired. She was greeted warmly by everyone and responded in kind. She had not shown resentment for being fired. In many ways, it probably ended up being a blessing in disguise. She was able to collect unemployment benefits. With that and the state assistance provided for her illness, she could focus on her health without worrying as much about finances. This was particularly important since Sherly had lost almost one hundred pounds in the first six months of her cancer diagnosis, and there did not seem to be signs of it slowing.

At an office visit, I asked her how things were going and what has been the most difficult part. She said, "It's been horrible, not being myself. My memory is like a ninety year old's. I'm forgetting the kids' birthdays. I can't even take a shower by myself." Although Sherly struggled with fatigue, poor balance, loss of appetite, and a host of other symptoms, it was the lack of independence and needing to rely on someone that was causing her the greatest distress.

"Is Scott helping you at all?" I asked, fully expecting the answer to be no.

Instead, Sherly said, "Scott has been the biggest help ever. He's taking kids to school, he's cooking, he's cleaning. I'm always on the couch, and I feel so helpless and useless all the time. I don't know how I would manage without Scott." Right then, my entire perspective of Scott as some parasitic, deadbeat boyfriend changed. I realized that I had harbored unfounded notions of Scott all these years. I had not allowed myself to consider the possibility that Scott was doing the best he could but faced his own set of challenges and limitations.

Sherly continued, "It's like Scott and I are doing it all by ourselves. The rest of the family helps, but they only do it when they remember." Sherly laughed bitterly, "Everybody would be there if there was a party at my house with beer, but they're not there when I need help with other things. I have an aunt who walks by the house every day. She never knocks on the door to see if there is anything she could do to help with cleaning or whatever. I find it very frustrating. If it doesn't affect them directly, then it's on the back burner."

"Is there anything I can do for you, as your doctor or your friend?"

"You could help me get a hospital bed," Sherly said. "Every time I lie flat, acid comes up my esophagus, and I choke. I can't eat anything. Do you know I'm wearing jeans I haven't been able to wear since elementary school?"

I promised I would get that hospital bed for her. I, the staff, and my church have been praying for her. Sherly has a long road to travel before she gets through all of this. But with the help of her doctors, the friends and family around her, and her own stubborn tenacity, I am confident that Sherly will beat this cancer.

Amber and Sherly in the office

Before and after chemo

Left to right: Jeremy Bryson, Jayden, Sherly, and Scott

The Importance of Physicals

Han Nguyen came to my office in 2008, after her primary care doctor died suddenly from cancer. She had heard through the grapevine of the closely-knit Vietnamese community that I was just about the only other Vietnamese-speaking physician in the state.

As is true for many middle-aged Asian women, Han had aged very well. It was hard to believe she was 60. She was a petite lady at barely over 100 lbs and not even five feet tall. Because she dyed her hair and avoided sun exposure, she looked more like a woman in her 40's.

When Han came to the office, she was already on medicines for high cholesterol and osteoporosis. High cholesterol in the Vietnamese population has increased dramatically as traditional Vietnamese foods with fresh ingredients get replaced by a more American diet. This phenomenon has been seen with just about every culture immigrating to the U.S., and Vietnamese immigrants—more importantly, the next generation—are no exception. Han's osteoporosis was mostly due to her menopause and lack of estrogen for eight years as well as her small frame. The two risk factors greatly increased her chances of developing osteoporosis, but she was being appropriately treated with medicine.

I addressed her chronic medical problems when she came in for the initial appointment, but I also encouraged her to make an appointment for a complete physical. Han did not show much enthusiasm for doing it. Her previous physician never addressed preventative care. Han only came in for acute problems or when her medication ran out. She could not remember the last time she had anything resembling a physical, and her last female check was much more than a decade ago. At my gentle insistence, she relented and agreed to come in.

The following month, Han came in for the physical. She was pleased that it wasn't as difficult as she thought it would be, even though it was quite thorough. Han was particularly apprehensive about the Pap smear.

Vietnamese women are very modest about their private parts, and she was uncomfortable with the thought of me as a man being down there. Also, she and her husband had not been sexually active since her change of life, so she hadn't exposed herself to anyone in quite a long time. I assured her it would be OK, and my nurse held her hand through the Pap. She was actually surprised at how little discomfort there was. I thanked Han for coming in for the physical and told her I would call her with the results.

Han's blood work came back all normal, but her Pap smear results were alarming. The interpretation read: "High grade malignant neoplasm. The cytologic features favor a poorly differentiated adenocarcinoma with focal squamous differentiation." Translated into vernacular, it seemed that I discovered an extremely aggressive cancer of her uterus. I called Han immediately and left a message that it was urgent that she come in right away for an evaluation and discussion.

Han got my message, and the next day she and her husband were in the office. I sat them down and spent an hour with them, discussing my findings. Uterine cancer was uncommon, especially considering Han had none of the signs of cancer: abdominal pain, post-menopausal vaginal bleeding, or weight loss. In fact, she had been feeling healthier than ever. Han had a number of questions, including how long she'd had the cancer. I could not answer that, because I did not know the extent of the disease. It was likely just plain dumb luck—although some might call it providence—that Han had her Pap smear and I found the cancer.

I spent the bulk of the office visit going over the action plan. Han needed an extensive evaluation by a gynecologist. Han needed a colposcopy, where a piece of the cervix is taken for testing. She needed an endometrial curettage and biopsy, in which a long-handled spatula is inserted into her uterus to scrape her uterine lining and get cells. And she needed a CT scan of her abdomen and pelvis. I told her she would likely need surgery after we figured out how far the cancer had spread. Han lived several towns away but came to me because I spoke Vietnamese. Therefore, I did not know any specialists in her area. I called the hospital and a gynecologist in their home town, and I helped them set up an appointment. Because their English was so poor, I gave the office all the information and acted as the translator.

Because of the severity of the pathology report and my insistence that she proceed as soon as possible, Han was seen by the gynecologist only three days after the diagnosis. The results were both puzzling and concerning. The cervical biopsy did not show any cancer, and neither did the endometrial curettage. The CT scan was the concerning part. There were lesions in the liver and throughout the inside of her abdominal cavity, free fluid in her pelvis, and a 6 mm nodule in her right lung. It looked like Han might have cancer throughout her body.

Han was referred from the gynecologist to Dr. Xun Clare Zhou, a sub-specialist in gynecologic oncology. Dr. Zhou reviewed all the data to date, examined her, performed another colposcopy, and sent Han for further testing. Because no cancer cells could be found, Dr. Zhou wanted Han to go for a biopsy of one of the lesions in her liver or lung found on the CT scan. That would help determine what type of cancer they were dealing with and how to go about tackling it.

Han came back to my office a week after her endometrial curettage. She was still in quite a bit of pain after all of her tests, and she still had profuse vaginal bleeding. I talked to Han and her husband about the mixed results of the tests and the need for the biopsy.

"I am NOT going for anything!" Han replied emphatically.

I was dumbfounded. "Why not?" I asked.

"I was doing just fine before all of this started," Han replied. "I didn't have any pain, I wasn't having any problems. Now I'm in terrible pain, and I haven't stopped bleeding yet! I don't want to do any other tests or surgeries that will make me even worse. I don't even know if it's going to help at all."

I told Han I understood that she was in pain, but the tests she had done were necessary, as was the upcoming biopsy. If she didn't proceed, everything she had done up to this point was for nothing. Still, Han wouldn't concede. I excused myself out of the room and called Dr. Zhou, explaining what the patient had decided. I asked Dr. Zhou to guess about the possibility of treatment and cure, considering there was no definitive diagnosis yet. Dr. Zhou said if the cancer was responsive to treatment, there was a 25% chance of cure after surgery and chemotherapy. But all of that hinged on getting the biopsy and determining the source of the cancer. In the end, Han reluctantly agreed. Relieved at Han's decision, I told Dr. Zhou and had her arrange the biopsy with the patient.

I thought Han was all set for her appointment with Dr. Zhou, so I focused on other patients who required my attention. About a month later, I received a call from the oncology office. "Hi, Dr. Han, this is Clare Zhou. We still haven't heard from your patient Mrs. Nguyen. Do you know what's been going on with her? I thought she was going to call me." I told Dr. Zhou that I thought everything had been taken care of but that I would get in touch with Han and find out what was going on. I called and left messages for Han to come in, but I got no response.

More than six weeks after Han's last appointment with me, she came to the office, and the only reason she did so was because she had run out of her blood pressure medication. When I asked her about the cancer and her plans, she said she didn't have any abdominal pain, and she hadn't called the oncology office yet. I again had a very long discussion with her and her husband about how it would be too late if she had abdominal pain before seeking treatment. Lack of abdominal pain did not correlate with disease severity.

Still, she was resistant to having surgery. I encouraged her to consider the surgery, since the only other option was death in six to nine months. We had an extensive discussion about the probable surgical course as well as the survival rate. Although it was not high, it was better than zero, which was what she was facing without treatment. Han put up quite a fight, including saying, "Well, if I die, then I die!" It was only through my persistence and her husband telling her that he would help her through the post-op course that she finally relented and agreed to contact the oncology office.

This time, Han did go for the pre-surgical consult. Dr. Zhou was concerned that with so much time that had lapsed, with such an aggressive tumor it would be better to perform surgery outright rather than doing any preliminary biopsy. Based on the exploratory surgery and pathology results, they would decide if Han should get a chemotherapy regimen or if the cancer was too advanced, and hospice was the only option. At the least, Dr. Zhou would take out as much tumor as she could to buy Han a little more time. At the end of the visit, Han signed consent for removal of her uterus, ovaries, fallopian tubes, lymph nodes, and omentum. Once the surgery was done, Han would have precious little left of her insides. And that was only the beginning. Han had to then go for chemotherapy, either intravenously or administered directly into her abdominal cavity through a port.

Whatever the case, Han would be dealing with a very difficult couple of months.

Dr. Zhou called me after the extensive surgery. Han had an extremely rare and aggressive cancer of her omentum, the flap of tissue overlaying her intestines and separating them from the abdominal muscles. The cancer had wrapped itself around her ovaries as well as invaded many of the lymph nodes in her pelvis. Based on this, she was at Stage IIIC, only a hair's breadth away from the dreaded Stage IV cancer. As it was, Han still required six months of multiple chemotherapy agents by IV and directly into her abdominal cavity. The treatment caused her to lose all of her hair, and she lost a great deal of weight, doubly dangerous for her since she started at only 106 lbs.

Through a great deal of care from the oncology team, a superb physical therapy program, and the 24-hour care of her devoted husband, Han started gaining her weight and her strength back. After finishing her chemotherapy, her hair started to regrow. The most amazing thing was that Han beat the odds. Before the surgery, Dr. Zhou gave her no more than a one in ten chance of surviving, especially considering Han procrastinated for two months before getting treatment.

Six months after her surgery, Han went back to work, with great fanfare and applause from her co-workers. She sees Dr. Zhou every few months and has been cancer free for four years and counting. Every time Han comes to my office, she has a big smile on her face and never fails to thank me for saving her life. I particularly enjoy the fruit and sweets she brings as tokens of gratitude. She also says she talks about me all the time to anyone who will listen, how I "forced" her to go for the surgery even though she didn't want to, and now she's alive because of it.

Han's story is actually bitter-sweet. Two years before her diagnosis, her husband's skin started darkening noticeably, developing large blisters that would heal darker than before. I sent him to a dermatologist, who diagnosed him with pemphigus, an auto-immune skin disease. None of the treatments given were successful, so he resigned himself to having dark skin.

During Han's chemotherapy and recuperation, while she was feeling stronger, he was getting weaker. He came to my office multiple times for a nagging cough and back pain, and multiple courses of antibiotics did not work. He ended up being admitted three times over the course of a month and received every diagnosis from pneumonia to tuberculosis. Nodules were seen on his CT scan, but a fluid collection of his lungs showed no cancer.

He finally had a direct lung biopsy at his last admission, and that did reveal lung cancer. He was treated with six rounds of chemotherapy to shrink the tumor. When receiving the chemotherapy, his skin came back to its normal color. The doctors determined that his dark skin was actually an outward manifestation of the cancer and not pemphigus as originally thought. So, his cancer had been growing for more than two years.

Han and her husband switched roles. While he had taken care of Han during the first part of her chemo, she took care of him at the last part of his. The cancer had been growing for too long, so all the chemotherapy and treatment could not save him. Four short months after Han felt well enough to go back to work, her husband died.

Han has said to me, "See, I listened to you, even when I didn't want to, and I'm alive. You told my husband all the time to quit his smoking, and he never listened. Now, he's dead. I tell all my friends to come to you and follow what you have to say if they want to live long."

Han Nguyen in 2013

The Bearer of Bad News

When Viktor came to my office for his new-patient physical, he looked like a model of health. In his 40's, he had not needed a doctor through his entire adult life. During our pre-physical interview, he relayed to me that he had actually climbed Mount Everest nine times, six of those with his wife.

Since it is my experience that men do not go to the doctor for a "general checkup" without at least something pressing on their minds, I asked Viktor what prompted him to come in for a physical. He then told me that a week prior, he noticed a rapidly growing lump in the left side of his groin. It was not that painful, but it did concern him a bit. He and his wife were devoted to each other and had two daughters, so a sexually transmitted disease was very unlikely. I assured him that I would inspect this area at the end of my exam.

The entire exam was completely normal until the end. Sure enough, I found an irregular firm mass in his left pubic region, at the base of his penis. Although I had my concerns, I kept them to myself and suggested Viktor go for further testing. An ultrasound of the area confirmed the presence of a solid mass, but the finding was nonspecific. I sent Viktor for a biopsy of the mass, and my worst fears were realized. Viktor had a very aggressive cancer arising from the base of his penis, which is a very rare cancer. In just the few weeks that it took to diagnose this cancer, it had already increased in size. Not only was the cancer destroying the penile root, it seemed to involve all the surrounding structures as well.

We quickly involved physicians from multiple specialties: urology, oncology, orthopedic surgery, and even oral surgery. After many meetings, it was decided that radical surgery was the best course of action. Apparently this type of cancer is very resistant to chemotherapy or radiation, so there was no way to shrink the cancer to preserve tissue. Viktor was facing removal of his entire penis, his bladder, and probably his pubic bone. Oral surgery was involved because a flap of his cheek might need to be harvested to rebuild any remnants after surgery. Without a bladder or penis, a pouch would need to be formed and urine diverted to it for Viktor to catheterize on a regular basis. Since the cancer was so aggressive, there was no guarantee the surgeons would be able to get all of it. But even if they did, it was clear that Viktor's life would never be the same again.

Less than three months after I first saw him, Viktor was back in my office for his pre-operative evaluation. The haughty, arrogant man I first met who had literally been at the top of the world was gone. This man had pain etched in the corners of his eyes. His voice trembled as he spoke. Viktor was wearing a picture of his two daughters around his neck, a new addition since his cancer diagnosis. Unconsciously, as if to remind himself of the precious gift of life, Viktor's hand would drift to the pictures as he asked me his questions.

Viktor wanted my opinion on the information so far, seeking the perspective of a physician with a holistic point of view rather than that of a specialist. As he continued to question me, his queries started to get more and more specific. He even asked me how many millimeters of margin around the cancer I thought the surgeons would take. I answered his questions to the best of my ability, but eventually, I just had to tell him I didn't know. Viktor was asking questions that were way beyond my specialty, and I had to tell him I just could not answer him. Although Viktor was asking questions about the surgery, what he was really asking was, "Am

I going to live? Am I going to be all right? Am I going to see my daughters grow up? Am I still going to be a man after this is all done? What is my quality of life going to be like?"

I had to stop Viktor and tell him that I did not have any other answers for his questions regarding his cancer or surgery. "Viktor, at some point, you are just going to have to trust the surgeons into whose hands you have placed your care. They know what they are doing, and they are doing everything in their power to save your life and maximize your function. Think of the surgeons as the lead climber on a hike to the summit of Everest. They know where to place the ropes and crampons. If you slip and fall, they will catch you. Just as you trusted the lead on your climb, trust these surgeons to take care of you." My explanation seemed to sink in.

When Viktor wanted to ask "just one more question," I thought to myself, "Oh man, what is it now?"

"What do you think about meditation and Buddhism?" Viktor asked me. "I've been trying to meditate more. My wife is from Nepal and is a Buddhist."

I was raised Buddhist but decided to make Christianity my faith path when I was in my teens, so I had a very good understanding of both faiths. I encouraged him to continue to meditate and find his center. I told him I saw in him a humility that I had not seen before. He replied that he had a totally different perspective on life and what was important.

When I left the room to prepare his pre-op paperwork, my medical student stayed with him to give him someone to talk to and listen to his story. Fifteen minutes later, as I was putting the finishing touches on the forms, Viktor and my medical student walked out of the exam room. Viktor's eyes were red from tears, but his countenance was lighter. There was still fear on his face, but there was also hope.

Viktor gave us each a long hug and thanked us for our time. He smiled tremulously as I handed him the forms, and he said, "I think I'm going to beat this, Doctor." Viktor walked out of my office, more ready to face the next phase of his life.

Grounded

Ron Iacobucci thought the power was off.

It was August 23, 1994, just after his lunch break. Ron was working for his father's company, putting in large underground water mains for the town of Groton, Connecticut. The pipes were huge, requiring excavation of deep trenches and then the lowering of each one-ton section of pipe. Ron was in the trench disconnecting the nylon sling used to cradle and lower the pipe into the trench. The long boom and stick of the excavator was pointed up, close to some low-hanging power lines. This shouldn't have been a problem, because standard protocol called for electricity to be turned off for the section of power lines the crew had to work under. But for some reason, the wires were still live. The boom was just close enough to the power line for an electrical arc to form, which welded the boom to the power line. Unknown to Ron and the rest of the crew, the entire excavator became a huge electrical conductor.

Ron was oblivious to the danger as he was leaning against the metal pipe while unhooking the nylon sling, because the nylon served as an electrical insulator. Ron did OK until he happened to shift his weight for better leverage. In doing so, he came into contact with the bucket of the excavator. The stored up electricity found the path of least resistance, going from the power line, through the excavator, into Ron, and down into the earth. Ron literally grounded the circuit. One hundred forty amps at eight thousand four hundred volts went from Ron's left hand to his right leg, traversing his heart and the rest of his body along the way.

The moment Ron's left hand touched the bucket, there was a blue flash. Ron had an instant of pain and pressure, but it vanished as quickly as it came. Then he felt like he was free falling, like cold air was going through is body. It felt like an eternity. *What happened? Where am I? What's going on?* Ron thought to himself. The next thing he knew, everything was white—the floor, the ceiling, everything. Ron looked around, but he could see nothing. He could feel his body but he could not see any part of it. Ron started hearing voices, but he could not make out any words. The voices, soft at first, started getting louder and louder, but he still couldn't understand anything. It sounded like several voices at once, like a huge conversation that was loud but without any yelling.

Ron realized at that point that it was not a dream, but he still did not know what was going on. "Am I dead?" Ron asked, but received no answer. He had no clue that he was just electrocuted. "I don't want to die," Ron said. His body lost its balance, and Ron felt like he was falling again, with the wind passing through his body. In the far distance, against an encompassing backdrop of white, Ron saw the black dot of a pin hole. It suddenly looked very close, but his hand couldn't touch it. As Ron watched, the hole got bigger and bigger, while the voices got quieter and quieter. When the hole got larger, Ron felt like he was being sucked through the hole, and everything was passing by very quickly. Although the experience was extremely vivid, he couldn't make out anything except a lot of colors. Like a water ride at Six Flags, Ron found himself bouncing around and shot out the hole.

When he came to, Ron took a huge, deep gasp like he had not breathed in a long time. He found that he was curled up, with his head lying against the trench box retaining the dirt wall. Ron heard someone say, "Oh my God, he's alive again." People were yelling to him not to move. His face was covered with blood, probably from where his head struck the trench box. Ron could smell the metallic tang of blood mixed with the distinctive aroma of cooked meat. His mouth tasted like his tongue was stuck on a nine-volt battery. Ron looked to the left and found his watch was melted around his left wrist, while his palm was fused onto the metal bucket. On the other side, his right leg had fused to the water pipe, the blackened flesh smoking. His left arm and right leg felt like they weighed a million pounds, and his whole body felt like he had been punched by a hundred people. All the while, Ron's father was going crazy above the trench, running around and crying hysterically.

Ron sat up and got very nauseous, immediately throwing up on himself. As he retched, he heard someone shout, "Stay still! The machine is still connected to the line. Don't move!"

Ron had only one thought: "I gotta get out of here." He got up on his unburned left leg, ripping off the palm and leg that were fused to the metal. When Ron put out his hand onto the side of the trench to steady himself, he was thrown ten feet back. The entire sides of the retaining wall for the trench were electrified. Ron staggered and hit the other side of the trench, again being thrown away by the force of electricity and the contraction of every muscle in his body in response to the electrical shock. Back onto the opposite side he hit and was again thrown back. Like a pin ball in a chute, Ron bounced from one side to the other until he fell face first into the dirt. When he looked up, he saw the menacing face of the excavator's bucket above him. Somehow, Ron managed to crawl from under the bucket through the dirt without touching the metal.

As Ron lay bonelessly on the ground, people swarmed around him, but the police did not allow anyone to touch him. The EMS was already there and put him in an ambulance. On route, they put monitors all over him and an IV into his good arm. The paramedics asked him questions like, "What is your name? What is your date of birth? Do you know your social security number?" They wanted to maintain his attention and to make sure he wasn't going into shock. Ron was completely coherent during the whole ride, answering all of their questions. Meanwhile, the ambulance careened through traffic, sirens blaring.

Ron was wheeled into the ER of Lawrence Memorial Hospital. His father had followed the ambulance and now stood over him crying. "I'm so sorry, it's my fault. I should have been there. It shouldn't have been you."

Ron said, "Dad, it's not your fault. It was an accident. I'll be fine."

"No, you're not. You might lose your hand." Ron looked down and saw his hand and leg swelling like grotesque balloons. Then he blacked out.

As Ron was regaining consciousness, he heard the doctor telling his father that they had to get Ron to Yale New Haven Hospital. The Life Star helicopter flew Ron to Yale. Landing on the roof of the hospital, the Life Star team tried to assure him that he was going to be OK. The double doors to the roof opened and a bunch of white-coated people ran towards him and took him inside.

The whole way to the trauma bay, Ron conversed with the doctor in the lead. Ron even managed to keep his sense of humor. While the nurses and techs were cutting off Ron's clothes, the doctor said, "Now Ron, I'm going to stick a finger up your rectum."

Ron quipped, "Why don't you stick up two. It feels better."

The doctor started laughing. "I can't believe you're still with it enough to be joking around. OK, I'm going to count to three, and you're going to go to sleep. One. Two." Ron never heard the three.

When Ron woke up, the clock read 2:15 AM. His nurse Mark was standing over him, smiling. "Glad to see you awake."

"How long have I been sleeping?" Ron asked.

"Three weeks, actually." Ron's eyes widened at Mark's revelation. "You've already had three surgeries. You've got a long road ahead of you." Mark sat and talked with Ron for long time, asking him what he remembered and about his life in general. Through the night, Mark eased Ron into a better understanding of his current state.

The next morning, Dr. Henry Spinelli walked into the unit. "You're a lucky guy, Ron. Not too many people would have lived through that, especially since your heart stopped. It's a miracle that you're alive. The only thing that saved you was that you were in such good shape and your body absorbed much of the electricity. We have a lot of work to do, but we'll get you out of here."

Tina and Rebecca were in charge of Ron's therapy, and they wheeled him into the debriding room. They lowered Ron into a large stainless steel tank and began cutting off his bandages. The first time Ron saw his arm, he almost passed out. His arm was pulled completely open, with all the muscles, veins, and nerves visible. The doctors had to do a fasciotomy to relieve the pressure in his arm. Ron's right leg looked like someone had melted his muscles like mozzarella cheese. In the warm water of the bubbling tank, the therapists used tweezers and scissors to gently remove dead tissue in his arm.

The daily ordeal of debridement went on for several weeks. After the debridement came the reconstruction of Ron's damaged tissue. Tendons and muscles were harvested from various parts of Ron's body to rebuild tissue that was destroyed. Joints were fused in his fingers and tendons rerouted to give him basic pincher grasping. Skin grafts from his unburned upper thigh were used to cover his left hand. In between the surgeries were many long hours of waiting, which was probably the most difficult part for Ron to endure.

Through it all, Ron's mother was there all day, every day. His friends and family came by to visit and break the monotony of the day. But for the entire month and a half of his hospitalization, Ron's father never came to visit.

Even after he was released from the hospital, Ron had to go back every day for continued debridements and therapy. Before Ron's accident, he was 230 pounds of solid muscle. While in the National Guard, Ron was able to outrun, outlift, and outclimb everyone in the entire company, including his superiors. He ran the mile in under five minutes and did over forty pull-ups at a time. After the accident, Ron shrank to 170 pounds, his entire body atrophied to the point where he could not sit up from weakness. His median and radial nerves were burned away, and he could not feel his fingers at all. Ron could not lift up his right leg from the nerve and muscle damage. He was told that he would have to wear a special shoe, and he would never walk right again. Now, Ron realized he really was grounded. He went from a twenty-two year old young man who was almost superhuman to someone who could not even walk or pick up a fork.

Through it all, however, Ron was determined to keep his spirits up. Never once did he start feeling sorry for himself or think about giving up. Ron continued at therapy, having to relearn every basic action of life— buttoning his shirt, picking up objects, walking, everything. He spent all day picking up one small object after another, made more difficult by the fact he could not actually feel any of the objects in his remaining fingers. For three years, this continued nearly every day. Ron felt like he was stuck in the movie *Groundhog Day*.

As Ron went through his surgeries and therapy, he found his mental processes and life priorities evolving. Since he spent so much time at the hospital and always went back to the same trauma floor, Ron got to know all the staff. Ron found himself more open with his feelings, sharing things that he wouldn't have shared before. It didn't matter what other people thought about him as much as what Ron thought about himself. He also realized that all the things he did in the past didn't mean nearly as much as his health. Without his health, he had nothing.

Through his accident and recuperation, Ron didn't really understand why he had to go through all of it. But over time, he came to the realization that the tragedy was really a blessing. It made him a stronger person. No future difficulty in life was going to be able to compare to the experience that he had. If he could make it through this, he could make it through anything. Nothing was impossible in this world if Ron put his mind to it.

Ron found greater compassion for people who have had difficult experiences. Physical scars do not change who you are. And sometimes, emotional scars were invisible but cut more deeply than physical ones. Because of his ordeal, Ron has gone out of his way to assist people who needed a helping hand, occasionally at great personal and financial sacrifice. Ron came to the realization that he was much more grounded, now in the positive sense. He had an emotional and spiritual maturity—a groundedness, if you will—that he had not possessed before his accident.

Finally, Ron was able to get to the point of forgiving his father for not being there for him when he needed him. From 1994 until 2011, Ron never spoke to his father about the whole ordeal, all of those years of surgeries and therapy. Ron came to the conclusion that his father did not visit because he felt responsible for the accident and could not bear the fact of what happened to Ron. Maybe it was because his father was burned himself as a small child and still bore the emotional wounds. Ron decided to write a long letter to his father in November 2011. In it, he wrote about how his father's absence from his life during his greatest time of need was terribly hurtful to him. But it wasn't entirely his dad's fault because his dad didn't have anyone to show him what it meant to be a good father. But his dad did teach him to strive and work hard, and he was thankful for that. Ron wrote that all the good qualities he had came from his father. Ron ended the letter telling his father that he forgave him.

Several weeks later, his father wrote back. "I want you to know that there isn't a day that goes by that I don't think about what happened to you." Since that letter, they both have taken steps to build their relationship.

Over four years and twenty-one surgeries, Ron was able to regain partial median nerve function and almost full use of his limbs. He continued to exercise and rebuild his body. Ron was able to get back to his rock-solid 236 pound, 5'8" frame. He now works as a personal trainer, helping everyone from housewives to Ironman triathletes reach their highest potential. His motto is, "I want you to be the best you can be." After all, that's what Ron strives for every day.

Ron at 18 in the National Guard

Ron in his home gym today

Ron and his bull mastiff Takoda

Laughter is the Best Medicine

Amber was one of my teen patients. She was sweet, but not extremely smart. As I was examining one of her ears once, I said offhandedly, "I can see all the way to the wall on the other side."

"Really? You can do that?" Amber said in amazement.

****

Tan was a new patient to the office, and he was filling out his paperwork with my nurse Sherly.

"So why are you here to see the doctor?" Sherly asked.

"The doctor needs to check on my little brother."

"Oh, so your little brother is the patient? Well, then I need to have him fill out—"

"No, I'm the patient." Tan corrected her.

Sherly was wondering if it was the Vietnamese accent or some other language barrier. "So you're the patient? You just said Dr. Han needed to check on your little brother."

"I'm the patient," he insisted. He then both looked and pointed down. "He needs to check on *my little brother*."

A look of recognition dawned on Sherly's face. "Oh! Well, finish that form, and Dr. Han can talk to you about your little brother."

****

"Doc, how do I find out if my testosterone is low?"

"You do a blood test. Why would you think your testosterone is low, Rafael?"

"I haven't been as interested in sex lately. I'm only having sex three times a week. It's not my new girlfriend, because she's hot."

"That's a pretty good amount, Rafael," I told him. "The average couple only has sex once or twice a week."

"I thought maybe it was because my young son is living with us now. And my girlfriend's daughter is also in the apartment."

"Rafael, if you have two young kids at the apartment and you're still fitting in sex three times a week, then you're doing really well."

"I don't know. I thought there was something wrong with me because with my old girlfriend, we were having sex five times a day."

"Five times a day?! What did you do, have sex twice in the morning, once at lunch, and twice before dinner? Did you ever leave the bedroom?"

"Oh, you'd be surprised, Doc!"

****

An elderly woman came in with a long list of problems. One after another, they kept on coming. More than half an hour later, I was still slogging through her medical issues. I exhaled deeply and said, "Boy, you're making me work hard today!"

She looked at me and pointed to the computer I had been furiously typing on. "What do you mean you're working hard? All you're doing is hitting those buttons over there!"

****

When Cathy came in to my office for her physical at the age of 23, the last thing she expected was a breast lump that ended up being breast cancer. She took the devastating news fairly well, considering it was a very aggressive form of cancer that necessitated a complete mastectomy. She dealt with the loss by maintaining an excellent disposition in life and a great sense of humor.

Cathy's mom came in for her appointment, and I asked about Cathy. She said that Cathy was doing well, and that she had just gotten a breast implant since her radiation treatment had completed. I asked her if she decided to get an implant that was much bigger than the other breast, so that way, she could be the human version of a fiddler crab.

As Cathy's mom was checking out, I relayed to the front staff what I had said. They proceeded to berate me mercilessly for being so callous. Cathy's mom then said, "Oh, that's nothing. Her dad told her for Halloween, she had the perfect costume as 'The UniBoober.'"

My office manager Mike said, "I should have known. And here I was accusing Dr. Han of being callous. I had forgotten what sort of family he was talking to!"

****

When patients see me enter the exam room in my white lab jacket and my stethoscope around my neck, there is instant recognition and an expectation as to what will shortly transpire. But, some patients seem to forget that I am just a normal guy who lives in town, does grocery shopping, and in general goes about his daily life just like anyone else. So, when a patient sees me out of the context of the office, there can be a disconnect and period of confusion until recognition sets in.

No one exemplified this better than Larry. I was at Home Depot renting a piece of equipment, and Larry was behind the counter helping me to check out. We went through the usual questions, initialed all the appropriate spaces for rental and insurance, and processed my credit card. Suddenly, Larry stopped midway through the transaction, stared at me for a while, and said, "Say, do I know you?"

Had Larry not paid attention to the credit card he had in his hand? "Yes, Larry, you know me. In fact, I've seen you naked. I'm your doctor."

****

Eduardo came to the office for a pre-employment physical as a migrant worker. He spoke only Spanish, and so I muddled through my history and physical. "No problemas. Todo está bien," he assured me.

Things were going very well with the physical, I thought. Almost too well. I got to the reflex test and had him sit on the edge of the exam table. I hit his knee, and he kicked. I hit it again, and he kicked. I swung my hammer again, but I stopped in mid air, and he kicked!

He looked at me sheepishly. "Hey, no cheating on the exam!" I told him. He didn't try "helping out" again, and the rest of the exam went without further incident.

****

A young Vietnamese couple came to the office, embarrassed and distraught. I brought them into the room and asked what was going on. "We, um, lost our toy," the husband said.

"What?" I was speaking their language, but I still didn't understand what he was saying.

After several minutes of questioning, I got the whole picture. Earlier, they were talking to another couple who were good friends of theirs. The buddy was raving about a particular sex toy that both made him last longer and enhanced her sexual pleasure. The friend allowed my patients to take this thing home for a test run.

Unfortunately, in the midst of their lovemaking, this toy slipped off him because he was not nearly as well endowed as his buddy. They looked everywhere, and they could not find the thing. "I think it's stuck in my stomach," the woman said.

I assured the couple that that was a physical impossibility. I had her put on a gown and did a thorough exam. Sure enough, I found the escapee toy. It looked like one of those wiggly monsters kids put on the heads of their erasers, but bigger. It was wedged in between the poor woman's cervix and vaginal wall. No wonder the couple couldn't find it.

I told her to relax as I got a long pair of forceps and grasped the toy. With an audible squelching sound, the rubber monster popped free from its confines. I rinsed off the toy and dropped it into a biohazard bag, giving it to the husband.

I didn't want to know what happened to the toy after that.

FAITH

"Seeds of faith are always within us; sometimes it takes a crisis to nourish and encourage their growth."

~Susan L Taylor, writer, journalist, and former editor-in-chief of *Essence* magazine

A Fighter

Minnie Teal, a 57-year-old black lady, has been seeing me for the past five years. Several years ago, she was hit by a dump truck, leaving her with constantly severe neck, back, and shoulder pain. She had been unable to work, and easy household chores like sweeping the kitchen were barely manageable.

As one might expect, her disability caused depression and anxiety. Shortly after she started coming to the office, she confided in me that she had crying spells through the day and felt very lonely. She was unable to work, and she had no income. Her husband was employed, but because of his busy schedule, Minnie was left home alone with nothing but her pain and her negative thoughts. A doctor had told her earlier she might be depressed, but she was unwilling to take any medicine at that time. Since I had developed a good relationship with her, she was willing to reconsider taking medicines. I gave her an antidepressant and added that issue to the chronic pain therapy I was treating her for.

Minnie was sent to numerous back and neck specialists for her pain. She was treated with physical therapy, chiropractic care, and finally daily narcotics to keep her pain at a manageable level. Just when she thought she was settling into her current state, life threw one more thing to send her condition once again into a tail spin.

For several months, on top of her daily pain, Minnie had bouts of severe fatigue and lethargy. This further limited even the minimal work she was able to do. On top of this, she had the sensation of her throat closing up on her. This feeling had actually happened in the past, and a gastroenterologist had to go in and dilate her esophagus to allow her to eat solid food without discomfort. Because of these previous episodes, Minnie thought her throat closing was a benign issue. She did not consider bringing up these symptoms to me during her routine visits. However, her deteriorating condition was brought to my attention through a different avenue.

Minnie was sent for an MRI by the orthopedic doctor to assess the bulging disks in her neck. The disks did not look worse than before, but the radiologist noted some very concerning findings. The radiologist saw a significant number of large lymph nodes throughout her neck and near her collar bone. These were not in the last MRI a few years ago. The radiologist stated in the report that although this could represent some sort of reactive swelling from an infection, a cancer such as lymphoma could not be ruled out. Because of Minnie's prior history of smoking, she was definitely at higher risk of cancer. I had my nurse call her and have her come in for an urgent visit.

The orthopedic doctor had briefed her on the findings of the MRI before she got to my office, so she was not surprised when I told her about the large lymph nodes and what they might mean. She was actually surprisingly calm. "I had a feelin' some-en' weren't right with my body when I felt my throat closin' up on me. I got this whirrin' in my head like it was flyin' around. That's when I was aksin' myself what this was goin' on in my body," Minnie told me in her typical non-grammatically-correct but honest speech.

In spite of all of this suffering and now the possibility of cancer, Minnie clung to her devout faith. "I'm not worried, Doc. My faith is up here." She lifted her hand above her head. "It's not down here." She dropped her hand to her lap. "God knows I've been doin' the work of the Lord, an' I've been praisin' Jesus. He's gonna see me through. He always has before. And God knows I'm a *fighter*! Ya see, I gots too much work left ta do here!"

Minnie and I continued our conversation about her faith and her physical ailments. She agreed to go to the surgeon for a biopsy of her lymph node to get a definitive diagnosis. Through the entire visit, Minnie maintained her composure. There was a peace about her that I rarely saw in someone facing devastating news.

At the end, I asked her if I could pray with her, and she readily agreed. I took her hands in mine, and she held on tightly as we both bowed our heads. I prayed for an extra measure of strength for her. I asked God to send His angels to minister to her. I prayed that all of her doctors would have wisdom and knowledge to know how to diagnose and treat her. I prayed for a miracle and for complete healing if it was cancer and in His will to heal her. I prayed that she would be a witness of God's love and peace to the people around her.

Throughout the prayer, Minnie expressed agreement with me by saying, "Yes Lord! Praise Jesus! Hallelujah," under her breath. When I got done praying, I let go of her hands, and we held each other in a long hug while she thanked me.

Minnie made an appointment with the surgeon, and no matter what the results reveal, I know she has already been a minister. Minnie ministered to me by showing amazing courage in spite of extreme adversity. She showed me it is possible to trust God instead of blaming God when life doesn't go the way you think it should. Her faith stirred up my own faith, which, honestly, had been fairly shaky.

And she didn't minister to just me during that office visit. My medical student was present in the room through the entire encounter and prayer.

We were all touched by the presence of the Holy during that time. It might have been the first time my medical student got to see the reality of living the Christian life. Being a Christian is not the picture of Jesus in flowing robes and long hair, with a light behind Him and bunnies at His feet. Being a Christian is living a life of difficulty and pain, and yet knowing there is a meaning and a purpose higher than we are. There is One who is in control, even when it is not the sort of control we would choose.

I will continue to pray for Minnie. I'm sure God will enjoy having her in heaven. But I'm selfish. I think there's still too much for her to do here on earth yet!

Minnie Teal

Standing on the Head of a Pin

"Be anxious about nothing. But in all things, with prayer and supplication, with acts of thanksgiving, let your petitions be made known to God. And so shall the peace of God, which exceeds all understanding, guard your hearts and your minds in Christ Jesus." *Philippians 4:6-7 (CPDV)*

As Stella puts it, "I was always a nervous little girl." Living seventy-five years and experiencing a fair share of difficulty could do that to someone, I suppose. Stella's parents were born in Poland and came to the U.S. as a young couple, and Stella, the youngest of eight children, was born shortly after. The family was very poor but happy. Stella's early childhood was spent in the shadow of World War II. As for most people growing up in that era, Stella learned the value of saving, hard work, and planning for the future. However, all that planning could not prepare her for everything.

Stella met and married Paul when they were both young. She knew early on that her husband had "a blood problem," but it did not affect their ability to have and raise a family. Things seemed to go well for many years as Paul worked at Pratt & Whitney. It was not until later in life that his blood disorder started to cause problems. He became easily fatigued and quite weak as his kidneys started to fail. Even kidney dialysis did not improve Paul's overall health, so he ended up in the hospital. Before he got much better or could even walk, the hospital discharged him to a physical rehabilitation facility. He was in rehab for months without making any progress, so Stella finally took him home.

As Stella prepared the house for her husband, she asked herself, "Can I deal with this? Can I take care of him? Can I really give him his baths?" She was not sure if she would be able to handle it. But Stella had been helping her husband through his declining health for the previous four years, and she learned to deal with it. All she knew was that he could not stay in the rehab facility a minute longer.

Paul was ecstatic to go home. He remained bedridden and very sick, but at least he was at home with the woman he loved. Stella took care of him through the last year of his life. She hid her growing worry and anxiety from Paul, but it was taking a toll on her own body.

Although she definitely had some chronic medical problems, Stella was nevertheless a fairly healthy woman. She took her medicines regularly. She came in for her appointments as scheduled. She avoided the lifestyle choices that could adversely affect her health, like smoking or excessive alcohol intake. Those aspects of her health made her an easy patient to care for. Unfortunately, Stella's anxiety manifested itself as physical symptoms. I sometimes had a difficult time reassuring Stella that her symptoms were caused by anxiety rather than a serious medical condition. At the same time, I had to make sure she really didn't have a medical problem that should be addressed. Anxious people still get sick, after all.

Stella scheduled a visit once for swelling in her legs. She had a six-hour bus ride, and by the end, her feet were tense and swollen. After she got up and moved around, the swelling improved and eventually resolved. Stella happened to mention her swelling to her granddaughter, who was starting nursing school. Her granddaughter told her that leg swelling was a symptom of congestive heart failure, which caused immense worry for both of them. Stella's physical exam was normal, and she had no other signs of heart failure. Still, it took a good bit of convincing that the swelling was a completely normal occurrence known as dependent edema. I myself get it all the time on long plane flights for my medical mission work.

A few months later at her routine follow up, Stella complained of continued anxiety. She felt jittery, shaky, very tense, and on edge. When I asked why, she couldn't tell me. As far as she could tell, she didn't have anything particularly stressful going on. Despite this, she was wound up. Food would get stuck in the middle of her throat. She had to swallow extra hard and drink water just to get it down. It definitely happened more when she got very upset. And then to top it off, she had several days of a stiff neck that worsened as she went through the day. All of her symptoms definitely sounded related to anxiety, and the entire exam was normal. To alleviate her fears, I sent her for a swallow study to evaluate the "stuck feeling" that she was having.

The swallow study went well and only showed a small Zenker's diverticulum, an outpouching from her esophagus. It was not uncommon, and unless it was large, it did not pose a problem. The nurse called Stella and told her that I thought there was nothing to worry about. Stella was not satisfied with this, however, so she made an appointment to go over the results in detail. I sat down with her and explained that I wasn't that concerned about the Zenker's diverticulum.

Stella looked at me with worry lines on her face. "But what if turns into cancer?"

I patted her hand in reassurance. "Stella, it won't become cancer. If you start bringing up a lot of undigested food, I can send you to get surgery to fix the problem. But it's so small that I doubt you're going to have any problems," I tried to assure her. I also offered her a referral to a gastroenterologist, but she didn't want to go to any other doctors. I assured her that if she was concerned, I would always be here to help her. It seemed that the knowledge that she had a safety net was enough to alleviate some of her worries.

One day, Stella came to see me for a five-day throbbing headache at her right temple. "I think my right eye is puffier and maybe drooping a little. What if it's a brain tumor?" Stella jumped to the worst-case scenario, even if the possibility was remote.

"Stella, brain tumors are really quite rare. I doubt you have a brain tumor. Let me take a look at you." After her examination— which was completely normal—I prescribed some prednisone and did a blood test. As I sat and looked at her, I could tell there was fear and anxiety in her eyes. I noticed she was wearing a gold cross, which prompted me to ask, "Stella, do you come from any sort of faith path?"

She replied, "I am Catholic. I believe in God."

I hesitated for a second, and I told her, "I don't usually do this, but I feel led to share a passage from the Bible with you, if you'll let me." She nodded assent.

I read the verses from the Book of Philippians to her. She put her hand to her heart and said softly, "Thank you."

I shared with her the mental image I got when I looked at her. "Stella, it's like you're standing on the head of a pin. As long as things are *just right*, you can balance yourself and feel stable. But if any outside force were to nudge you just a little bit, you get unbalanced and threaten to topple over.

"True peace comes from within and is not dependent on external circumstances. You are standing on the head of a pin. I want to give you a firm foundation to stand on. No matter what the world or life throws at you, it shouldn't shake that peace you have inside you. Even if you did have a brain tumor—which I assure you I seriously doubt—that should not change the peace you could have."

I told her to take the medicine I gave her and come back in a day or two for me to re-evaluate her headache and go over the lab test. I gave her homework for the next visit. She needed to find the Bible passage I gave her and read it several times, letting it sink into her soul. She had me write the passage down so she could reread it and look it up. As she got off the exam table, I took a step toward her and gave her a tight hug, which she gratefully returned.

A few days later, Stella came back as promised. Her headache was improved but not gone. The test came back with reassuring numbers. I gave her some other pain med samples and told her to let me know how she did through the week.

She also did her homework. She looked up and rewrote the Philippians 4:6-7 passage. She had never seen that passage before, so it was a very nice discovery. I had her recite it a few times during our office visit, and I encouraged her to memorize it and incorporate it into her heart. My hope for her was that she would be able to break free from the constant anxiety about the "what ifs" in life. Worrying about all those "what ifs" was robbing her of her ability to enjoy each day. At seventy-five years old, Stella deserved to enjoy every day of life given to her. Of course, that could be said of everyone, no matter their age.

Stella and Paul in 2000 in Long Island, NY

Stella in 2013

Consequences

Bill's childhood shattered into a thousand pieces when his father, a well respected police officer, pulled his car to the side of the road and shot himself.

There was no note, no indication of what might have led his dad to take such a drastic and irrevocable action. Maybe to escape the ghosts at home, or maybe for some other reason, but shortly after their dad's suicide, Bill's brother Mike enlisted in the Marines at nineteen. That left Bill, only fourteen years old, to support his mother, who was a nervous wreck and could barely leave the house. Bill went to school and then worked two jobs to help pay the bills.

On nights and weekends, Bill released all of his pent up anger and frustration by drinking, smoking, and partying. With no inclination towards learning, Bill barely graduated from high school. Instead, he was much better at losing his temper, fighting, and getting in trouble. Bill was one of those surly drunks who made rash decisions and turned on friends. On one of those drunken nights, Bill was arrested for breach of peace after fighting in the middle of Main Street. The police officers took him down to the station, but they let him go. They knew his father had been a cop, and it was a show of kindness to his mother. Bill, like so many teenagers, didn't recognize grace when it was extended to him. That trip down to the station did not do much to curb his wild behavior.

Shortly after squeaking through high school, when Bill was nineteen, he was drafted into the Army during the Vietnam War. With Mike already in the Marines and Bill as the sole supporter of the house, he did not have to enlist. But, Bill *wanted* to go. He told his mother and his friends he wanted to fight for his country, but what he really wanted was action and adventure and a way to be recognized. In 1966, Bill entered eight weeks of Boot Camp and then infantry training in Ft Hood, Texas. Bill's advanced infantry training was done at Ft Leavenworth, Kansas, where he trained in escape and evasion maneuvers and actions to take if he were captured. At the completion of his training, Bill and the rest of his division of over 1200 men took the 27-day voyage to Vietnam.

The ship landed in Vang Thao in the Mekong Delta. As he disembarked, Bill was both nervous and excited about what the next year would bring. The command center was sprawling. There was order to the camp, but not nearly as regimented as Bill had seen stateside. The first couple of days were spent splitting everyone up into their companies and platoons, receiving their gear, and getting briefed on the current situation. Bill was named point man for his platoon, so he was always going to be in the front. Bill was glad he joined the Army, and now he was going to be the first man to see the action. It took less than two months for Bill to regret his decision.

Vogan was one of the guys in Bill's platoon and the same age as he was. He had straw blond hair, several shades lighter than Bill's. Vogan was 5'9" to Bill's 6'1" lean frame. Vogan proudly talked about his fiancée and shared pictures of the house they were going to buy together.

Two months into their tour of duty, the platoon was crossing through a field. Bill was at his usual place in front at point, and Vogan followed several yards behind him. As Bill waded through the tall grasses, he heard a loud explosion behind him. The guys behind him were screaming, "He's hit!

He's hit!" Vogan had stepped on a land mine and triggered it. Vogan's body was ripped to shreds, but the worst of it was the massive head wound. Bill ran back and found Vogan sprawled in the grass, his eyes unfocused and glazed. And then Vogan looked up directly at Bill. His mouth curled into a bemused smile as the light went out of his eyes. It was the first time Bill had seen a person die, and he knew he would never forget it for the rest of his life.

A week after Vogan's death, Bill's platoon was sent on a seek-and-destroy mission. The group was walking along in a rice patty, with Bill at point. Suddenly, a *Việt Cộng* soldier stood up out of the rice patty barely thirty feet away. Bill froze like a deer in headlights. The VC had him dead to rights and pulled the trigger of his AK-47 automatic rifle. Miraculously, the rifle jammed and didn't go off. The VC soldier threw his weapon down and started running.

When Bill saw the soldier running away, his brain kicked into gear, and he started running after the enemy. While he was running, Bill fired his M16 automatic rifle, hitting the soldier a couple of times. Wounded, the soldier's pace slowed down drastically, and Bill caught up to him. Bill was yelling and screaming at him, the memory of Vogan being blown up the previous week coming back in vivid detail. This soldier became for Bill the embodiment of the entire war. Bill emptied the whole magazine of the M16 into him, getting him back for his friend, like this man was personally responsible for Vogan's death.

As the magazine ran through its bullets and fired blanks, Bill had to force his finger off the trigger. He was shaking and crying. Somehow, the soldier was still alive after being riddled with bullets, but it was clear his death was close. Bill stood over the man he had just shot, watching for several minutes as the man's life slipped away.

Bill had just killed his first human being, and he knew that, like Vogan's death, this memory would be etched into his mind forever. Still standing there over the body and shaking, Bill knew he had to get a grip on himself. He was a soldier, and he had a job to do. Legs wobbly from the physical and emotional exertion, Bill went back to point. The platoon continued on their mission, but it took several days for Bill to get back to feeling normal.

That soldier was not the only man Bill had to kill. By his third, he didn't feel anything. Killing the enemy became a part of everything else. Bill found himself thinking, "I killed this one; I'm alive. I'm alive; I killed this one."

There was one time, however, when Bill was proud about *not* being a party to killing someone. One day, his platoon came across a *hooch*, little more than a tiny shack of a tree house in the jungle. Inside was a small middle-aged Vietnamese man, terrified at being surrounded by a group of American soldiers. The man had no weapons and no identification, but the lieutenant in command of the platoon was convinced the man was a VC sympathizer.

The lieutenant turned to the men and said, "Come on boys, we're going to blow him away." He dragged the pleading man against the wall of a dike and the troops clustered on the other side. The lieutenant told the men to take aim and shoot him. Bill raised his rifle along with everyone else, but he did not aim it at the man. Instead, he shot his rifle into the ground in front of the captive, while the other bullets hit true. Bill could honestly say that he was not an accomplice to that man's death. Bill didn't believe the man was VC anyway. He was probably just someone trying to escape both sides of the fighting but ended up in the wrong place at the wrong time, and he paid for it with his life.

In June 1967, Bill received his Purple Heart for being wounded in action. As usual, Bill was at point, walking along a trail with banana leaves in the way. Bill lifted up one of the banana leaves and triggered the pin on a homemade explosive, sending shrapnel through his whole body. He was transported to base camp, and medics took out as much shrapnel as they could. There were pieces that were lodged so deeply that the medics couldn't remove them. Bill would have metal inside him for the rest of his life.

Bill stayed at base camp recuperating for three weeks, and then he asked for one week of R&R in Bangkok before going back to duty. When he came back and was asked to take point again, he flatly refused. Bill had had enough of being the first person shot at and tripping traps. Bill finished his tour of duty in Vietnam in November 1967 and got back home in time for Thanksgiving.

Bill found adjusting back to civilian life extremely difficult. He felt like no one cared about him. There was no fanfare, no parades. His friends were curious about his experiences, but their questions only alienated him further. Did he rape any women? Did he kill any women or kids? "No!" Bill yelled at them. His friends should have known him better than that. Bill was already traumatized by the killing and death he had seen during his tour of duty, and questions like that from his friends only made him feel worse.

To run from his demons, Bill turned once again to drinking, smoking, and using pot. He found a bright spot in his life when he met Bonnie at a disco tech in New Haven. Bill got her number and then called her a couple of days later. They started dating and were engaged in six months. Bill and Bonnie got married in September 1969, and their son Darren was born four years later.

Although Bonnie saw the kindness and goodness in Bill's heart, she also experienced his flash-in-a-pan temper. When things weren't going his way, Bill would "go off" and start swearing. Bill had always had a temper when he was younger, but it worsened because of his time in Vietnam.

On top of that, Bill suffered from post-traumatic stress disorder. He had flashbacks of situations in Vietnam, where everyday situations brought back vivid memories of his war experience. Driving along wooded highways in Connecticut, Bill spent more time staring into the forest for possible communist soldiers than paying attention to the road. Bonnie finally convinced him to seek psychiatric treatment at the VA hospital. Bill didn't feel like it helped much, because they just gave him high doses of Xanax, which made him feel drugged.

Through this time, Bonnie supported her husband as much as she was able. She got Bill a job working for her father as a truck driver delivering oil to residences. This job paid their bills for thirteen years until Bill decided to try his hand at being a small business owner. He opened a tobacco shop in Branford. For four years, Bill struggled with trying to maintain a steady profit. Although there were some good years, mostly the business barely scraped by. Finally, Bill decided he couldn't keep the doors open anymore and closed the shop down.

As Bill informed his customers about the closing, one of his regulars who was a lieutenant at the nearby prison encouraged him to consider becoming a correctional officer. Bill thought it was a good idea because of his military experience. The problem was that the prison environment was too similar to the exclusive club mentality of Bill's military days. Although Bill had kept his drinking and partying to a manageable level through his marriage, the prison brought it all back.

Bill started hanging out with his fellow CO's, then he started drinking with them. At times Bill stayed out all night, coming back home and giving

Bonnie some half-hearted excuse. And then Bill began having affairs with the female officers. Bonnie found out the whole truth because one woman kept on calling the house. Bonnie confronted Bill and asked him if she was his girlfriend, which he admitted. In an effort to salvage the marriage, the couple tried counseling, but it didn't help. After twenty years of marriage, Bill and Bonnie divorced.

After the divorce, Bill was no longer tied down and did as he pleased. If Bill wasn't working, he was drinking, smoking, spending time with women, or all three at once. In an ironic repetition of fate, Darren lost his father emotionally at about the same age Bill was when his own father committed suicide. Bill was more interested in partying than going to Darren's little league games or school activities. Bill tried occasionally to talk to Darren or give him money, but the relationship just was not there. Because of his selfishness, Bill missed out on his son's formative years and young adulthood.

Through this time, Bill continued as a corrections officer at the prison. It was the fall of 2007, and Bill was six months away from twenty years on the job and being able to retire with a full pension. Bill was driving home and felt like he couldn't catch his breath. Every time he breathed in, it was like someone was stabbing him in the back. Bill crawled up the stairs and labored to the phone, dialing 911. "Help me. I think I'm dying," he said into the receiver before he blacked out.

Bill woke up once in the helicopter on the way to Yale. He was strapped down and hooked to every portable machine imaginable. He could still hear multiple voices as he faded from consciousness.

Bill was aware of very little that happened afterwards. He remembered always wanting ice chips. The morphine was like the nectar of the gods because it took away his pain. He could have sworn there was a car parked right in the middle of the ICU. Through all of it, Bill felt like he was passing from one dream to another. Life barely seemed real. When he woke up, two months had passed.

What Bill did not know until later was that the stabbing sensation in his back was his aorta ripping apart. Because of Bill's poor lifestyle habits, especially his smoking and drinking, his blood pressure elevated while the wall of his aorta weakened. Much like leaving the spigot open on a garden hose, the pressure formed a bleb in his aorta, developing into an aneurysm. The wall of Bill's aorta finally gave out and ripped open, spilling blood with every beat of his heart.

Most people with aortic dissections die within minutes and never make it to the hospital. Somehow, Bill hung on to life. When the surgeons opened up his chest, they found a pool of blood around his aortic arch, with the dissection extending down his aorta and into the subclavian artery of his left arm. For three hours, the team of surgeons kept Bill on cardiopulmonary bypass while they repaired the dissection with multiple grafts. To minimize his body's oxygen demand, they supercooled Bill's body down to 19° C (65° F) while they worked on him. During the surgery, they also had to remove several ribs and most of Bill's left lung. The surgeons did as much as they could, jump-started his heart, and closed him up.

For the next two months, Bill was in the ICU fighting for his life. Countless times, the team thought it would be Bill's last day on earth. Bill developed multiple infections, with pus draining out of his chest, requiring several rounds of antibiotics. Every time they tried to wean him off the ventilator, Bill decompensated and had to be put back on. He was intubated for so long he needed a tracheostomy. Due to lack of oxygen during the dissection and surgery, Bill had a stroke and could not speak normally or fully move his left side. His kidneys failed several times. He couldn't eat and was wasting away, so a gastric tube was placed to put some nutrition into him. Somehow, against all the odds, Bill started pulling through.

Bill then spent several months going through rehab, relearning how to walk, speak, even breathe. Each step seemed insurmountable. But through the help of friends and family, especially Darren, Bill did start to improve. Eventually, Bill was able to be discharged for outpatient care. During his hospitalization, Bill received one last incredible piece of news. Word had spread about Bill's condition, and correctional officers from all over the state donated their sick leave and paid time off. The donated time was enough to make up for Bill's last six months of work, allowing him to retire with a full pension and medical benefits.

After his hospitalization, Bill was brought to my office by Darren, who had already been a patient for several years. Although Bill had been through rehab, he was still very weak. Gradually, Bill's stamina improved, and he was able to do more than just getting from his bed to the bathroom. For the next year, I met with Bill very regularly to assess his cardiac status and the health of his remaining lung. Bill stopped smoking and drinking because he knew it would kill him. He took his medicines as prescribed and started the process of eating right and exercising.

Along with his physical health, Bill worked on other aspects of his life. At Darren's urging, Bill moved into the lower level of Darren's split ranch, which he converted into an apartment for his dad. Father and son worked together to rebuild, and at times create from scratch, ties that should have been formed twenty years before. Back then, Bill was not ready to appreciate all that he had. But now, with a new chance at life, Bill savored every moment spent with his son and grandchildren. Darren on his part took the difficult step of forgiving his father for abandoning the family and not being available when Darren was going through his own problems. They were both determined to make the present and future better than the past.

Like many people faced with a near-death experience, Bill started considering the spiritual part of his life. While Bill was estranged from his family, Darren had been coming to terms with his own anger, depression, and anxiety by seeking spiritual input. After Bill moved into Darren's home, he started going to church with his son. Bill was sure that some of the congregation were thinking, "What's Bill doing in church?" Being from a small community, they knew of Bill's decades of loose living. But Bill found no judgment from the people at church. In fact, he found them to be very caring and easy to talk to. This unconditional love allowed Bill to find some healing in his own life. Bill continued to seek spiritual understanding, and in September 2008, he decided to get baptized.

Since then, life has continued to be a daily struggle. Bill's legs are still messed up, and he can't walk quite right. With only one lung, he loses his breath and gets tired quickly. But he's biking, trying to lose weight, eating healthier, and getting stronger. He comes in regularly for his office visits, and he takes all of his medications. Mentally, Bill feels better, but he still gets depressed at times. When he starts feeling sorry for himself and all the things he has lost, he reminds himself that he's the luckiest person around because he could have died back in 2007.

Now, every day is a gift. Standing on his back deck, Bill still stares into the forest at times, half expecting a communist soldier to jump out from beneath the underbrush. But those days are long past, and Bill knows he's surrounded by love. There's nothing to fear from behind the leaves anymore.

Dong Tam Base Camp, April 16, 1967

Mekong Delta, June 27, 1967

Bill and Darren at his bachelor's graduation from the University of Connecticut

Swimming Against the Current

Patrick "Smitty" Smithson was again in for a follow up visit, and nothing had changed much since his last office visit. Frankly, nothing had changed much for Smitty over the past seven years that I had been taking care of him, and that was why I was annoyed. I was tired of dealing with the same old things, doing everything I could think of to help Smitty get to a better, healthier place in his life. Nothing was working.

In his fifties, Smitty was much further than "middle age" based on my projection of his life expectancy. Smitty was 278 lbs on a 5'9" frame. One might say he was too short for his weight. His obesity was a major contributing factor to his high blood pressure, high cholesterol, and pre-diabetes. Even Smitty's low Vitamin D was caused by his obesity, since the extra fat was sucking all of the Vitamin D right out of his blood stream. With all of these risk factors, I knew that chances were high that Smitty would not live to see 70, particularly due to the fact that both of his parents had heart issues. In spite of these risks, nothing I said was able to break through Smitty's inertia of inactivity.

When asked about whether he was trying to exercise more, decrease his food intake, and lose weight, Smitty's answer was almost always the same. "No, I didn't." That's it. Just a vacant stare with glassy eyes and, "Not really." Once, I actually got more than three words out of Smitty regarding his lack of exercise. "I don't have time. I get up early to go to work, and I don't get home until late."

Since I took care of Smitty's wife and their adult children, I knew his answer was not entirely truthful. Smitty left for work at about 7:30 AM. Although there were definitely times when he got home at 9 PM, usually he got home from work by 6:30 or so. It was a clear case of lack of motivation, not true lack of time. But Smitty's occasional late night gave him an excuse to not exercise any other day either.

Unfortunately, Smitty's lack of motivation was not limited to his lifestyle habits. His wife Cheryl had seen me multiple times for stress and anxiety complaints, mostly because she didn't see Smitty doing anything to foster their relationship. Although they had been married for over twenty-five years, for the past five years, it seemed more like a roommate relationship than a healthy marriage. Cheryl shared how they hadn't had sex for at least two years, and they hadn't slept in the same bed for at least that long. Smitty would go for weeks without even touching her once. Cheryl tried talking to him about the issue, but he didn't respond, and he didn't change his pattern of aloofness. Knowing what I knew about Smitty, I believed her.

"The thing is, I know he loves me," Cheryl told me one day. "He's always been very good to the kids, which I'm grateful for. But I need more than that." Cheryl's eyes welled up, and she dabbed the tears from the corner of her eyes as she said, "I love him, but I don't think I've been in love with him for a long time. I've really thought about getting a divorce, but I don't want to do that to the kids. I know he loves me, but it's just not enough. I need someone to hold me and support me. Smitty doesn't know how to express himself in any way.

"There's this guy, and he treats me so nice," she continued. He's interested in me, and he smiles at me so differently than the way Smitty looks at me. It makes me feel bad and dirty inside, but damn it, I want to be loved and held." Cheryl started to weep openly.

I knew Cheryl wasn't someone to throw away twenty-five years of a relationship on a whim, but I could also tell that she was not getting what she desperately needed at home. She needed someone to love her and care for her, someone whom she could trust. Getting Smitty to really demonstrate his love for her would go far to bring healing for both of them. I knew Cheryl had been up to this point unsuccessful in getting Smitty to change, so she was going to need my help.

When Smitty came in for his annual physical, I asked him about his sexual history, as I do for all patients. He confirmed what Cheryl had told me previously, that they had not been sexually intimate for a number of years. When I asked why that was the case, he said, "She doesn't seem that interested."

"When was the last time you asked, and what did she say?" I asked him.

"I haven't asked in over a year, but when I did, she didn't want to," Smitty responded.

"So you stopped there? You hadn't had sex for a long time before that. You asked once, and she said 'No,' and that's it?" Smitty's only reply was to look back at me.

Because of my previous conversation with Cheryl, I asked my follow up question. "Smitty, how often do you show affection to your wife? I'm talking like a non-sexual but intimate touch."

"Not much," he conceded. I personally knew that the answer was closer to zero.

"So why don't you?" I asked.

He responded, "I'm just not good at showing that sort of thing."

I told him, "You can't expect Cheryl to be interested in sex if you don't show her that you care about her and give her intimacy in non-sexual ways. There is an emotional component to sex for most women that needs to be addressed before, during, and after sex. And frankly, I think more important than you two having no sex is you two not expressing intimacy to each other at all.

"Have you heard of the Five Love Languages?" Smitty shook his head. "The Five Love Languages detail how people give and receive love. For your wife, one of her big things is touch. Showing physical affection is a big way that Cheryl shows her love and knows people love her.

"I have homework for you, if you're willing to take it. I want you to find some way every day to touch your wife in an intimate, non-sexual way. Put your hands on her shoulder as you're walking by. Give her a little pat on the back, or maybe a quick kiss. Don't ask for or expect sex, but if your show of affection leads to other things, don't shy away from it either."

"I can try that," Smitty responded. We made an appointment for another three months, and he left the office.

Three months later, Smitty was back. His weight was exactly the same. "So what did you do?" I asked him.

"I've been walking for 30 minutes during lunch three times a week."

"Congratulations!" I exclaimed. "That's great! It's a good start to weight loss. But if that's the case, I'm curious why you're exactly the same weight as before."

"I do well for breakfast and lunch, but I'm eating too much for dinner," Smitty replied.

We talked about weight control as a balance between how much one puts in and how much one expends. It didn't do any good for Smitty to do that walking if he was going to gorge during dinner. So, I suggested really paying attention to his portion sizes during dinner to make the exercise count.

"What about the non-sexual touching?" I asked.

"I did good for two weeks, and then I stopped." When I asked why, he responded, "I just went back to my old habits." And when I asked what he meant by that, he said, "When I get home from work, I just want to unwind by watching the TV for a couple of hours."

"Smitty, is your relationship with your wife important to you?"

"Sex just isn't a top goal for me," he responded.

"I wasn't talking about sex. I was talking about your general relationship. If sex isn't your top goal, what is it? What do you want? Life and relationships are like being in a river with a current. If you're just floating, you're going to be washed out to sea. If you want to just stay still, you have to expend energy to swim against the current. And if you're already down the river and want to get back, it's going to take even more effort." Smitty nodded in understanding.

"Have you heard of the Bible verse, 'Where your treasure is, there your heart shall be also'? Isn't it interesting that it's not the other way around? It doesn't say, 'Where your *heart* is, there your *treasure* is. Smitty, your most precious treasure is your time. Where you choose to spend your time, there your heart will be as well. If you make the conscious choice to spend time with your wife and show her that you care about her, I think you will find, amazingly, that your heart will follow. If you wait for your heart to lead, you will spend your time at the TV, wondering why your family is falling apart."

Smitty concurred, "A guy at my men's Bible study group said almost the same thing you did. He said if we say our families are so important to us, then why do we spend all of our time at work or doing our own thing? Family is supposed to be at the top, but it gets the bottom of our time."

"See," I pointed out, "he and I both agree. Now you just need to follow. The problem is that you, my friend, are resistant to change. You're a creature of habit, set in his ways. You're like the Lotus-eaters from *The*

Odyssey, who ate the narcotic lotus plant and spent their lives sleeping through everything.

"I'm here to help you, Smitty. But I can't walk the path for you. You have to do that yourself."

"I think writing down my goals is a good start," he said. I thought it was a great idea, so I gave him that as homework. I also encouraged him to go back to trying to show affection to his wife. I look forward to getting a positive report when he comes back to the office.

Through the Fire

It was after high school, while Gordon was studying at Manchester Community College, that he realized he did not want to live any more. He was unhappy, with zero direction in his life. He lived in a dysfunctional family. His father was in a marriage he did not want to be in and with kids he didn't particularly love. Gordon felt absolutely no connection with his dad. He had no male role model, not even any other close relationships. He felt unloved and unwanted. There was really no reason to live any longer.

As Gordon was sitting in his car, he decided he would end his life by slitting his wrists. He took out the knife he found in the car and cut across his wrists. The knife was too dull to bite deep enough to puncture his artery, and he could not cut through his tendon. He was also unsuccessful at slitting his throat. So, Gordon found leftover gasoline, poured it on himself, and ran his car off the road to pass off his death as a car accident.

Gordon swerved his car off the road and down the rocky embankment. He flipped the car, catching it and himself on fire. Witnesses to the scene got out of their cars to help, but the fire was so intense that they could not even get near.

While Gordon was hanging upside down in the car, burning and waiting to die, he felt a hand on his shoulder. He then heard a clear voice in his ear, which he could only say was from God. "Just get yourself out of the car, and I'll be with you forever." In response to that urging, Gordon smashed the glass with his hand and crawled out of the car. Just at that point, the EMS arrived and took him away.

Third degree burns covered forty percent of Gordon's body. His left ear was burned off completely, along with some of the left side of his face. Burns encompassed his neck, left arm, chest, and thighs, all the way to the muscle underneath. He had large patches where the skin was black parchment overlying fat that had melted and fused to the tissue underneath. And of course, Gordon's hand was slashed in multiple places from the window glass that he had to break through. In spite of the life-threatening injuries, Gordon had no feeling of pain: all the nerves to the skin had been burned away along with everything else.

The EMS rushed Gordon into the critical care unit at John Dempsey Hospital in Farmington, and vast amounts of fluids were pumped into his body. Without skin, Gordon had no ability to protect against heat loss or fluid evaporation, so he was put under thermal blankets. He was intubated to protect his airway. Antibiotics were started to minimize the chances of infection. The doctors did everything they could, but Gordon did not respond to treatment. At the end of the day, the priest was called in to read Gordon his last rites.

Miraculously, he did not die. Because Gordon's faith background was not clear, the priest was called back in to baptize him. Unexplainable by medical science alone, it was after that baptism that Gordon really began responding to treatment. His vital signs stabilized. His kidney function, which had been dropping, started to level out and then improve. His lungs stopped filling with fluid, and his breathing became less labored. After weeks of fighting to save his life, Gordon's doctors were able to stabilize him enough not to fear he would crash and die.

After the critical care management came the lengthy process of recuperation. Gordon had to be placed in constant traction because his extensive burns caused contractures in his muscles and joints. The nerve endings around the injured tissue sent nonstop signals of PAIN. Gordon felt like he was still on fire. There were times when the slightest touch or movement brought agony.

In spite of this, every day his limbs and joints had to be stretched, or the contractures and scarring would be irreversible. Gordon also needed dozens of surgeries to break adhesions, reattach muscles and tendons, and apply skin grafts. For each skin graft, small patches of unburned skin from various places on Gordon's body were harvested and carefully placed over burn areas. Both areas would be allowed to heal until the donor site was healed enough to give another patch to cover a burn area. It was like playing a huge game of jigsaw with Gordon's skin.

Doctors and nurses frequently commented how Gordon's burns were the most extensive of anyone they had seen who survived. Gordon was told that it would be years before he would be able to walk. But with a commitment to hard work in spite of the pain, a good attitude, and— Gordon would say—the help of God, Gordon got better much more quickly than anyone anticipated. After only a few months of rehab, he was able to walk unassisted. Gordon's skin, although very tender and sensitive, was healing nicely. He was then moved from John Dempsey Hospital to the Gaylord Rehabilitation Hospital in order to finish his rehab.

Gordon's months in Gaylord were some of the best times for him. He was happy and sociable, making friends with all the nurses and therapists. When he was not doing his own rehab, Gordon visited other wings of the facility. He spent the most time in the quadriplegic wing, helping the patients eat, moving them around to sunny windows, or just sitting for hours talking to them about their lives. Eventually, Gordon got strong enough to go home. A year and a half after his attempted suicide, Gordon returned home to his family.

Eighteen months was a long time, and the family had changed greatly while Gordon was recuperating. Unbeknownst to him, Gordon's father had moved out of the house shortly after the accident and started another family with a different woman. He took both the car and his paychecks along with him. That revelation explained to Gordon why his mother and sisters hardly ever visited him in the hospital: they simply had no way to get there. Gordon arrived home to a house behind on mortgage payments and without food or heat. Gordon's father had cut all ties with him, and to the day he died in 2010, Gordon never spoke to him again.

To help the family make ends meet, Gordon took two part-time jobs. During the day, he collected money from cars at the highway toll booth. At night, he worked in a restaurant. Before his accident, Gordon had experience working in restaurants, starting as a dish washer and over time moving all the way up to a management position. After the accident, Gordon had to start from the bottom again as a dish washer.

This time around, however, his body was not nearly as well equipped to deal with the stresses and hazards of the restaurant industry. Gordon found his body could not adjust to sudden changes in temperature. He got quickly overheated in hot environments; while in cold temperatures, his skin became brittle and quite painful. The skin grafts would break down and open up, and his left arm had lymphatic drainage oozing all the time. The thicker scars cracked and bled. These open wounds made Gordon vulnerable to infections, worsened by his lowered immune system. Gordon had to go to the hospital multiple times for rapidly progressing infections that led to the point of liver and kidney failure.

Throughout all of this, Gordon had to continue working to help support the family. He took prescription pain meds to help with his constant pain. This led to a dependence on narcotics, not just for pain but as a means of escape. Addiction to alcohol was not far behind. And for ten years, Gordon kept up a cocaine habit. He was incredibly depressed about his lot in life, but he had to continue for his family, because they had no one else.

Gordon was part of the working poor, making a hair's too much for state assistance, but not enough to climb out of the hole. When he tried to get counseling for his depression and substance use, he was told that based on his income, a fifteen minute counseling session would cost $100. Gordon had to choose to put food on the table for his mother and sisters instead.

Gordon began coming to the office in 2007. I took over his care, which up to that point was barely managed by Gordon's recurrent visits to the ER. Gordon detailed to me his frequent skin infections, his insomnia, and his depression. Little by little, we managed each of his concerns. Gordon started on a regimen of meticulous skin care with multiple over-the-counter and prescription medications. I addressed the insomnia and high blood pressure. And for his depression, I treated him with medication and in-office counseling.

Over time, all of Gordon's medical problems improved, with the exception of his skin. Gordon had continued in the restaurant industry for twenty years after his ordeal, and his sensitive skin just could not take any more injury. Every few weeks, Gordon was back in the hospital with a severe infection, or at least in my office with an arm or leg that was swollen and beet-red, oozing yellow fluid. We both knew that Gordon could get into serious trouble very quickly if this pattern continued. I then worked with Gordon to apply for and receive federal disability.

After he was granted disability under the Social Security Act, Gordon did not just sit at home doing nothing. In fact, if anything, he was busier than ever. He started volunteering for Head Start, a kindergarten and pre-K school for underprivileged children. There, he found positive role models and was amazed by the dedication of the staff.

Gordon began going to conferences on communication, family skills, leadership, learning styles, teaching styles, and how to connect with people. He fell in love with the idea of life-long learning and helping young people get the resources they needed to succeed in life. Gordon went to the Neighborhood Academy, signed up for the Citizen's Emergency Response Team, and attended the Citizen's Police Academy. By participating and volunteering his time, Gordon started to feel positively about himself and his town. He felt it was his responsibility to make a positive contribution to the world and his neighborhood in particular.

Gordon received a scholarship to the Phoenix Society's annual World Burn Congress for burn survivors. There, he received training on how to present the case to enforce a federal policy requiring sprinkler systems to be installed in all new residential construction, including single family housing. Currently only a handful of states enforce this policy, and Connecticut is not one of them.

At home, Gordon is pursuing an associate's degree in business office technology, with a medical specialty. Classes in medical coding and medical insurance claims will allow him to be certified in both those fields and re-enter the work force with a higher paying and more stable job.

The aspect of Gordon's life that has brought the most comfort and meaning to him has been his spiritual journey. Although Gordon experienced a divine presence in the burning car and near-miraculous healing through his ordeal, he only had a passing curiosity about spiritual matters. When Gordon came to my office, I mentioned offhandedly that he should consider examining the spiritual part of his life and look into how that might bring him greater fulfillment. At that time, I did not know how Gordon came to be burned or the brush with divinity that he experienced. But because of my gentle urging, Gordon started to more seriously consider this aspect of life.

Gordon started visiting many churches and religions in the months following our conversation. In truth, I had no idea how much of an impact my words made on him. After searching for himself and speaking to missionaries who came to his door, Gordon found the most resonance with the teachings of Joseph Smith. As a public commitment of his faith, Gordon was baptized in June 2011 into the Church of Jesus Christ of Latter-day Saints. In the past, Gordon would deal with his depression by drinking and using drugs. After his conversion, Gordon found comfort and peace in going to church, reading his Bible, and fellowshipping with church members.

I asked Gordon what he has learned through his life experience. This was his response: "I have learned not to hang on to your past because you can't change it. I have come to realize that everything we do, whether good or bad, affects the people around us. When I was living irresponsibly, it affected people. When I started being a positive influence in the community, my outlook on life and even my personal health improved. I was shocked to find out that people who I looked up to and admired actually saw what I was doing and were inspired themselves. It makes me feel like I haven't gone through all of this for nothing."

Gordon and his friend Shirleen at her birthday party, June 2012

Gordon with his friends Eilyn (far left) and Shirleen, June 2012

Gordon

Laughter is the Best Medicine

Nancy tottered into the office for her physical, dragging along her oxygen with her granddaughter helping her out. I stood directly at her side, with my mouth as close as I could get to her right ear without invading her personal space.

As I asked her questions and typed, I kept on having to repeat myself. Nancy would look over at her granddaughter and ask, "What did he say, Cindy? I couldn't hear him." Cindy would then have to repeat my words back.

I finally said with some humor in my voice, "Nancy, you should really get hearing aids."

She said, "They won't fit."

"What do you mean they won't fit?" I asked.

Nancy replied, "I got glasses. I got oxygen. And I got teeny tiny ears. Everything already falls off my face as it is. If you want me to get hearing aids, you've got to get me bigger ears."

****

"Boy Albert, you're really thin!" I commented.

Albert responded, "If you think I'm thin, you should see my wife. She's the exact *opposite*. When we stand next to each other, we look like the number ten."

****

I found Pastor Harry to have high cholesterol on his lab work and asked my nurse Tina to give him a call.

Tina picked up the phone and dialed. "Harry, Dr. Han noticed that your cholesterol was a bit higher than he'd like. I guess you'll need to stop those fatty foods and treats." Tina paused as Harry responded. She laughed and said, "I'll definitely tell him."

Tina hung up the phone and turned to me. "He told me to tell you, '*Well* now, wait a minute. Remind him that I'm a pastor, and I'm limited in the vices that I can have.'"

****

We have a patient in the office with a very distinct laugh. It sounds exactly like a horse braying. The sound echoes down the hall, and without any other indication, I know Bradley is in the office.

Bradley told me that one time, he was in a restaurant with a couple of buddies. They were cutting up, and Bradley started laugh-braying. The waitress nearby heard the laugh and thought Bradley was choking, so she ran over. She grabbed Bradley from behind, yanked him out of the chair, and started to perform the Heimlich maneuver.

Bradley was so startled he couldn't say anything, while his buddies were falling out of their seats in uproarious laughter. It took a bit of convincing for the waitress to believe that Bradley had been laughing and not dying in front of her.

****

During my residency training in Roanoke, Virginia, I saw a man who brought his child to the clinic for cough and runny nose. The child appeared to have a simple cold, and I prescribed some cough syrup. Knowing that cigarette smoking often lowered the immune system and made a person more susceptible to viral and bacterial infections, I asked the father if he smoked.

"Naw, I don't smoke," he replied sincerely in a deep southern accent. "But my wife, she smokes like a fish!"

****

"I'm sorry I'm running late. There was a last-minute patient," I explained to Andy and Renee, two drug reps who call on me and with whom I was having lunch at a sushi bar.

"No problem, we understand," Andy said as I scooted myself into the booth. They were in the middle of a rep conversation which I didn't want to interrupt, so I busied myself quietly by picking up an edamame pod from the bowl in the center of the table.

I popped the pod into my mouth, bit down...and found it was empty. The edamame had already been eaten. Apparently, the reps had gotten to the restaurant early to have their own meeting and passed the time by ordering the edamame. The edamame came out in a full bowl along with an empty bowl for the shells. After they finished with the bowl, they piled the bowl of leftover shells on top of the empty one, leaving only one bowl in the center of the table.

I pursed my lips, made a face, and took out the used edamame pod out of my mouth. Waggling it in front of the reps I told them, "I'm just glad I really know the two of you well."

****

Leslie suffers with chronic pain and one of the few things that helps her is a TENS unit, which delivers a steady electrical charge between the leads placed at each side of her back. The small current helps relax tightened muscles and bring pain relief.

Leslie was having chest tightness one day and went to the ER. When they tried to do the EKG, the heart rhythm looked like nothing the doctors had ever seen. Fiddling with the leads and machine seemed to do no good. It was only after several unsuccessful attempts at getting an EKG reading that Leslie considered mentioning the TENS unit strapped to her back.

****

I ask all of my teen patients if they have started being sexually active. During a school physical I asked this question to a young man, and his reply was yes.

"OK, how many people have you been sexually active with?" I asked.

"Well, not with anyone else," he replied. "Just myself."

I told him he could be active like that all he wanted.

EXTRAORDINARY LIVES

"Each of us has an inner dream that we can unfold if we will just have the courage to admit what it is. And the faith to trust our own admission. The admitting is often very difficult."

~Julia Cameron, author of *The Artist's Way*

Before the Dawn

Mary really never understood why her mother did the things she did. For one thing, Mary's mother left her to be raised by her father's parents. Mary was so young when that happened that she didn't even have memories of her mother during childhood. It didn't help that Mary's father wasn't in the picture either. But Papa Henry and Ma Jeffie were enough parents for Mary through her young years.

And then as inexplicably as she had left, Mary's mother returned to town when Mary was ten. She decided to take Mary away from the grandparents. Although Mary was confused about the change, she was excited, too. Her mother was back, and she wanted to take her home!

Very quickly though, whatever hopes Mary had for an ideal life were destroyed. Papa Henry and Ma Jeffie had provided a loving home and stability. Mary received none of that with her mother. Maw had a boyfriend, and that relationship produced Mary's brother. When that relationship didn't work, Maw found another guy, and therefore another child. That didn't go so well either. Maw burned through relationships quicker than tinder lit with a match. Before Mary turned fifteen, she had four baby half-brothers and sisters from three different fathers.

None of the men stuck around for any length of time, so the responsibility fell on Mary to care for the four babies. From when she was ten years old, Mary had to feed the children, clean the house, wash the clothes, and do all the household chores. She woke up practically at the crack of dawn to care for the multiplying family and then walk to school to get there by nine AM. Then Mary had to rush home right after school to clean the house. God forbid she didn't get everything done, or her mother would "do a job" on her. Maw would walk in and see something out of place, stomp through the house to get the switch, and chase Mary, yelling and whipping her with the switch. Maw was indiscriminate in her whipping; Mary would carry scars on her face from those switch whippings for the rest of her life. Mary felt like little more than a slave.

Slaves can be sold, and that is what Maw did to her daughter. When Mary was fifteen, Maw arranged her marriage to a 25-year-old man from church she barely knew. If Mary *had* known what Dave was like, she would have never agreed to the marriage, no matter what Maw said. Dave came from a privileged background, and he was used to getting what he wanted. Dave took Mary to his bed after the wedding, and Mary lost her virginity to him. Mary's first sexual experience was a horrible one, worse than any beating she had received from Maw. Dave had no consideration for the young girl who was now his wife. He had a need, and Mary was the one who was supposed to sate it. By the time he was done, Mary was weeping.

Right after the marriage, Mary's husband started to physically and emotionally abuse her. His weapon of choice was the back of his hand, and he used it freely. To her credit, Mary did fight back, but what chance did a fifteen-year-old girl have against a man who towered over her? When Dave wasn't hitting her, he found ways to subjugate her emotionally, using ugly and demeaning words. And through it all, Dave demanded that Mary fulfill her "wifely obligations." Frequently. Only a few months into the marriage, Dave got Mary pregnant. Mary was sixteen when she gave birth to her daughter.

If Mary thought Dave would change now that he had a daughter, she was mistaken. Dave continued to spend his days carousing and his nights forcing Mary to sleep with him. Mary was not even recovered from her incredibly difficult first pregnancy when Dave got her pregnant again. But Mary's young body could not handle such an extreme stress. At seven months, the child had to be forcibly delivered and only lived four days.

Dave, however, was relentless. A few months later, the cycle started again with another pregnancy. Mary was barely eighteen and eight months pregnant with her third child. Throughout the pregnancy, she still suffered physical abuse and emotional neglect. Mary then stopped feeling any movement from the baby. At home alone, Mary delivered her stillborn boy. The next door neighbor came over to the house because she heard the screaming, and she found Mary unconscious, surrounded by blood and a dead baby. Mary regained consciousness late the next day and buried her child.

Another year, and another child. Mary was nineteen, and this time, she was able to deliver a strong, healthy boy. Mary was now caring for her three year old and a four month infant, and Dave was continuing to abuse her. Mary knew that Dave was incapable of changing, and she would likely die if she remained with him. Mary had to make the heart-wrenching decision to give her children to Dave's mother, because she knew Dave had no interest in the kids. With nowhere to go, Mary had to move back in with her mother.

Mary found work and sent money to provide for her two children. She ended up meeting a man in the neighborhood, got remarried, and moved out of state. They had a daughter and a son together. However, Mary's luck with men remained abysmal. While she worked, Willie spent all the money gambling. Mary was pregnant with their third child when he was arrested for burglary and sent to prison. Mary packed up the two kids and moved back home with her mother, just in time to deliver her youngest daughter.

Mary was now responsible for five children: her oldest two living with her ex-mother-in-law and the younger three living with Maw and her.

Mary tried to make things work out with her mother as much as she could, but Maw did not have the parenting skills to deal with Mary and the kids. Mary finally had to leave her three kids with Maw so she could move out by herself and find jobs to support everyone. Mary worked three full-time jobs, sleeping two hours a night. Every bit of money she had, she sent back to Maw.

Mary went where she heard there were jobs, and that took her over a thousand miles from home, landing her in Hartford, Connecticut with $20 in her pocket. Through a set of circumstances Mary would call providential, she found a place to stay and a job three days later. In between her regular job as a maid she washed and ironed shirts for the men at the department store to make extra money. It seemed no matter how much money Mary sent home, Maw was always asking for more. Mary didn't find out until years later that Maw was keeping the majority of the money for herself instead of using it for the kids. Nevertheless, Mary saved every extra penny she earned, and a year later she brought her youngest daughter up to Connecticut to live with her. Seven months later, she got the other two.

Mary and her three younger children spent the next several years comfortably and happily, even if they had very little money. Truly, the kids never knew they were poor until the youngest daughter went to college. Mary always made sure that they were well fed, well groomed, and well dressed every day. Mary had a gift for stretching a dollar to its farthest limits and make thrift store purchases look like department store treasures. And of course, Mary did not forget about her two eldest children. She still sent money back to Dave's mother to ensure they were well cared for.

As Mary approached fifty, she became friendly with Emmett, a man from church. That friendship blossomed, and the two got married. With Emmett, Mary found the husband who finally deserved her. Emmett treasured and practically worshipped his wife. Mary had never learned how to drive, so Emmett taught her. He made her start taking care of herself and buy herself things she enjoyed. One day, Mary came home after shopping all day, bringing home gifts for all the kids and her husband.

"So what did you get for yourself?" Emmett asked.

Mary looked down. "Nothing. There was this one hat I kind of liked, but I decided not to get it. It wasn't a big deal."

"Oh, yes, it is," Emmett informed her. Emmett bundled Mary back into the car, drove her to the store, and made her go in and buy herself the hat. From that moment on, Mary had a soft spot in her heart for a nicely crafted hat and over time built an impressive collection.

For two years, Mary's life was just short of bliss. She had three of her children with her and a husband who adored her. Because of the support Emmett gave her, Mary decided to go back to school to get her GED. But Mary's time of happiness was tragically short. Just after two years of marriage, Emmett had a massive stroke. Emmett, a shell of his former self, languished in a nursing home for another eight years before he died. With the responsibility of the kids and caring for Emmett, Mary could no longer afford the time that the adult education classes required, so she dropped out. She still had to make a living for the family, so she decided to go to hairdressing school.

Mary's heart was broken, though, so she couldn't focus. She had nervous breakdowns and couldn't stop crying. Mary's condition got so severe that she wasted away to 85 lbs. She ended up in the hospital multiple times due to severe depression. She underwent a total of seven courses of ECT, "electroconvulsive therapy," otherwise known as shock treatments. After the treatments, she had holes in her memory and difficulty making new ones. Her psychiatrist told her that she would not be able to complete hairdressing school and likely would never be able to work a steady job again. Despondent, Mary could only see one way out. She wrote a note to her children, took an entire bottle of pills, and lay down in bed to die.

After what seemed like only minutes to her, Mary opened her eyes to find herself in the hospital, waking up from a week-long coma. Somehow, Mary started picking back up the pieces of her life. She got herself together by thinking, praying, and reading a multitude of books about mental and emotional health. She decided at that point that she was never going to let anyone or anything in life get her down like that ever again. She started seeing both a psychiatrist and a therapist, which really helped her process the tragedies in her life.

Although Mary survived her suicide attempt and started the healing process, life was not ready to give her a break or cut her any slack. Shortly after her recovery, Mary discovered that her daughter, who recently graduated from law school, was developing a serious psychiatric condition. Dorothy, who had always been sweet and friendly, became argumentative, disagreeable, and controlling. Mary also found out that Dorothy was lying to friends and family in an attempt to turn them against her mother.

Because of Dorothy's convincing words and her ability to mix just enough truth with fiction, many of Mary's close relationships became strained. The situation got so unhealthy that Mary spent almost all of her time in her bedroom, a virtual prisoner in her own home. Mary confided with her physician and friends about her difficulties, and eventually, Mary had to ask Dorothy to move out of the house. It was one of the hardest things Mary ever had to do, because she felt like she was turning her back on her own flesh and blood. But Mary knew it was the right thing to do, because Dorothy's presence was poisoning Mary and the siblings. From a distance, Mary watched through the years as Dorothy's psychiatric illness landed her in one hospital after another.

In spite of all the challenges with Dorothy, Mary kept her promise to herself and God that she would start finding ways to give back. Mary started by volunteering at the hospital that gave her virtually free medical and psychiatric care. For years Mary willingly helped in whatever capacity she could throughout the hospital until a ruptured disk curtailed her ability to walk. In honor of her husband Emmett, who served in World War II, in 1975, Mary joined the VFW, the *Veterans of Foreign Wars*. And in 1990, she joined the American Legion, the nation's largest wartime veterans' service organization. In both organizations, she devoted countless hours helping veterans and their families. She served as a chaplain for six years, officiating at memorial services. When her illnesses prevented her from being on her feet, she wrote cards to sick members or the families of deceased members. And for the past 25 years, Mary has served as a volunteer driver for the annual Greater Hartford Open golf tournament, now known as the Travelers Championship. Apparently, Mary is always in high demand because of her age and experience as well as being the only black woman chauffeur.

For more than thirty years, even though she has not held a job or contributed to the GDP, Mary has striven to make her life a positive impact on others. Life has not made it easy for her though. Mary has continued to experience her share of struggle and tragedy. She's had numerous medical problems for which I have been treating her for over a decade. Her son had a serious heart attack. She was at her grand-daughter's side and watched her die at 44 from complications related to AIDS. Yet through all of this, Mary manages to keep a smile on her face. Most people who know Mary would never guess that she spends the majority of every day in moderate to severe pain or that she carries emotional burdens that would cripple most everyone else.

One way that Mary has been able to get beyond her hurts is to find forgiveness for her parents. When her father got sick and died, she traveled over a thousand miles back to her home town to bury him, a man she barely knew. Why? Because she felt like it was the right thing to do. And then when her mother got sick as well, Mary was the only one of the children to be at her side. For years, Mary traveled back and forth between Connecticut and her home town, helping Maw as she slowly declined.

During the time Mary cared for Maw before she died, she had the chance to reflect on all the ways her mother had treated her so poorly through her life. "So why did you do it? Why did you treat me that way?" Mary asked.

All Maw could say was, "I don't really know." Mary never got a straight answer from her mother.

But although she was terribly hurt, Mary never got angry. She did not allow anger to poison her heart. Instead, she felt pity for her mother, who likely never found the love she was looking for all her life.

Anyone walking into her tiny four-room efficiency would see that for herself Mary has found overwhelming love, mostly from her extended family. Mary boasts about her five children, the nine grand kids, the twelve great-grandchildren, and even a five-year-old great-great-granddaughter. Pictures of all of them line every wall and horizontal surface in the apartment. Interspersed with these pictures are ones of friends who became like family, many of whom have passed on.

A person meeting Mary for the first time might notice her crisp attire and elegant headwear. Or she might be drawn in by Mary's wise eyes and commanding presence... or be captivated by her precise speech and broad knowledge base... or maybe her laugh that seems to fill the entire room with warmth and joy. From top to bottom, Mary exudes an air of confidence, a feeling that she has seen it all and could not be fazed by anything. Mary carries herself like a woman who has been financially successful all her life and is now enjoying her golden years. No one would guess that she was a high-school dropout on state assistance for the majority of her life.

So what is her secret? I asked Mary just this question.

She responded, "Don't ever give up. Just keep facing things. I remember my grandmother saying to me long ago, 'The darkest time is just before dawn.' You never know, but you just gotta keep trying. Never, ever, stop."

Mary and a friend at a VFW function in 1994

Mary at a friend's house in 2002

Mary in 2013

Not a Linebacker for the New York Giants

Gary Kissman started his life on April 11, 1956 behind the proverbial 8-ball. Dr. Fisher at Manchester Memorial Hospital brought Gary into the world at only 29 weeks and weighing three and a half pounds. Because of his severe prematurity, Gary's body was not capable of regulating his temperature, breathing, feeding, or other autonomic functions. Many babies born at 29 weeks do not survive more than a few weeks; this was especially true back in the 1950s. To give him a fighting chance, the doctors started Gary in an incubator and gradually moved him to the neonatal ICU. After a month or so, Gary was ready to leave the hospital.

Gary's parents noticed there was something wrong with him when he was five months old. He was not hitting any of the normal physical development milestones an infant should meet. At six months, Gary still couldn't sit up. His limbs were weak and floppy. He had no trunk strength. His growth was stunted. Albert and Alva brought their son to the doctor, who diagnosed Gary with cerebral palsy. Because of Gary's prematurity and difficult first few months of life, his brain did not form the motor neurons and connections to his limb and girdle muscles. They were told that at best, Gary would live his life in a wheel chair.

Gary's parents would not give up on their son. They cared for his every need, and they treated him like any other boy. When Gary was seven years old, he lived in a neighborhood where there were a lot of kids. Even though Gary could not join the kids physically as they played baseball, he still went

387

out and watched them play. That introduction to baseball became a life-long passion for Gary.

As his parents watched Gary with the neighborhood kids, they knew that Gary longed to be a participant in life and not just a spectator. The next year, they enrolled Gary into a summer camp for the disabled. Counselors teamed up with campers, helping them at bat and racing them around the bases in their wheelchairs. That summer was a pivotal point for Gary. He realized that he did have limitations, but that did not mean he could not enjoy life to the fullest.

One of Gary's greatest limitations was his leg weakness. Gary could not transfer himself in any way because his legs could not hold his weight without his knees buckling. Gary had to wear a lower-body brace that went from below his knees to his pelvis. Because of the constant use, the pelvic straps for the brace dug into his sides, causing pain.

Gary decided to get a knee fusion. With his knees permanently fused in a slightly bent position, he could help with his transfers and be able to stand without worrying that his knees would buckle. In 1964, when he was nine years old, Gary spent several months at the Shriners Hospital to get his knees fused and go through rehab. Gary vividly recalls having the cast on and having nurses flip him over like an omelet every four hours to prevent pressure ulcers and bed sores.

Because of Gary's limitations from his CP, he physically could not get to school. His family could not arrange for a bus to come out to the house and take Gary to school, so Gary's mother had home schooled him from first to third grade. After Gary's surgery and rehab, he was in a better position to be more independent and access the available public transportation. At eleven years old, Gary went to school for the first time, entering fourth grade.

Gary remembers facing the first day of school not knowing the first thing to do. The administrators were uncommonly sensitive to Gary's needs and assigned a teacher to lead him through the first day. The other kids accepted Gary right away. They fought over who would push his wheelchair to the next class. As was typical of Gary's gregarious personality, he made friends with the entire school by the end of the first few weeks. Gary continued in school and got along well with everyone he met. Year after year went by, and in 1976, Gary graduated high school from Bacon Academy in Colchester, Connecticut.

Gary was used to excelling, or at least holding his own, in high school. After graduating, he expected that he would find a job. However, Gary received no assistance for employment placement. When he asked to be in a job program at the employment office, he was put in a corner and left there for the entire day. No one came by to help. After four days, Gary asked his father to stop taking him down to the center.

Gary ended up staying home, being cared for by his mother. Things went well for a few years, but tragedy struck. Alva found a lump in her breast, and further testing showed it was aggressive breast cancer. After only a year of struggling with the disease, Alva died in 1981 at only forty-eight years old.

Gary recalls the year or so after his mother's death as a very dark time for him and his father. Albert spent most of his time crying, and when Albert wasn't crying, Gary was. It was a depression that both of them found difficult to surmount. Albert had served as a Manchester police officer, a dog warden, and finally as a foreman at Pratt & Whitney. Being fifteen years older than Alva, he was up for retirement shortly after her passing. Before learning of her cancer, Alva had thought that at retirement, Albert would help shoulder some of the responsibilities of caring for Gary. But with Alva gone, Albert had to do everything.

For the next sixteen years, Albert took care of his son full time, without any help from state agencies and barely any help from family. Typically, Gary was kept busy with two hours of morning exercises, and then Albert read the newspaper to him. Of course Gary was fully capable of reading and in fact did a lot of reading himself. But Albert reading the paper to him was a father-son tradition the two developed, and it was a precious time for both of them.

After breakfast and washing up, Gary joined his father on whatever errands needed to be done for the day. Albert would just throw Gary over his shoulder and took him in the car wherever he went. Sometimes, Gary would join his dad by using his wheelchair, and other times, he would just wait in the car for his dad to come back.

Gary didn't just go on short errands. Albert made sure his son got to enjoy life. They travelled together to Vermont. They went to ball games and had ice cream. They joined their entire extended family in Disney World for a family reunion. Gary still vividly recalls seeing the U.S. Olympic basketball team play in Hartford as well as going to the 1992 Olympic trials for boxing in Worchester, Massachusetts. Maybe it was because of Gary's love of all things sports, or maybe it was his attitude of refusing to back down from anything, but Albert called Gary his "little lion."

Albert took care of Gary until Parkinson's disease, Alzheimer's, and emphysema set in. It got to the point that Albert could not care for himself, much less address Gary's daily needs. Albert enlisted the help of a private home health agency, who helped with both of their needs for a few years. And then suddenly, the caregiver decided to go on a vacation and ended up never coming back to the house. The two men had more needs than ever, and they did not know where to turn. When they asked their extended family, no one wanted to help. The family suggested a nursing home for the two of them, just so someone else would deal with the situation. Albert sent up prayers that God would send some sort of help for them.

Help came in the form of an angel. Gary's cousin Paula stepped up, and she agreed to move into the house and take care of both of them. While Albert still retained his mental faculties, he taught Paula how to take care of Gary. At the same time, Paula helped Albert with his declining health. For almost two years, Paula shouldered the responsibilities of caring for the two men. When the Alzheimer's and Parkinson's got severe and Paula could no longer adequately care for both Albert and Gary, she had to make a tough choice. Paula had Gary's dad placed in a nursing home. After being in the nursing home for less than two months, Albert developed aspiration pneumonia. He died shortly after at eighty years old.

Paula started caring for Albert and Gary in 1997. After Albert passed, the estate was placed in a trust fund for Gary. Paula continued to live in the house and care for her cousin. She tried working per-diem hours during the day, but Gary really required more than full-time care. Paula applied for payment for a maximum of 25 hrs a week through the state's personal care attendant (PCA) program. In addition to Paula's stipend, the state provided a social worker as well as other helpers totaling around fifty hours a week. Paula survived by getting things on sale and becoming the queen of coupons, typically saving $60 a week on groceries.

Through the years, Paula and Gary have settled into a daily routine. Paula wakes Gary out of bed at 5:30 AM for a quick sponge bath to deal with any of the night's soiling. Three days a week, Gary gets a whole shower. After dressing comes breakfast. Gary then does stretching exercises on the floor and his standing table, which takes him to mid morning. The afternoons are filled with a range of activities, including Gary driving his electric wheelchair around the neighborhood with a person at this side.

Gary also takes the transit bus to go shopping, or visits a friend to watch a ball game.

Gary has had to face and overcome many challenges through his life, most of them physical. Simple activities that non-disabled people take for granted represent daily challenges: feeding, positioning his legs, using the commode. Paula had to find Gary a cup that was tall enough and heavy enough not to topple over, along with long straws for Gary to drink by himself and give him more independence. Before Paula started taking care of Gary, Albert would hold the urinal the whole time Gary was urinating. Paula did not think that was appropriate for her to do, so she needed to come up with an alternative. She took the cover of a tub of margarine and folded it in half. The folded cover helps keep Gary's privates down, and any urine that splashes is contained by the cover. Gary and Paula call it the *pee pee shield*. Paula's close attention to detail and thrifty ingenuity have helped maximize Gary's quality of life.

Gary and Paula always keep their eyes open for advancements in equipment to assist Gary with his disability. The standing table gives Gary a surface to lean on and helps provide a prolonged stretch for his hamstrings, back, and neck. And while he is leaning on the table, Paula has Gary do hand exercises to keep up coordination and finger suppleness.

The most beneficial piece of equipment Gary has acquired is his electric wheelchair. This allows him to reposition himself during the day as well as move around the house and outside independently. In spite of Gary's obvious disabilities, he still feels like there is little he can't do with the help and aids he has.

Gary started coming to the office in 2003, and he has been a joy to take care of ever since. We both have rolled over the bumps Gary's CP has presented to him. When I gained his permission to tell his story, I asked Gary how he views the world differently from non-disabled people. Gary said, "I appreciate things more than other people. I try to understand other people and be in a good mood all the time. I'm out there some days, but aren't we all?"

Paula chimed in, "Gary is very patient. I don't think I've ever seen Gary in a bad mood. He'll talk to anybody—at the grocery store, at the bank, in your office. There isn't anyone he can't talk to."

I asked Gary whether he felt like his CP has opened or closed doors for him. Gary responded, "Opened doors. People accept me very well. Those who don't, miss out, because they could have been my friend."

"Isn't there anything you wish you could do, but you can't because of your cerebral palsy?"

Gary replied, "I wish I could go back to Disney World. That was a great time with my family, but we don't have the money for it now. And don't laugh at me, but I always wanted to be a linebacker for the New York Giants. I could also see myself as a shortstop or second base for the Yankees because you're always in the action."

Gary might not be built like a linebacker or a shortstop, but knowing him, I can guarantee that he's always in the action anywhere he happens to be.

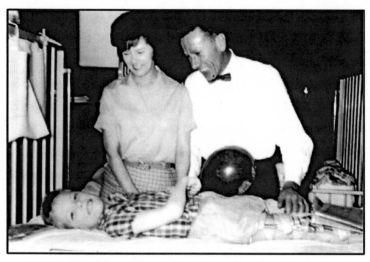

Gary with his parents at Shriner's Hospital, 1965

Gary in his house in the 1980s

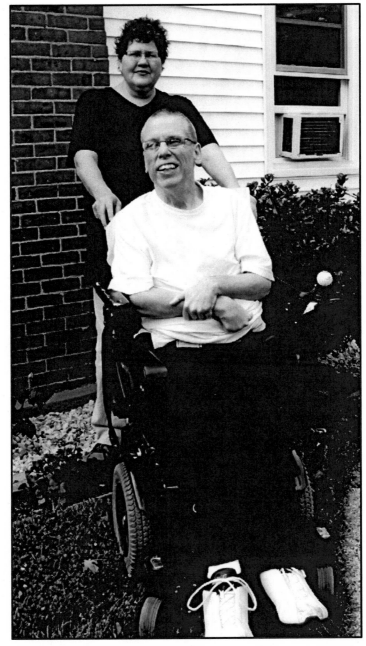

Gary and Paula

Finding the Strength

Karen thought life was just perfect when she married her high school sweetheart Greg a year after graduation. But a sweetly romantic courtship and engagement quickly turned sour after the marriage. It seemed Greg had a very different viewpoint from Karen about the balance of power in the relationship. Karen thought she was getting a life mate who would walk with her. Greg instead made it plainly clear that Karen was more like his property, and what he said and did was law. Karen was able to maintain a semblance of independence through her job and the steady income she earned. But when Karen got pregnant and decided to stay home with Aimee instead of going back to work, what little respect Greg showed Karen vanished. "You are nothing. I am king." Karen heard those exact words from Greg more times than she could count. In many ways, the mental abuse was more difficult to bear than had it been physical. Bruises heal, but the constant ridicule stayed with her.

Two years after Aimee, Karen was pregnant with Lisa. Greg dropped Karen off at the hospital and drove away. Through fifteen hours of labor, Greg neither came to the hospital nor called. Lisa was born without her father present. In fact, Greg only came back to the hospital to pick up Karen and the baby. It was at that point that Karen knew that things would never change. Karen struggled to maintain her family for another three years, but it was no use. She filed for divorce and moved out with the kids.

While separated and waiting for the finalization of the divorce, Karen met her best friend's brother, Russ, who was incidentally going through a divorce himself. There was chemistry from the start, and the two started seeing each other. They knew they were right for each other, and within the year, they decided to get married. It was a busy year for Karen. She was married, separated, met Russ, divorced, engaged, and then remarried. The whirlwind did not end after that. Less than six months after the wedding, Karen was pregnant with Darren.

Karen and Russ were the heads of a very blended family: Lisa and Aimee from Karen's first marriage, Nicole from Russ's first marriage, and Darren from their life together. They were in love, and the kids all got along fabulously. Things this time really were perfect. But one month after Darren's first birthday, Russ died in a tragic drowning accident.

Russ's death devastated the family. Karen was heartbroken beyond words. She had just lost the most extraordinary man she had ever known. She was completely overwhelmed; she had no idea how to find the strength to do what needed to be done. Karen found that she could not grieve and concentrate on the needs of her children at the same time. So, she stuffed the feelings way down deep, and she told herself that she would come back to them another time. Eventually, the kids dealt with their father's death, and Karen carried the family through. Every now and then, the feeling of loss would come upon her, and Karen would cry. But she did not allow herself to grieve for long because it hurt too much. She couldn't stand the pain, so she kept pushing it back down.

Karen did not realize that she made a major mistake in thinking that she could bury her grief without serious consequences. Although on the outside, Karen seemed to be doing fine, her heart was still terribly wounded by the loss of her husband. In the small town, everyone knew of Russ's death and constantly asked Karen how she was doing. The sympathetic looks and pity even a year after the death regularly opened up the painful wounds that were just under the surface. Karen finally couldn't take the smothering environment anymore and moved away.

Roy came into Karen's life during this time of emotional vulnerability, and he swept her off her feet. He was caring and considerate. He seemed to be able to say all the right things at the right time. Karen so needed someone to hug her and tell her, "You're doing a good job." She fell for him, hard. When they initially got married, Karen never imagined what a terrible alcoholic he was. Karen considered herself a rather intelligent person, so how could she have made such an error in judgment?

When Roy drank, he insulted Karen mercilessly. After a while, Roy did not abuse her with just words. He would shove her, or push her down, or grab her hair, but he was very careful not to beat her or leave any marks that others could see. The repeated verbal and physical harassment terrified her. But every time Karen got up the nerve to stand up to him and tell him she was leaving, Roy gave her flowers, apologies, tears, words of love and "never again." And of course Karen forgave him, thinking, "Maybe he'll change now." But things of course did not change. They only got worse.

Karen was stuck in a classic co-dependent relationship. She was emotionally and physically worn out, feeling trapped in her own house, in a prison of her own making. She was in a desperate situation that was spinning out of control, like a ship being dragged to the bottom of a whirlpool. Every moment of each day was consumed with deadening anxiety. This lead to panic attacks which started taking over every aspect of her life. Karen started having symptoms of numbness and fatigue, but tests came back negative. The symptoms persisted, along with some new ones, but subsequent tests were normal as well.

One morning, Karen woke up and thought she was losing her mind. She felt terrified, in such a state of anxiety that she wanted to run, but to where, she did not know. Karen called Roy at work and asked him to come home and take her to the doctor's office. At the doctor's office, she found the courage to confide with him about the abuse she was experiencing. Her physician listened intently to Karen's story and said, "I want you to go into the mental health unit at the hospital."

"You must be kidding! I'm not crazy," Karen replied.

"I know you're not crazy," Dr. Brown soothed. "*You* know you're not crazy. But I'm worried about you. If you don't get away from him, he will destroy you. Once you are out of his environment, you will be able to start sorting out your thoughts and feelings and start making decisions on your own."

Dr. Brown consulted a psychiatrist colleague who agreed to see Karen the next morning. After a lengthy talk, he made arrangements for Karen to be admitted that evening to the inpatient behavioral health unit. Karen spent a total of five weeks in the unit. She started a regimen of medicines, group therapy, and individual counseling specifically tailored for those who have experienced psychological mistreatment. Karen listened, wrote a lot of notes, talked a lot in class about feelings, and cried a lot explaining them. For the first time in almost a decade, Karen gave herself permission to grieve over the loss of her second husband, Russ.

Through the inpatient program and the caring staff, Karen found the path to make herself emotionally healthy again. During the stay, Karen came to the conclusion that Roy could not stay in her life anymore. For the five weeks while she was in the unit, Roy used access to the children as a way to exert control over her. Although the hospital allowed several hours each day for family visitation, Roy rarely took the children to the hospital.

On weekends, patients were allowed to go home if they were signed out by a responsible person. Karen cringed every time Roy deigned to come and play the role of the "responsible" person, signing Karen out for the weekend. She didn't say anything because she loved and needed that time with her children, but Karen found that she was becoming less and less afraid of him. She realized she had rediscovered the strength inside herself. She saw how weak and pathetic Roy really was, and inwardly, she laughed at him.

Halfway through her treatment, Karen discovered a friend in Doug, who had just entered the program because of an impossible marriage. They realized it was easy to talk to each other, and they each helped the other gain perspectives regarding their situations. Karen finished the program at the same time as Doug, and they promised to keep in touch.

When she went home, Karen found the strength to stand her ground, and she made herself crystal clear about what she expected from Roy. After that declaration, Roy did not utter an unkind word to her again. Karen then started the divorce process, kicking Roy out of the house. Karen again had a home filled with love. She knew that she now had the tools to mend her heavy heart over time.

Although Karen's heart and soul were finding healing, her body was not following suit. The unexplained symptoms of numbness and fatigue continued, worsening through the years instead of improving. Karen's periods of extreme fatigue interfered with shopping, cooking, cleaning, and planned activities with the kids. Karen would be walking and suddenly one of her ankles would give out, dropping her to the ground. In a short span, Karen had three severe sprained ankles and had to use crutches. Then she found that just taking a morning shower left her so exhausted that she had to sit for twenty minutes afterwards just to get her strength back. Karen's entire life was affected by her limitations.

Towards the latter part of the 1980s, Karen's condition worsened to the point where she could no longer drive. She could not transport her children to their various activities. She had severe pain in her spine, tailbone, arms, and hands. Her arms and legs would frequently go into spasms that left her debilitated afterwards. She finally could take no more of this. She saw a neurologist and basically demanded an MRI. The neurologist reluctantly acquiesced.

One week later, Karen received a call from the neurology office. "Karen, the MRI showed an abnormality in the white matter of the brain that is consistent with Multiple Sclerosis. There's not really much that we can do for you." He hung up the phone with a click.

Karen was so shocked she couldn't even speak. Tears poured down her face as she tried to absorb this devastating news. The thought of facing MS and the callous way the neurologist broke the news to her led Karen back into a state of deep depression that lasted for three years. She didn't feel like doing anything. She was no longer interested in doing the craft work and gardening she enjoyed. She spent many days sitting around, or sometimes not even getting out of bed.

One of the few things that kept Karen from giving up was her relationship with Doug. They had kept in contact after their three weeks in the hospital together. Karen divorced Roy, while Doug did the same with his wife. Their friendship helped them through the process, and it turned into a romance. Even after her MS diagnosis, Doug stayed committed to her. He was in it for the long haul. A year after Karen was diagnosed with MS, Doug proposed to her. With Karen leaning on a cane and her kids and close friends around her, Karen tied the knot with Doug.

Karen's MS continued to progress, robbing her of her ability to walk, and then to move. Forced into a sedentary lifestyle, Karen went from 130 lbs to over double that amount. When I took over her care from my step-father in 2001, Karen was already confined to a wheelchair as a quadriplegic. She could just move her right hand enough to steer her electric wheelchair. Doug served as her sole care giver. Every morning,

Doug performed Karen's bathroom and hygiene needs. He then transferred her to her electric wheelchair, where she spent her day. Doug gave her morning meds with breakfast, feeding her each bite of food. For the afternoon meds, Doug taped them to the door frame so that Karen could slide the wheel chair over and peel them off with her teeth. A glass of water with an extra long straw was available for Karen to swallow the pills. Karen then spent the day by herself in the house. When Doug got home in the evening, he changed Karen's undergarments, made dinner, and fed her. They would have a few hours together watching TV, and then it was time for bed.

In addition to the standard medical problems for anyone in mid-life, I also addressed the particular challenges Doug and Karen faced because of her MS. Loneliness and depression were constant issues she and I discussed. And of course there were the physical symptoms of her MS— muscle and joint spasms, leg swelling, and skin breakdown. Doug, meanwhile, experienced back pain from lifting Karen every day. She weighed almost 280 lbs because she was unable to do any activity. And then there were issues that they struggled with as a couple. How could Doug avoid caregiver fatigue? How could Doug be the one to change Karen's soiled undergarments in one moment and then be the husband and lover in the next? What sexual position could they use to accommodate Karen's physical disability? Although Karen had no motor control, her sensation was exquisitely intact, and she was a very loving, affectionate person, fulfilled by physical and intimate contact. These issues and many more we navigated to give Doug and Karen as rewarding a life as any other couple.

In December 2007, on a way to a party, Doug and Karen suffered a major car accident. Doug got through with minor injuries, but Karen had severe chest trauma. She was taken by Life Star to the hospital, and her heart stopped twice on the way. For three weeks, cardiologists monitored her in the hospital. While there, her case came to the attention of the MS Society president, Susan Raimondo. Susan helped arrange visiting nurse help for four hours a day, paid by the MS Society. She then helped to enroll Karen into the state's pilot program for disabled citizens under 65. The program provided funding for a total of eight hours a day.

Even with all of the extra help, Karen has had more than her fair share of major medical issues. In November 2009 she developed a blood clot in her leg and had to be put on Coumadin. A month later at Christmas, she was gravely ill from severe pancreatitis. In July 2011, Karen started acting strangely. She became lethargic and then unresponsive to questions. Doug called 911, and Karen was taken by ambulance to the community hospital. She was found to have a subdural hematoma on her brain, likely from the Coumadin. Karen was then transferred to the tertiary care hospital to control her bleeding and seizures. Although she was stabilized and sent home, Karen had recurrent symptoms. The subdural hemorrhage subsequently led to multiple admissions to the hospital and finally a craniotomy to relieve pressure on her brain.

Karen has had MS for 31 of her 63 years. In spite of the mountain of challenges Karen has faced, she continues to keep a smile on her face. She told me once, "I'm really a little girl, trapped in this body. See, look, I'm wiggling my toe." I reflexively looked down, and of course her toe wasn't moving. Karen had a glint of amusement in her eyes. "Yeah, I know, it's not moving, but I'm telling it to. And just to let you know, I might not be able to move, but I can *feel* everything!"

Karen has this advice to anyone: "Go with the flow. Cry if you have to, and try to keep a positive attitude."

Karen in 1987

Karen and Doug at their wedding, July 30, 1989

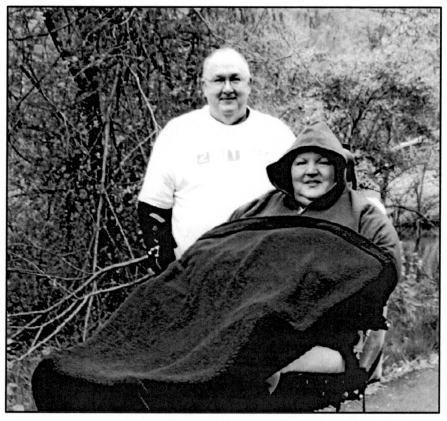

Karen and Doug on the MS Walk 2012

Left to right: Aimee, Lisa, Darren, Karen, and Doug; Christmas 2012

An Unexpected Blessing

Paul and Nancy were so excited they could barely contain themselves. The day had finally come. After a long struggle with infertility and use of Clomid to induce ovulation, Nancy was at term and ready to deliver. Four-year-old Jonathan was going to have a baby brother!

The delivery went without a hitch. Nancy was able to deliver naturally, and the baby boy—they decided to name him Steven—cried right away, with an Apgar score of 9, only one point off from perfect. At a bit over seven lbs, Steven was a good size baby. Everything seemed wonderful. It was only upon closer inspection that one could notice Steven's almond-shaped, close-set eyes. Steven had the eyes of an Asian baby, but his parents were Caucasian. He also had low-set ears, a flattened nasal bridge, single palmar creases in his hands, and inward-curving little fingers. The sum total of the physical exam pointed to only one thing, and genetic testing confirmed it. Steven had Trisomy 21, commonly known as Down Syndrome.

Paul and Nancy were devastated. Nancy was only 32, well under the age when the risk for Down Syndrome started to climb. When Nancy found out, she was almost in a catatonic state. Her dream and vision for her family was destroyed. The family was already facing a multitude of stresses, and the thought of Steven not being the perfectly healthy baby boy they were expecting was almost too much to bear. The couple met with the Human Genetics team, receiving extensive counseling regarding the diagnosis and cause of Down Syndrome as well as the implications for the future. They were also hoping to have another child for a total of three, but now had to consider the risk of having another Down Syndrome baby. Although the possibility of giving Steven up for adoption was presented to them, they never considered that as an option.

Steven and the family were enrolled into several programs, including the Early Intervention Program, the genetics clinic, and the Down Syndrome Congress. Steven did well at first, feeding well and doing the things that babies do. But at the seven-week check up, it seemed he was not gaining as much weight as he should have. Nancy had been noticing that Steven was having difficulty breathing while he was eating, and he might have even turned a little blue. Plus, he was spitting up after feedings. More than just a simple dribble, the formula would shoot out of his mouth and nose. Burping him and keeping his head up helped somewhat, but the problem worsened over the next several months. Finally, further studies confirmed that Steven had duodenal atresia, a narrowing of his intestines, preventing him from passing and digesting food. Even after surgery to bypass the narrowing, Steven could not eat well and had to be fed through a gastric tube.

Steven's intestinal issue was just the beginning of a series of major medical problems that threatened his life at every turn and shook the faith of his parents. Right before the intestinal surgery, the surgeon suggested Steven see a cardiologist because he was turning blue. Cardiac studies showed he had an "AV canal," a large hole in the center of his heart. His oxygenated and spent blood was mixing together, and he was not getting enough oxygen when he was nursing. This explained why Steven had been turning blue. Steven was suffocating every time he tried to feed, which of course affected his lungs as well. A month after the intestinal surgery, Steven still could not be weaned off the ventilator.

When Steven was transferred to Boston Children's Hospital for heart surgery, Xrays noted a mass growing in Steven's chest. That turned out to be a huge cyst in his chest wall that required removal even before cardiac surgery could be done. At seven months old, Steven was again prepped for surgery. For several hours, the team of doctors worked to repair all the broken parts of Steven's body. They were successful, but Steven was severely weakened by the ordeal. He remained in the ICU for three weeks. He required heart medicine, oxygen, and a diuretic. Steven spent the next several months recuperating from the surgery. Three months later, he continued to require a gastric tube to provide his nutrition. Still, the cardiologist agreed to release Steven early so he could have his first Christmas at home. Steven came home on Christmas Eve with his gastric tube, his oxygen, and medication. The portable oxygen tank weighed more than he did.

Still, children, even those with Down Syndrome, are incredibly resilient. Steven did get better, and he far exceeded the expectations of all of his doctors. He started growing and communicating more. Steven entered school—one of the first Down Syndrome children in the town to do so—and made friends. He was a handful for his parents. During one of his doctor appointments when he was seven, the physician called him "exuberant." Steven got along fabulously with his older brother Jonathan as well as his younger brother David, who was born a year later and did not have Down Syndrome.

Nancy transferred Steven's records to my office after having a good experience as my patient. He was now twenty years old and doing very well. Other than some minor illnesses, hernia surgery, and dental surgery, Steven did not face any life-threatening medical problems. Steven lived every day enjoying life.

Steven walked in for the first office visit with a big smile on his face. He had thick glasses framing his dark, almond-shaped eyes. He was shorter than his brothers, but average for a young man with Down Syndrome. As was typical of many Down patients, he had a large tongue and a small jaw, which made his speech a bit difficult to understand. His mother was used to hearing her son, though, so Nancy interpreted anything I didn't pick up on right away. It was actually a very easy visit, with just a bit of a sore throat and athlete's foot. I gave him some medicine and did not expect him back until his annual physical.

Steven ended up coming back sooner than I expected. His school called Nancy because Steven had fallen several times. He would be fine and then suddenly get all clammy, have a racing heart, fall to the ground, and get confused. Because there were multiple episodes, the school suggested Steven get examined. I could not find much on the exam, but because of Steven's extensive cardiac background I sent him to the cardiologist. They found electrical abnormalities in his heart, likely from all the surgery he had when he was younger. Steven ended up getting a pacemaker placed in his chest, the youngest patient in my office to need one.

For all of the challenges Steven presented to the family, Nancy would be the first to say that he has been an unexpected blessing, one they would never trade for an "easier" child. Steven has a gift for enjoying life, which tends to keep Nancy grounded. When he turned twenty one, Nancy asked him what he wanted for his birthday party. "Beer!" He replied happily. Well, he was 21, so Nancy had no reason to refuse him. Steven generally has a pleasant, cheerful disposition, no matter what happens. He shows compassion even when a person is being mean, and he doesn't harbor ill will for any length of time.

Steven always speaks his mind. There is no need to guess what he is thinking. Once, Nancy's sister had to stay with them for a week after foot surgery. She took Steven's room, while he moved in with David. He tolerated it, but he didn't like it. When she came back for a few days to visit, Steven wasn't going to have her overstay her welcome. They walked in the door from an errand and found Steven had packed all of her bags and put them at the front door. "Go home," he told her matter-of-factly. Nancy and her sister couldn't help but laugh.

Steven is very concerned about others and their well being. During a Special Olympics swimming competition, Steven stopped and stood up in the middle of the race. Nancy couldn't figure out what was going on. What happened was that Steven noticed that he was way ahead of the other swimmers, so he wanted to wait until they caught up to him. Once they did, he started swimming again. Steven was not nearly as interested in being the first and winning as he was with the camaraderie of the event.

Steven is also keen on the girls, and man, did he know how to butter them up! He took a shine to one of the lifeguards at the pool where David worked. As she was turned away while cleaning the pool, he came up to her underwater and grabbed her legs, laughing uproariously. None of the people at the pool did much swimming that day because they were too busy watching Steven's antics with his favorite lifeguard.

It isn't just girls who Steven gets along with. He brings joy with him wherever he goes, lightening the hearts of the people around him. He has a loud boisterous laugh and no such thing as an "inside voice." Everyone he meets becomes an instant friend to him. There doesn't seem to be anyone whose heart he cannot melt.

Steven has always been a very affectionate person, especially to his mother. Nancy says, "God knew I needed a lot of hugs, so He gave me Steven."

Nancy asserts that the life lessons Steven has taught her could fill many books. Steven has shown her that a lot of the stuff we deal with on a daily basis is not as important as showing love for one another. She told me, "From when he was a baby, Steven would look at you with these eyes of wonder, that there was so much beauty in the world. He sees it as a good place filled with kindness and love. He's full of life.

"I've said this to a number of people: Steven may be mentally retarded, but he's not stupid. He's a very visual learner, and he picks up on things really quickly. Just because people are different does not mean they are not capable in some way. He's shown me the possibilities in life."

Even though he had Down Syndrome, Steven was included in the regular sixth grade class. During the year, a new student transferred to the school. The teacher had a rough time with this new student because of a difficult transition. Still, the teacher noticed the student was kind to Steven. That recognition of the student's compassion for Steven fostered compassion and patience in herself as she dealt with the frustrations of the new student. Over time, the student adjusted and did very well in class.

Steven has also taught Nancy to follow her heart. When Steven was a toddler, he wasn't really "toddling" because he couldn't walk. Still, it was about the right age for him to be potty trained. When she asked the "experts," they all told her that he was too young, that he couldn't do it because of his Down Syndrome. She did not listen to them and worked on potty training Steven anyway, and he did very well.

Nancy has learned to honor her commitments. Don't promise something you can't commit to. When she tells Steven she's going to do something and doesn't do it, it crushes his spirit. So, Nancy is careful to follow through on her promises, or not make the promise in the first place.

Paul and Nancy have worked hard to give Steven a rich set of life experiences. He has gone to school since childhood. He's been involved in the Special Olympics with various sports as well as other camps. He gets to drink beer, but in moderation of course. He has a girlfriend who he's quite taken with. When he gets older, he will likely work, have a job, and have a say on how he spends his earnings. As Nancy has said, "He's entitled to as full a life as anybody."

Nancy shared with me a poem by Emily Perl Kingsley called *Welcome to Holland* which helped her tremendously as she was facing the possibility of raising a Down Syndrome child. You might plan all your life of going to Italy, but sometimes, life takes you to Holland. It's not a worse place, just different. Life does not always lead you down the expected path you plan on taking. Sometimes, the unexpected path is better than the one you had actually planned.

Steven at his brother Jonathan's wedding, August 2009

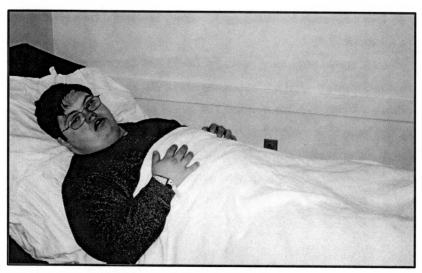

Steven at the hospital, March 2007

Steven as a brand-new uncle, April 2012

Laughter is the Best Medicine

"Gladys, you need a tetanus shot."

"And why is that?"

"Well, you're eighty years old. You haven't had a tetanus shot in more than ten years. You don't want to step on a rusty nail and get lock jaw."

"Some of my family might think that would be a good thing," Gladys quipped.

****

"Your physical is due in a month," I told Felix.

"Are you sure? I think I just did it."

I looked through the chart. "Nope, it's been just about a year. In fact, I made you turn your head and cough, and I gave you the finger. I guess the memory is still fresh on your mind."

Felix looked at me in anticipated discomfort. "Aw Doc, do we have to? You know, you would think with all the technology we have these days, there would be something better than a finger up my ass to examine my prostate."

"There is," I replied. "Two fingers."

****

Oscar and Francine came in as usual for their routine appointment. Although married sixty years, they still liked having their separate exam rooms for their visits. I started with Francine first, but it was taking a bit longer than usual. I decided to let Oscar know I hadn't forgotten about him.

I knocked on Oscar's door and poked my head in. "I'm going to take care of the missus, and then I'll come in to see you."

Oscar responded, "*I* take care of the missus. You just take a look at her."

****

Even after almost ten years of taking care of my patient Reginald, I never realized how much of a racist he was. The first clue I got was when he refused to take anything but brand-name Lipitor rather than generic for his elevated cholesterol. When I asked him why, he said, "Don't you know those generics aren't made in America? They're stealing good American jobs. And who knows what those Indians are putting into those pills."

At another office visit, we happened to talk about different races and nationalities. Reginald said, "Hey, I have nothing against black people. I just don't think I could ever be friends with one. They're just too different."

I wanted to ask Reginald if he ever noticed that I wasn't white. His explanation clarified things immensely. He said, "I think Orientals are the smartest people. If I had a choice, I'd always go to an Oriental. All of my doctors are Oriental."

Well, how could I argue with that line of reasoning?

****

I'm usually pretty good at keeping on time at my office, but that day, I was running very behind. Joanne had come in for a quick blood draw to check her low thyroid levels. I rushed into the room, said a cursory hello, apologized for keeping her for so long, drew her blood, filled out the slip, and bid her farewell.

The next day, Joanne's test result came back as zero, which was impossible. I looked more closely at the test result, and then I called her.

"Joanne, I got your results back, and I have good news and bad news. The good news is, you don't have a prostate. The bad news is, in my haste I circled the PSA rather than the thyroid levels. We have to redraw your blood for the thyroid test."

Thankfully, Joanne was very forgiving and had a good sense of humor. She came in for her redraw, and thankfully her levels came back normal.

****

Cheryl was seeing me that day for a knee injury that occurred a few days earlier. Apparently, she had to take her dog, a 50 lb lab, to the vet. Although it was raining heavily, she decided wearing flip flops was sufficient. It was an unwise decision, as her foot slipped out of the wet flip flops and caused her to twist her knee badly.

She came in to the office with crutches and a knee brace. After taking off the knee brace, she struggled to pull her pants leg up for me to examine her knee.

"Why don't you drop your pants instead? It would be much easier that way."

"I'm not going to drop my pants for you," she replied.

"Why not?" I asked curiously.

"I'm going commando. I'm not wearing any underwear!" She finally confessed.

"TMI," was all I could say. Too Much Information.

After a bit of work, she was able to shimmy her pants up beyond her knee for me to examine it.

****

My office routinely sees patients of multiple backgrounds and nationalities. I converse easily in three languages and can say a few words and phrases in many more.

One day, a young black couple came to the office as new patients. I could tell by their accent that they were of an African nationality. "What country do you come from?" I asked.

"Kenya," the husband replied.

"And what is the predominant language of Kenya?"

"Swahili," he answered.

My receptionist interjected, "Well *there's* a language you don't know, Dr. Han."

Instead of objecting, I took a deep breath and sang, "*Viumbe vyote vya mungu wetu/ Na mfalme wetu/ Pazeni sauti/ Na mfalme wetu.*"

The couple excitedly said, "Oh, that song is very well known in our country! We have sung it many times in church."

Tammy looked at me with her mouth open. She then laughed and said, "I should know better by now not to say you can't do something."

****

When I take a sexual history, I keep all of my questions very open ended so I don't assume anything. A young man came in, and I asked him if he was sexually active. "No," he said.

"When was the last time you had sex?"

"Last week."

"Last week? What happened?" I asked.

"I broke up with my girlfriend," he replied.

"So you had sex with your girlfriend, and *then* you broke up with her?" I pressed.

"Of course. It was break-up sex."

"Look," I told him. "You're sexually active."

"Yeah, well, I haven't gone a whole week without sex in a long time," he replied.

****

During my residency, cell phones were available but not in common use, and the main method of communication was by pager. Every resident had one, and I rarely went anywhere without it on me. And when you were on call, you had not one but two pagers.

I was relaxing at a bar having a drink one night when a guy sitting next to me started to make small talk. "So, are you a drug dealer?" He asked half-jokingly.

"A drug dealer? Why would you think that?" I replied.

"Well, I noticed your pagers, so I was wondering if you were a drug dealer."

"I guess you're right. I am sort of a drug dealer. I'm a doctor."

"Get out of town! Are you serious?" He guffawed.

"Yep. I'm serious. I'm in the residency program in town."

With the ice broken and once he got over his embarrassment, Mike introduced himself. We spent the rest of the night chatting away.

Fourteen years later, Mike and I are still together.

CPSIA information can be obtained at www.ICGtesting.com
Printed in the USA
BVOW02*0918220813

328538BV00001BB/1/P